SHORT
ROUTE
TO
CHAOS

SHORT

CONSCIENCE, COMMUNITY,

ROUTE

AND THE

TO

RE-CONSTITUTION OF

CHAOS

AMERICAN SCHOOLING

Stephen Arons

University of Massachusetts Press

AMHERST

Copyright © 1997 by Stephen Arons

Printed in the United States of America
LC 96-51512
ISBN 1-55849-077-9 (cloth); 078-7 (pbk.)
Designed by Jack Harrison
Set in Trump Medieval and Gill Sans Ultra Bold display by dix!
Printed and bound by Braun-Brumfield, Inc.
Library of Congress Cataloging-in-Publication Data

Arons, Stephen.
   Short route to chaos : conscience, community, and the
re-constitution of American schooling / Stephen Arons.
      p.   cm.
Includes bibliographical references and index.
ISBN 1-55849-077-9 (cloth : alk. paper).
—ISBN 1-55849-078-7 (pbk. : alk. paper)
1. Public schools—United States.
2. United States. Goals 2000: Educate America Act.
3. Politics and education—United States.
4. Christianity and politics—United States.
5. School choice—United States.
6. Community and school—United States.
7. Educational law and legislation—United States.
I. Title.
LA217.2.A78   1997
371.01'0973—dc21   96-51512
                                    CIP

British Library Cataloguing in Publication data are available.

This book is dedicated to the memory of my earliest teachers,

> *Leon Arons,* who taught by example the importance of careful thought, personal courage, and bad puns.

> *Annette Trenner Arons,* who taught by example the value of creativity, wit, and generosity of spirit.

> *Mickey Trenner,* my older brother in fact if not in law, who taught me how to fish, and why.

Contents

Acknowledgments

The intellectual and personal debts I owe in connection with writing this book are beyond repayment. But I must at least attempt to acknowledge some of them.

First and foremost, I am grateful to Ada Luz Medina, without whose patient support, encouragement, insight, and inspiration of the spirit, this book would have been neither started nor completed. And to my very good friends and most honest critics—Charles Lawrence III, Walt Senterfitt, Bob Seidman—my endless gratitude and immediate release from any responsibility for the flaws in this work. I owe a great deal also to Steve Sugarman, Tyll van Geel, Perry Amsellem, Gary Lamb, Rosemary Salamone, Sonia Nieto, Charles Hamilton, Leonard Liggio, Sara Lawrence, Milton Cantor, and Charles Tsarnas, who helped more than even he could know. And Ben, you saved me at the finish line.

For research fellowship support, I am indebted to the generosity of the Earhart Foundation. Bruce Wilcox provided the early and continuing confidence that was so essential to this work; Ella Kusnetz and Pam Wilkinson made a manuscript into a book with extraordinary attention to detail and helpful editorial suggestions. I had able research assistance from Tami Paluca-Sackrey, Barbara Morgan, Joe Scott, Luke Cebula, Rhys James, Shawn Casey, Pamela Young, and Amy Hanson.

Finally, I am grateful for the inspiration of Robert Bolt, who in writing *A Man for All Seasons* brought Sir Thomas More back to the discourse over public life. Bolt died in February 1995, leaving to every reader a powerful and enduring legacy about the clash of power, law, and conscience.

Prologue

In 1535, Sir Thomas More was beheaded on orders of King Henry VIII after a trial based on false evidence. More's offense to the English crown had been his refusal to acquiesce in Henry's divorce from his first wife and in the Act of Supremacy. By that act, Parliament had made Henry head of the Church of England, and the church independent of the pope in Rome.

Thomas More was a man of sharp wit, powerful intellect, and an enormous appetite for life. He had a wide-ranging reputation as a successful statesman, an accomplished lawyer, an honest judge, and a skilled political adviser. For several years a favorite of King Henry, he had been appointed lord chancellor in 1529 in recognition of his service to the crown. In sixteenth-century England and abroad, More was regarded as "a man for all seasons." In the eighteenth century, Samuel Johnson defined him as "the person of the greatest virtue these islands ever produced."

Yet More was put to death, not for any action taken against Henry, but for adhering to his own most deeply held beliefs. In the face of the status, wealth, and power which the king offered in his effort to secure More's support for the divorce, More stuck to that small part of his "self" that transcended politics, material well-being, and family life. He would not, to put it simply, sacrifice his conscience to Henry's power.

In 1960, 425 years after More's beheading, Robert Bolt wrote *A Man for All Seasons*,* a lively and thought-provoking play about More's conflict with Henry VIII, and a powerful vehicle for inquiring into the role of conscience in modern life. Bolt's play is concerned as well with the meaning of individualism and community in a mass culture, with the place of civil disobedience in an age of rules, and with the relationship of common persons to the heroes they survive. Bolt's More has "an adamantine sense of his own self." This sense of self is an attribute essential to More's moral compass, but it is criticized by his enemies as mere selfishness, "a shrill incessant pedagogue about its own salvation."

Early in act one of the play, Sir Thomas is summoned by the then-lord chancellor, Cardinal Wolsey, to a discussion about efforts being made to secure a dispensation from the pope so that Henry might divorce Catherine of Aragon, who had borne him no male heir. The king intended to marry Anne Boleyn, whom he was sure would give him a son. Wolsey seeks More's support for applying military pressure on the pope in order to have the divorce granted, belittling the "horrible moral squint" with which he claims More views matters of state. More, a Catholic perhaps more devout than the cardinal, will have none of it, though Wolsey appeals to the good of the country, to the fear of civil war if there is no male heir, and to Sir Thomas's sense of duty to the crown:

> *Wolsey:* All right, regrettable! But necessary, to get us an heir! Now explain how you as Councilor of England can obstruct those measures for the sake of your own, private, conscience.

> *More:* Well . . . I believe, when statesmen forsake their own private conscience for the sake of their public duties . . . they lead their country by a short route to chaos.

In this statement about the heavy cost of ignoring private conscience in public affairs, as in the rest of More's life and in the play which is a memorial to it, there lies a warning of considerable significance for late twentieth-century Americans. When conscience is disparaged by public officials, and every day made less and less relevant in the lives of ordi-

---

* Several brief quotations used in my prologue and epilogue are drawn from Robert Bolt, *A Man for All Seasons* (New York: Random House, 1962).

nary citizens, the result is likely to be disastrous, both for individual liberty and for the life of the society. The government that uses political power to hold private conscience hostage may indeed be mapping out a short route to chaos.

At the time, More's warning might have seemed paradoxical to Cardinal Wolsey; and it may, in spite of the lessons of history, still seem so today. For in seeking to influence More, Wolsey—like many a modern government—had already said, "your conscience is your own affair." Moreover, the cardinal's professed goal was to avoid chaos, not enhance it. He had sought to have More ignore his conscience only in this one matter of state, to keep it to himself so that the establishment of an enduring order—the Tudor succession—might prevent the ultimate chaos of civil war.

But More regarded his conscience as something he could not ignore —even for reasons of state—without sacrificing his own being. Near the end of the play, when More's daughter, Margaret, visits him in jail shortly before his trial and execution, she urges him to save himself by swearing an oath to the Act of Supremacy: "Then say the words of the oath and in your heart think otherwise." To this More replies, "When a man takes an oath, Meg, he's holding his own self in his hands. Like Water. And if he opens his fingers then—he needn't hope to find himself again."

Conscience for More is thus a vital part of the self, as vital as water is to life. But it is also transcendent and larger than the self. It is at once part of an individual and larger than any one being. It expresses those beliefs, sometimes shared by or even defining a community, that an individual holds beyond the reach of government or any other temporal power. More's life is witness to the idea that conscience lies at the narrow intersection of the private self, the shared values of a community of belief, and those ultimate truths that an individual regards as transcending both.

But just as More saw the risk to himself in Wolsey's plan and in Margaret's proposal, he saw also the more general relationship between private conscience and the conduct of government. His paradoxical warning to Wolsey suggests that the government which is not built on respect for individual conscience will soon lose its legitimacy and effectiveness and will ultimately end in an explosion of conflict. In such a government, communities and individuals holding differing ideas of truth and ultimate meaning must seek to have their visions adopted as official belief, or they risk losing altogether both the sense of self and the idea of community. Wolsey's demand of More, however much intended to create order, was in fact likely to result in a chaos deeper than the cardinal claimed to fear.

A Man for All Seasons is laced through with these and other complex issues of private conscience and public power. It invites us to think about the importance of maintaining a balance between the use of government to attain the common good and the preservation of the individual liberties upon which a good life in common depends. It challenges our ideas of the process by which the common good should be defined, suggesting that what appears an expedient path to order and cohesion may in fact be a short route to conflict and meaninglessness. Its message is a prescription, not for the content of morality but for the conditions under which morality may productively be sought. It asks whether conscience, often disparaged as merely subjective, can ever be more than an inconvenience in a society in which power becomes the only currency of political life.

The England of King Henry VIII and Sir Thomas More was, of course, a theocracy. It joined the religious beliefs of the powerful to the power of the state. Since then a revolution has created in America—and elsewhere—a great experiment in constitutional democracy, in which the structure and principles of government are designed to empower the common people without enabling their representatives to tyrannize over the consciences of individual citizens or over communities of belief within the nation.

This understanding, that democratic majorities must be prevented from controlling the content of belief and communication in order to assure that democracy itself remains workable, is woven into the very fabric of the American experiment. The quintessential statement of these principles is found in the First Amendment to the U.S. Constitution, which protects conscience by securing the freedom of belief, expression, assembly, and religion, and by protecting the entire "sphere of intellect and spirit" from government coercion. Between More's time and Bolt's, the structure of political power and the importance of individual liberty have thus been redefined. But nearly half a millennium after More's death, and even in the relatively enlightened culture of constitutional democracy, the attempt of power to impose a self-serving order on unruly consciences can still propel a society along the road to chaos.

In a highly pluralistic democracy such as the United States—where there are so many differing communities of belief and where all are entitled to participate in shaping the common core of culture—the problem of private conscience and government power may seem even more complex and intractable. It is a problem which concerns not simply the powerful and the religious, but ordinary families and diverse communities as well. It is a problem not only of how to preserve the most fundamental individual liberties; but also of how to sustain the communities which give individual freedom its value. It is a problem for the grand issues of foreign policy and domestic tranquility, but also for the common schooling that constitutes, at present, a compulsory encounter between government-approved values and individual belief. It is a problem that forms the core of this book about the consequences of an ongoing and radical restructuring of American schooling in the 1990s.

In taking More's warning seriously and applying it to American school reform, "chaos" may appear an unduly frightening and heavy-handed term. More's warning may have overstated the likely result of a victory of power over conscience in a theocratic state, not to mention its result in the mundane world of schooling in a constitutional democracy. But any culture or institution that actively disrespects private conscience and is structurally antagonistic to the development of communities of shared conscience may end in self-destruction. Conscience may not be easily defined, understood, or institutionally respected. But the marginalization of conscience—whether in a buccaneering monarchy or in the education policies of a democracy—has consequences impossible to ignore. The trivialization of individual liberty, the collapse of internalized beliefs and the sense of self, and the disintegration of shared worldview and of genuine communities are surely the precursors of chaos, if not the thing itself. More's belief—that forsaking private conscience for the sake of public order leads by a short route to chaos—may be more important today than it was nearly five hundred years ago.

Bolt's portrayal of the conflict between single-minded power and ambiguous conscience is a prologue to what follows here—an examination of how the constitution of schooling may affect the rights of conscience and the vitality of community life. In Bolt's play, More's life is both inspiration and warning. For although More brought his own private conscience to the performance of his public duties, he paid the ultimate price for doing so. The price of conscience in public schooling, while of a lesser magnitude, is nevertheless too high, as this book seeks to demonstrate. Students—along with their families, teachers, and communities—should not be confronted daily with an educational institution that is structurally hostile to the development and exercise of conscience and that marginalizes or actively disrespects that small but vital part of the self.

Thomas More was betrayed at his trial by Richard Rich, who was rewarded in advance by the king for falsely testifying that More had revealed his opposition to the legality of the Act of Supremacy. In the first scene of Bolt's play, the young Rich had come to More seeking a place in King Henry's court. More, who saw Rich's thirst for status and power and his weakness of character even then, told Rich he should accept a post at a school instead. "A man should go," said More, "where he won't be tempted." More obviously did not anticipate politics in the United States, where the temptation to disregard conscience and undermine community has been turned into a governing principle of school reform.

SHORT
ROUTE
TO
CHAOS

Introduction

American public schooling has fallen upon hard times. Wracked by polarizing political conflict over its content; suffering from weak public confidence and self-interested corporate pressure; analyzed and reformed nearly to death by thousands of well-intentioned experts and hundreds of trend-driven reports; regulated, litigated, and overgoverned at every level; abandoned in the inner cities; undermined by tightfisted taxpayer revolts; preached to by the proselytizers of character education, family values, and political correctness; weakened by teacher-bashing, administrative overload, and massive resource and racial inequalities; and continuously subjected to the moralistic rhetoric of local and national demagogues—public schooling seems moribund.[1] One author's analysis is entitled simply *Public Education: An Autopsy.*[2]

Public schooling, of course, is no stranger to conflict. Since its beginning as an effort to moral-ize diverse children in a common school, compulsory schooling has been an arena in which Americans have struggled to define a common culture and to inculcate it in young minds. In almost every generation, parents, educators, communities of belief, and special interest groups have participated in a struggle over public schooling. They have sought to advance their own vision of the future and to secure their own position in the present. Looking backward to a history of individualism weakly restrained by collective needs and forward to the specter of social fragmentation and individual isolation, Americans seem perpetually predisposed to look to reform of the common school as a means to help create cohesion and unity out of self-absorption and diversity.

A repeating cycle of struggles over cultural turf, community boundaries, and freedom of conscience has characterized American school reform. But to judge from the reform-advocating reports that have punctuated the public school discourse from Horace Mann's *Twelfth Annual Report of the Secretary of the Board* in 1849, to *A Nation at Risk* in 1983,[3] all this feuding has improved neither the quality of schooling nor the character of school children. Americans have not only tolerated the politicization of public schooling, they have reveled in it and sought its spoils.

The periodic intensity of these school struggles reflects a curious fact. Much of what goes on in school touches on the deepest and most sensitive aspects of a child's development and of a parent's hopes. Yet when we send our children off to public school each morning, we are giving a large part of their day over, not to a village,[4] but to an institution beholden to a political majority and administered by a governmental bureaucracy. This reality of life in public schooling accounts for much of the history of school conflict. In fact, the history of schooling can be read as a seismic record of the constantly shifting ideological terrain underlying the institutional effort to educate the young in a pluralistic democracy.

The histories have titles like *The Great School Wars, Schooled to Order, The One Best System, Conflict of Interests, Education as Cultural Imperialism.* They chronicle struggles between Protestants and Catholics; among Americans who trace their heritage to northern Europe, the Mediterranean, Latin America, North America, Asia, or Africa; between scientific reasoning and spiritual faith; between the needs of industry and the idiosyncracies of individuals; between a bewildering, exhilarating diversity and a sometimes oppressive nationalism; between entrenched racism and the struggle for equality.

Of late, things have gone from bad to worse. The past decade has witnessed an increase in the passionate intensity with which these conflicts are conducted. Individual families, who may want nothing more than to be active in their children's schooling, have sometimes found themselves drawn into organized and intolerant efforts to control the content of schooling for every family's children. At the same time, bureaucratic pressures have made teaching less individually oriented and less based on intellectual discipline. Teachers themselves have been required to behave more like bureaucratic agents or police officers than independent professionals and stewards of the intellectual and moral development of children.

In public schools, the individual "sphere of intellect and spirit," once so carefully guarded by the U.S. Supreme Court, has been compressed almost beyond recognition. One civic group after another attempts to impose its vision of good education, and all join in a struggle over the one true morality to be adopted by public schools. The outcomes of the conflicts over curriculum, texts, tests, and teachers seem less and less like constructive compromises that knit communities together; more and more they resemble blood feuds, ideological wars, episodes of selfishness wrapped in the rhetoric of rectitude.

As constitutional protections for freedom of intellect and spirit in the schools become weaker, polarization and divisiveness have begun to take the upper hand. There are short-term winners and losers among the combatants in the school wars; but in the long run, the schools seem ever less satisfactory to the public. Large and well-financed organizations have arisen which seek to impose their views upon the public schools, and the education establishment has spared no effort or expense to maintain its grip on the schools. Gaining political and cultural power seems to be both the means and the ends for some of the crusaders in the school wars. Their exaggerated, oversimplified, categorical claims produce a public debate characterized much more by hot-button political strife than by intelligence, insight, or reasoned discourse, and much of the public seems to be simply saddened by the repetitive spectacle of public schooling turned into an ideological battleground.

That such destructiveness should arise from school conflicts is hardly a surprise, though the recent intensity of the conflicts may be. Fifty years ago, in a landmark decision involving individual liberty and public schools, the U.S. Supreme Court warned that the temptation to use schooling as a cultural battleground could ultimately undermine not only individual conscience, but public education itself.[5] The majority opinion made it eloquently clear that as long as government determines the ideological content of compulsory education, destructive battles over schooling will continue. And so they have.

Half a century after this warning from the nation's constitutional guardian of personal liberty and democratic self-government, American public education is being restructured by federal mandate. But it is being restructured in a way that threatens even more imposition on individual conscience, promises even more unnecessary and destructive ideological conflict, and will produce even more difficulties for the development of communities of belief in a culture of diversity. The problems of American public education as currently organized and administered are nearly overwhelming. This is clear to nearly everyone.[6] But the *Goals 2000:* Educate America Act of 1994—fashioned by the Bush and Clinton administrations and passed with overwhelming bipartisan support in Congress—is a classic example of how government-mandated education reform can become its own worst enemy.

Goals 2000 uses the creation of national and state content standards for public schooling as a means to increase vastly the power of state and federal authorities over every significant aspect of public schooling, from the content of courses and student examinations to the certification of teachers and the approval of textbooks. *Goals 2000* is comprehensive, centralizing, and insensitive to the diversity of goals that students, families, and communities bring to education. Through the use of federal grants and state regulations, it aims to bring every school in every school district in every state into conformity with politically prescribed standards of what should be learned by every child.

Goals 2000 was crafted by people of skill and good will with praiseworthy hopes for the future of public education. The creation of national and state curriculum standards under *Goals 2000* was an attempt to revitalize public education, to improve its quality, and to reduce the harsh and self-perpetuating inequalities of opportunity that bedevil both schooling and society. But the Act's effects cannot match its supporters' intentions, and it threatens to escalate still further the ideological conflicts that are already tearing public education apart. *Goals 2000* is a wrongheaded miscalculation of gigantic proportions that will further undermine public confidence in public schooling.

Goals 2000 has so fundamentally reallocated power in American schooling that it might justly be labeled a re-constitution of schooling. This re-constitution has been brought about without the benefit of either a formal amendment to the U.S. Constitution or the informed consent of the American people. And it is broadly inconsistent with the principles of constitutional democracy. Because the entire *Goals 2000* reform effort is centered on augmenting governmental mechanisms for the control of school curriculum, the Act will ultimately undermine some of the nation's most important freedoms and needlessly turn Americans against each other. To put the matter more directly, *Goals 2000*, though generally benign in its intentions, has so magnified the already considerable problems of public schooling that it is creating a new problem: Can public education be saved from public schooling?

Goals 2000 is a symptom as well as a cause of the decline of public schooling. It is a symptom of a long-term and deeply disturbing trend in school reform, a trend that cannot be reversed merely by repealing some of *Goals 2000*'s provisions or by reverting to the already-failed practice of local control of public schools. *Goals 2000* reflects an increasing public and professional willingness to let government rather than teachers and families determine the content and direction of education. This trend, and its consequences for conscience and community, threatens to set American public education on a short route to chaos.

Conscience and Community

The recent intensification of the school wars has been especially disheartening because schooling is one of the few face-to-face, participatory institutions in the society available to create the compromises of behavior and belief necessary to sustain community life. Schooling is a crucible out of which community cohesion may be formed and strengthened, or melted down and made useless. When voluntary compromise and reorientation come out of these struggles, community cohesion is strengthened, as is the quality of education taking place within that community. But sometimes an individual's conscience or a minority's deeply held beliefs prevent compromise. If such dissenters are nevertheless forced to accept the majority's will, polarization increases, community cohesion is weakened, and another round of the zero-sum conflict predicted by the Supreme Court becomes inevitable. The difference between the two contradictory outcomes is determined by the conditions under which schools operate and are governed.[7]

The importance of public schooling as an arena for generating a spirit of community essential in an individualist democracy has been powerfully stated by Benjamin Barber in *An Aristocracy of Everyone:*

> While society can cajole and hint and guide and suggest, the greater part of what transpires in the minds and hearts of the young is beyond it. This makes formal schooling, however inadequate, our sole *public* resource: the only

place where, as a collective, self-conscious public pursuing common goods, we try to shape our children to live in a democratic world. Can we afford to privatize *the only public institutions we possess?*[8]

We do need these public institutions to serve these public purposes. We need them desperately. But suppose that public schooling has been structured and governed in a way that makes attaining these public purposes harder rather than easier, and that *Goals 2000* exaggerates this problem still further. Suppose that Barber's goal of pursuing the common good is the right one, especially in a culturally diverse and pluralistic society; but suppose that our national experience tells us that we cannot attain the common good unless we deny government at every level the power to use public schooling to manipulate private conscience.

Suppose further that unless everyone is guaranteed freedom of choice in regard to the most fundamental aspects of schooling, the pubic school will continue to be more a source of conflict than a means to create community. And suppose that real community building must be voluntary—that coercion yields only conformity, disaffection, or at its most extreme, rebellion. Would we not then have to revise Barber's question so that it became, "Can we afford to politicize the truly private aspects of education—to give governments control over the development of spirit and intellect—if we expect to preserve *the only public institutions we possess?*"

The vast inequalities that characterize American public education further aggravate the difficulty of preserving common schools as the primary public institutions available for enhancing the sense of community. By failing to end inequality of educational opportunity, we have victimized the large number of children who live in poverty as well as the current racial and ethnic minorities who, within two generations, will constitute a majority of Americans.

To make matters worse, the current structure of schooling—which will be still further centralized as *Goals 2000* takes hold in the states— virtually limits the constitutionally protected right of school choice to the relatively affluent. Public schooling thus undermines and ignores the voluntary nature of community-building and leaves in place for most Americans only the corrosive effect that coercion has on the willingness of a diverse people to make the difficult compromises necessary to build a common life.

So although we may wish to use public schooling to define and sustain community, we may actually be creating a system of schools so overloaded with unnecessary conflict that it weakens both community and education. What the school wars tell us is that somehow we have been transforming a vital instrument for creating cohesion into a source of division and hostility; that there is something built into the structure of public schooling that undermines one of its most important functions.

The apparently endless school wars are also disheartening because among their most prominent casualties has been freedom of conscience in education—the individual liberty to follow an internal moral compass in setting a course for a meaningful and fulfilling life. As so many of the conflicts over the content of public schools demonstrate, a school system dominated by political majorities, operated by governmental bureaucracies, and vastly unequal in resources and in freedom of choice, cannot help being hostile to individual conscience.

The politicization of schooling that America has experienced pushes conscience to the margin. It teaches students, teachers, and communities the corrosive lesson that obedience to power is more important than being true to oneself. It demands that any family committed to acting on conscience for one child's schooling convince the majority of an entire school district to apply the same beliefs to all children. In the school wars tolerance is the exception, conformity is the rule, and conscience is usually dismissed as an administrative inconvenience, an attempt at polarizing the school, or a luxury unnecessary in the lives of common persons.

A school conflict may begin as an act of individual conscience, but it often becomes an ideological crusade. As a result, simple-minded slogans of intolerance and distrust make reasoned discourse difficult and threaten to crowd out the reflection and self-knowledge on which the survival of individual conscience depends. As these ideological battles heat up, some combatants in the school wars—sensing the ease with which public schooling can be politicized—exploit claims of conscience in an attempt to make whole school systems over in their own image. Others, realizing that it is power blocs and not individuals who are accommodated, join the crusade out of self-defense.

Ironically, families who insist on acting on their own deep beliefs in matters of schooling are frequently belittled, resisted as self-centered trouble makers, or dismissed as ideologically driven power grabbers. Attempts by teachers or students to deal with issues of character and conscience in school are often cut down in a crossfire of competing demands, if they are not first drowned in a sea of vague platitudes. Almost everyone understands the message implicit in a politically manipulated, bureaucratically operated, and grossly unequal system of schools—that most dissenters have no escape from the majority, and that private conscience is out of place in public schooling. Under *Goals 2000*, the cycle of turning individual acts of conscience into unnecessary, destructive, full-scale, ideological school wars will be magnified and extended.

Conscience may seem a mysterious, indefinable, and overly broad term to use in connection with school conflict. After all, conscience has been referred to as the rule of divine power, as an innate and universal sense of right and wrong, and as the foundation of upright character in the individual. It has been understood as inherited from culture, derived from individual experience, or produced when the idiosyncratic morals of individual parents are internalized in the superegos of their children. In a world characterized at once by cultural relativism and moral absolutism, there have been arguments about whether conscience is subjective, universal, or culturally specific, about whether conscience is necessarily related to religious belief or can be an integral part of the lives of nonreligious persons and secular societies. As institutions—including schooling—become more impersonal, bureaucratic, and inflexible, the contest between power and conscience has included disagreement over whether conscience is the ultimate expression of selfishness, the motive for selfless sacrifice, or an invitation to anarchy.

This book makes no attempt to sort out and discriminate among different understandings of conscience.[9] It does note, however, that much of what happens in school touches upon the development and expression of conscience, that many people involved in school conflicts see their concerns as rooted in conscience, and that in schooling freedom of conscience, however defined, is an American birthright. This book suggests that in public schooling as in other realms of life, Thomas More's prescription holds true. Conscience is that small but vital part of the self that ought to remain beyond the reach of *any* government.

In spite of all the debates, disagreements, and struggles that have surrounded the exercise of conscience, the centrality of conscience to the structure of a democratic society is also undeniable: democracy in America is based upon deeply held beliefs about the role of individual conscience in a system of self-government. The freedom of individual intellect and spirit at the core of conscience is central to achieving a just consent of the governed. It is the cornerstone of a political system based on popular sovereignty. It secures the sanctity of the individual person against the power of the state. It is the most reliable protection against majority rule becoming a tyranny of the majority. And it is an essential condition for sustaining community life in a constitutional democracy.

Repetitive and usually unnecessary conflict over issues of conscience in schooling has weakened public education and threatens to destroy it altogether. If public education is to be preserved, the level of conflict over conscience must be reduced; and what conflict remains must take place under conditions designed to foster compromise and resolution rather than divisiveness and ideological warfare. If public education is to be *worthy* of being preserved, neither our ability to redefine and maintain our diverse communities, nor our commitment to preserve the freedom of conscience essential to meaningful individual lives in these communities, can be sacrificed on the altar of government-driven educational reform.

A central purpose of this book is to expose the dissonance between the principles of constitutional democracy and the structure of American schooling. This dissonance has been evident and increasingly destructive under the regime of local control. It will be made still more destructive under *Goals 2000*, which, by trivializing conscience and undermining community, sets the nation on a short route to chaos.

I conclude that another path and a different destination for school reform must be found. This destination—more appropriate for a pluralistic society—recognizes that the most valuable education is based upon goals generated not by governments, but by individual learners and teachers and by the families and communities of which they are a part. This alternative path is already partly mapped out. Its signposts are the fundamental principles of constitutional democracy which inform our most valued liberties and protect the process of democratic self-government from excessive concentrations of power.

The early tone of this book may seem harsh, as befits a wake-up call for what a friend and colleague has called the "moral general audience." But in the end this is a search for common ground and common sense. It is undertaken with respect for those whose personal and professional labor is aimed at improving schooling at any level. But it is also undertaken with an understanding of how deeply schooling conflicts have polarized an already divided, troubled, and angry public. It tries to take into account how many voices are calling for abandoning a national commitment to children, for giving up on the ideal of universal public education, and for ignoring the long-term needs of a democracy based on the equal moral worth of all persons.

The usefulness of trying to identify common ground lies only in its potential for redirecting the public debate over schooling. There is no prepackaged school reform program or trendy political platform here. There is, however, a suggestion that the common sense of a diverse nation is still capable of creating an education system that benefits all Americans.

In writing this book I have tried to keep in mind President George Washington's admonition that "the basis of our political system is the right of the people to make and alter their constitutions of government." I take it that this right extends to the constitution of public schooling, an institution on which we annually spend in excess of a quarter of a trillion dollars. It is therefore my intention to suggest how the American people themselves—not limited by the current views of their political representatives, education experts, and constitutional courts, and quite apart from "politics as usual"—may achieve a reconstitution [10] of schooling adequate to strengthen both conscience and community in public education.

Chapter 1, "Education Headline News," sketches several of the local, state, and national conflicts over public schooling that grabbed headlines during 1993 and 1994, while Congress was considering and adopting *Goals 2000.* That was a time when the lessons taught by repetitive school conflicts should have had an impact on policymakers. The brief retelling of these stories is meant to anchor the reader in the complex mix of issues of conscience and community that fuels the school wars. I do not draw specific lessons from specific stories, but rather try to find, later in the book, more general understandings of the nature and significance of the many school conflicts that have bedeviled public schooling historically and that are likely to increase as *Goals 2000* takes hold in the states.

The headlines and the substance of these stories paint an unpleasant picture, one that is unflattering to most of the combatants as well as to the school structure that seems to make such continuing conflict inevitable. This is part of the message—that ideological and politicized conflict over the content of schooling brings out the worst in us, just as it undermines our most fundamental freedoms and one of our most important institutions.

But this is not a complete picture. Most of the individual families, teachers, and other educators involved in school conflicts come to them with the best intentions and the most sincerely held beliefs. They seek to educate the children in their charge and to play by the rules of public schools. Yet they and their goals are transformed, distorted, and made destructive by school systems that require majority approval for the exercise of individual freedoms.

A family's heritage, hopes, and expectations as well as its most basic beliefs and most tentative explorations are inevitably affected by the socialization process that takes place in every school. It has been said that "education in its fullest sense is inescapably a moral enterprise."[11] And so it is. Every parent and every teacher knows by heart that there is more to schooling than multiplication tables, social studies homework, standardized science tests, and the acquisition of job skills. There is child rearing, with all the intensely personal issues of belief that inform it. When these matters of individual conscience and moral concern become the involuntary stuff of government-centered politics, the results can be catastrophic.

There are, then, two accurate and interrelated pictures that can be painted of school conflict. One, seen from the inside, shows dissenting families, hard-working teachers, and individual schools struggling honorably and well to preserve or create their own vision of "the moral enterprise" of schooling. A second sees the conflicts from the outside and shows how even the most honorable purposes can be twisted, exploited, and turned into cannon fodder for school wars whose aims have more to do with political power and cultural sway than with quality education and individual aspirations.

I have written elsewhere, and I hope empathically, about the inside view of school conflict. In *Compelling Belief: The Culture of American Schooling*, I sought to display school conflict as seen by dissenting families, by home schoolers, teachers, religious and independent schools, and minority communities. I spent many hours with these people and came to view them as representing the best hope for reinvigorating individual liberty and community responsibility in education. I still believe that to be true. The evidence still supports that belief. But I also believe that the evidence for an unflattering, unpleasant, outside view of school conflict—and of its broad social destructiveness—is real. It is that view on which I focus here.

There is therefore something to offend almost everyone in chapter 1. Those who populated *Compelling Belief* are still present, but in the background, their deepest educational concerns overwhelmed by the increasing politicization of schooling. In the foreground are the many organizations and self-styled leaders who have been exploiting school conflict and the weaknesses in school structure. There are also the reluctant servants of a hidebound establishment protecting the status quo for its own purposes, and the proliferating experts and policy wonks whose good intentions help pave the road to chaos.

Chapter 2, "School Wars: The Education Empire Strikes Back," focuses on two of the most powerful combatants in the school wars, the Education Empire and the Christian Right. It attempts to show some of the forces and self-interest that led to the adoption of *Goals 2000*, and some of the conflict and opportunism that have been unleashed by this re-constitution of American schooling. Chapter 2 completes the picture of American schooling's undermining itself and tearing communities apart in an attempt to use the power of government to establish an official knowledge and an official morality for all children. It is an ugly and painful picture of what our public schools are becoming. But it is one we ignore at our own peril.

Chapter 3 introduces the content and structure of the *Goals 2000* legislation, the ultimate escalation of the school wars. The detail of how this legislation is structured is provided in spite of the fact that the law may be further amended or even repealed. This is done for three reasons: First, *Goals 2000* is in place and has already yielded a set of proposed national content standards, numerous organizations with a stake in establishing these standards, and the agreement of at least forty-six of fifty states to participate in the *Goals 2000* re-constitution of schooling. There is enormous momentum here.

Second, *Goals 2000* is a model, a template for each state's school reform efforts. It is a well-developed example of how governments at any level can gain, and are gaining, control of virtually every aspect of education without regard to individual learners, teachers, families, and communities. Were the federal law to be repealed tomorrow, so much has already been committed to this comprehensive, government-centered model of schooling that the repeal would have very little effect in the states.

Third, *Goals 2000* is the result, as well as the cause, of a fundamental shift in thinking about the nature of schooling in the United States. To understand the consequences of increasing the power of government over the education of individuals, the details of the current form of this wrongheaded thinking need to be understood. *Goals 2000* stands for something more destructive than it is by itself. To understand the underlying problem it is necessary to analyze its latest legislative manifestation.

Chapter 4, "Renouncing Our Constitutional Heritage," uses basic principles of constitutional democracy in the United States to analyze *Goals 2000.* These broad principles are evoked by discussing one of the Supreme Court's most significant and eloquent school decisions, *West Virginia v. Barnette.* The intent is not to suggest that *Goals 2000* violates the Constitution or to make a lawyer's argument that litigation could be used to correct any of the statute's myriad flaws. But *Barnette* is a powerful and concise constitutional discussion of the relationship among public schooling, private conscience, and the importance of community cohesion. Retelling that story helps to make constitutional thinking, as it applies to schooling at least, accessible to everyone. And using law in this way helps author as well as reader to adhere to the old adage, "law is too important to be left to lawyers."

Chapter 5, "The Legacy of Local Control," also uses the stories of major Supreme Court cases to help make constitutional principles a part of the public discourse about schooling. And like chapter 4, chapter 5 does not offer a discussion of the niceties of current constitutional law or suggest that new legal theories or more enlightened court decisions could make public schooling consistent with the principles of constitutional democracy. Quite the contrary. By the end of chapter 5 it begins to appear that the Constitution as presently written is incapable of dealing effectively with the problems of conscience and community inherent in a school system run by governments at *any* level.

The most vocal and well-organized opposition to *Goals 2000* has thus far come from the advocates of local control of schooling. But it is local control that has given us our current moribund public school system. Far from being a constructive alternative to *Goals 2000,* local control of schooling has been responsible for the some of the worst failures of public schooling—from racial segregation and massive resource inequalities to restrictions on the freedom of inquiry, the professionalism of teachers, and the liberty of families.

The debate between local control and *Goals 2000*, then, is like an argument about whether it is better to stand on the frying pan or in the fire. One alternative may be marginally better than the other, but both are unbearable for the same reason. To escape this pointless debate and pursue a more productive approach, it is necessary to understand what *Goals 2000* and local control have in common. Chapter 5 suggests that although *Goals 2000* intensifies many of the problems and conflicts in public schooling, it makes no sense whatsoever to respond to *Goals 2000* by urging a return to local control.

Chapter 6, "Conscience and Community," argues that the freedom of individual conscience and the importance of building cohesive communities are not mutually exclusive, but mutually dependent. Conventional wisdom and conventional politics have made these two principles into opponents, as if we could have one but not the other. But the dichotomy is artificial; and we must have both, or we shall have neither. Alexis de Tocqueville's extraordinary book, *Democracy in America*, provides guidance in reaching this conclusion.

The mutual dependence of conscience and community is a reality in schooling as it is elsewhere. Once this principle is considered, it becomes possible to imagine conditions under which schooling could enhance both conscience and community. Chapter 6 discusses these conditions along with their origin in the principles of constitutional democracy.

In Chapter 7, the simultaneous pursuit of conscience and community becomes the basis for conceiving a "Re-Constitution of American Schooling" to replace that adopted in *Goals 2000*. It is argued that ordinary citizens have the ability and the right to seize this constitutional moment in American education; that it is an opportunity to secure, equally and for everyone, both the freedom of conscience and the benefits of community in public education; that it is still possible to save public education from public schooling.

CHAPTER ONE

Education
Headline News

During the time when the 103rd Congress of the United States considered and adopted the Bush/Clinton Goals 2000 school reform plan, the following battles in the ongoing school wars made headlines.

Lake County, Florida, northwest of the bland and profitable fantasies of Disney World, was fertile ground for orange growing until the big freeze of the mid-1980s. Now it is a site where real estate developers try to squeeze profits from the construction of the American dream and where special interest groups used 1994 to sharpen their strategies in the battle for local control of American memory.

No skirmish in our endlessly seamy and seemingly endless school wars presents such a spectacle of superficial citizenship as that of the state and local governments of Florida going at each other over the official history of American culture. Reflecting on the ongoing struggle in Lake County and the national attention it received, one resident complained, "It's bad enough we're the laughingstock of Florida; now we're the laughingstock of the nation."[1] But there isn't much to laugh about.

This is a sad story, really, and too similar to scores of more sophisticated struggles to be dismissed as an attempt by uneducated conservatives to turn the clock back a hundred years. Like so many other conflicts over official history or science or culture in the schools, Lake County's has proceeded by seeding cynicism in young minds and polluting the public discourse. Its currency has been simplistic symbols, distorted by partisan passions and overly inflated by media hype. Headlines:

BOARD DEMANDS SCHOOLS TEACH AMERICAN SUPERIORITY
Associated Press/AP World stream, May 26, 1994

SUPERIOR-CULTURE POLICY TERMED A "DANGEROUS TREND"
St. Petersburg Times, June 3, 1994

On May 10, 1994, the Lake County School Board, bedrock of local control in a county of 165,000 residents, 23,000 public school pupils, and 1,400 teachers, passed a motion that declared with the force of law that American culture is superior to all other cultures, historically and in the modern world:

> In compliance with state law, the District School Board shall provide in-service training, media and instructional materials that explain and teach about other cultures. This instruction shall also include and instill in our students an appreciation of our American heritage and culture such as: our republican form of government, capitalism, a free enterprise system, patriotism, strong family values, freedom of religion and other basic values that are superior to other foreign or historic cultures.[2]

Up until this time, the reigning government policy controlling the content of what teachers teach and students learn about American culture in Florida's public schools had been determined by state law. In 1992, Florida Statutes, Chapter 92–100 had sought to foster multicultural education for a multicultural state by amending a number of state education statutes and declaring the intent of the legislative majority to be that "students are to develop an understanding, respect, and appreciation for the history, culture, and contributions of other groups, and eliminate personal and national ethnocentrism so they understand that a specific culture is not intrinsically superior or inferior to another."[3]

The local school board's 1994 prescription for teaching the true meaning of American culture and world history was in conflict with the state government's 1992 regulation; and the battle was joined.

BATTLE OVER PATRIOTISM CURRICULUM
New York Times, May 15, 1994

The author of the policy, chair of the county school board, defended local—but not state—restrictions on the intellectual freedom of teachers and students: "I don't need to visit other countries to know that

America is the best country in the world. Thousands of people risk life and limb every day to come to America because they know this is the land of the free."[4] But the freedom of thought and belief for which so many thousands risked their lives was not part of the local board's position about the one true meaning of American history. Nor was it part of the board's strategy for attempting to wrest control of *Official Knowledge* from the state.[5]

Another member of the 3–2 majority by which the school board had thumbed its nose at the state's multicultural education law also publicly defended her vote for the Americanism policy: "We need to reinforce that we should be teaching America first," otherwise young people who "felt our land was inferior or equal to others, would have no motivation to go to war and defend our country."[6]

CULTURE CLASH DIVIDES FLORIDA COUNTY
USA Today, May 18, 1994

The cultural concerns of Lake County's conservative Christian coalition on the school board were quickly and accurately interpreted by a trio of eighth grade history students, one of whom could "understand them wanting to teach us that the country is superior so that the country won't fall apart." Another "would go along with it just to make the grade in class." And a third student, who spoke as if he had been reading the history his elders apparently ignored, reasoned that, "Hitler taught the Nazis they are superior and you see what happened."[7]

Teachers, of course, were caught in this cultural cross fire. The state of Florida required them to propound one official truth about America while the Lake County School Board insisted on another, contradictory truth. One history instructor was "worried about how we can be factual and objective and still get the board's point across." Coming to the rescue of teachers was their union, the Florida Education Association/United (FEA/U), which filed suit on May 24, 1994, against the Lake County School Board. The union claimed on behalf of plaintiff teachers, parents, and students that the local ordinance violated the First Amendment rights of teachers and students, the Florida Code of Ethics for teachers, and the state multicultural education law of 1992. Though the suit vigorously attacked local restrictions on the freedom to teach and to learn, it unaccountably contained no challenge to the equally restrictive means employed by the state to enforce its multicultural curriculum.[8] The confusion deepened.

The Florida commissioner of education sought to find in this confusion a vagueness that would permit compromise, but to no avail. Three weeks after the filing of the teachers' suit, the commissioner wrote to the Lake County School Board urging them to "modify the language that references the teaching of American heritage and culture as superior to other foreign or historic cultures."[9] After explaining that the greatness of American culture lies in the fact that it "is truly representative of the world's cultures," the commissioner sought to convince the chair of the Lake County Board that the belief in cultural superiority could be imposed by means other than the disputed cultural superiority policy.

He pointed out that state law authorizes local boards to "require patriotic programs" and that the daily pledge of allegiance is "required to be said . . . in our schools."[10] The state's highest education officer thus attempted to fashion a compromise in which the proponents of multicultural education would have their view imposed by one law and the proponents of Americanism would have their view enforced by another. Presumably neither side would have to confront the contradiction between the two laws, and only students and teachers would remain conflicted about which truth the government required them to adopt.

The local board would have none of it. Perhaps it seemed to these Christian fundamentalists that the compromise suggested to them was akin to the compromise between Genesis and Darwinian evolution proffered to their forebears in the 1920s—a perfectly practical way to avoid a symbolic battle which they were eager to fight for ideological reasons.

Some outside observers thought that they saw right to the heart of this apparently unresolvable conflict. The Lake County policy is "close to racism," said one Florida professor. Another lauded the state multicultural education law that the local policy was meant to defy and stressed the need to "level the playing field between the oppressors and the oppressed." Arguments about who had been oppressing whom then, and about who was indoctrinating whom now, began to get heated. But it wasn't the freedom to teach or to learn that the good people of Florida wanted to argue; it was the official history of the United States. All the disputants paraded their loyalty and touted their patriotism, but there was very little agreement on the nature of the nation to which that loyalty and patriotism applied.

LOVE IT OR HATE IT SCHOOL POLICY COMMANDS ATTENTION
Orlando Sentinel, May 22, 1994

Tempers got short. A member of the Lake County School Board, who had voted against the cultural superiority policy, attacked the board's majority: "These are people with no experience and no education . . . who want to wrap the Bible and the flag around themselves, who don't believe in public education and are trying to undermine the system."[11] The Board's attorney argued that multicultural education deprived students of "important political and societal values . . . central . . . in shaping American culture." He claimed that fears concerning the seeds of prejudice being planted in young minds or the suppression of certain ideas when teaching history were "imagined fears . . . hypothetical . . . totally unfounded from a simple reading of the policy in question."[12] An attorney for the teachers' union, who attended a number of the board's public meetings, observed later that, "it was clear that the Board held the public in contempt. . . . It was a holy war. . . . Reasoned discourse and discussion were not on this Board's agenda."[13]

The suit by the teachers' union only managed to confuse things further, for it claimed both that teachers had the right to teach unimpeded by official government pronouncements about truth and that the state legislature's pronouncement of truth was superior to the local board's. The circuit court judges of Lake County were not eager to sort out this mess. Each of the three elected judges who could have been assigned to the case recused himself on the grounds that he had children in the Lake County public schools. Their actions were an indicator of how nervous even the most judicious person can become about getting caught on the wrong side of a battle between ideological crusaders. Though a judge from a neighboring county was assigned to hear the case, the matter never came to trial.

In September 1994, a new front opened in the Florida battle for local control of national history. A slate of Lake County School Board candidates committed to repeal of the "Americanism" policy sought and received substantial support and assistance from the Florida Education Association/United, the teachers' union that had filed the suit against Lake County's version of political correctness. Each of FEA/U's candidates was successful in the primary election, with the result that after election day in November the dominance of the Christian coalition on the board was ended. In December the newly elected majority took the first steps to rescind the disputed policy. By mid-January 1995, the shift in policy was finalized, and the state's version of political correctness was all that remained. The FEA/U, which had filed a motion holding the litigation against Lake County in abeyance while elections were pending, then withdrew its suit.

The political battle to determine the official truth of American history and to impose it on the public school students and teachers of Lake County was fought on five fronts—in the Florida state legislature, in the state Department of Education, in the public meetings of the local school board, in the circuit court in and for Lake County, and in a 1994 election campaign that will not be remembered for its civility or common sense.

It is hard to say who won. One politician's family values are another's political correctness; and teachers have merely traded in one political supervisor for another. But it's easy to see that whichever group of ideological crusaders wins a battle like this, what is lost is of far greater magnitude than what is won. The public loses respect for its school leaders and for the political process in general. Neighbors become enemies, and, as they do, communities begin to come apart. Freedom of intellect and belief—the liberty of students, teachers, and families to explore their individual versions of truth, meaning, and useful education—are tarnished by the corrosive struggle for power over school curriculum. Public school politics becomes, not a laughing matter, but a laughingstock with tragic consequences.

"POLITICALLY INCORRECT" WHITE MALES OUSTED FROM HISTORY GUIDELINES   *Chicago Tribune,* October 26, 1994

PANEL UNVEILS STANDARDS FOR HISTORY RELEASE COMES AMID OUTCRIES OF IMBALANCE
Education Week, November 2, 1994

UP IN ARMS ABOUT THE "AMERICAN EXPERIENCE" HISTORY CURRICULUM GUIDELINES PLAY DOWN TRADITIONAL HEROES AND FOCUS ON NEGATIVES, CRITICS SAY
Washington Post, October 28, 1994

When the ground of political struggle over the official truth of American history shifted in 1994 from local control to national standards, the story was sadly the same. The players generally wear suits, and some have graduate degrees or have held high office, but, otherwise, differences between the Lake County crusades and the fight over federal certification of national school standards in history are hard to find.

When Lynne Cheney read the national history standards proposed for adoption by the federal government pursuant to the Bush/Clinton[14] *Goals 2000: Educate America Act* of 1994, she felt "flimflammed."[15] Cheney had been chair of the National Endowment for the Humanities (NEH) during the Bush administration. In 1992 she signed a grant for more than half a million dollars for a group at the University of California at Los Angeles, the National Center for History in the Schools, to define what every K-12 student in the nation should know about American history.[16] Apparently Cheney felt swindled because it didn't appear that her own version of American history would ultimately be imposed on the nation's teachers and students. In a *Wall Street Journal* article entitled "The End of History," she vowed to undertake the "formidable task" of trying to prevent the work of the National Center for History in the Schools from being certified as official knowledge by the National Education Standards Improvement Council (NESIC), an arm of the federal government created by the *Goals 2000* legislation.[17]

The Cheney crusade became serious in a hurry. In December 1994, it was reported that the Reader's Digest Association would fund an alternative standards panel that would review and critique any proposed national education content standards. Cheney seemed to be trying to create a kind of conservative shadow government to do battle with the education establishment over certification of an official history of the United States.[18] Even if national certification of content standards were abandoned, Cheney's private certification panel and others like it could operate as the private certifiers of Americanism, as had been done in the 1950s in the entertainment industry, when only politically approved thoughts and expressions could survive in public.[19]

Putting the nation's colleges and universities in her sights along with its elementary and secondary schools, Cheney's *Wall Street Journal* article advised those who would join her crusade that they would have to "go up against an academic establishment that revels in . . . politicized history. . . ." With the fury of an ideologue scorned, she wrote, "We are a better people than the National Standards indicate," and she warned that, unless her crusade were victorious in the battle for defining American history, "much that is significant in our past will begin to disappear from our schools."[20] She later added, "and then from our minds, and from our knowledge, and from our hearts."[21] Lynne

Cheney, the Bush administration, and their ultraconservative backers had not gotten what they paid for. Rush Limbaugh agreed, saying that the proposed national history standards should be "flushed down the toilet."[22]

The drafters of the U.S. history standards, who had already heard and presumably taken account of the historical interpretations of many scholars, teachers, business people, and interest groups, were prepared to fight back. Cheney's *Wall Street Journal* article acted like blood in the water, and the media feeding frenzy made the conflict front-page news for weeks. The resulting fight was hardly America's finest hour.

Gary Nash, noted UCLA historian and codirector of the American History Standards Project, called Cheney "a bean counter." "She wants to see how many beans Harriet Tubman has, and who has got no beans. There are an infinite number of beans."[23] Because "counting how many times different subjects are mentioned in the document yields telling results," Cheney's *Wall Street Journal* article included one graph indicating that whereas the history standards mentioned Harriet Tubman six times, they mentioned Ulysses S. Grant only once, and that while the KKK received seventeen mentions, Thomas Alva Edison did not receive even one official nod. The tone used by the writers of the standards did not please their benefactor either:

> The authors tend to save their unqualified admiration for people, places, and events that are politically correct. . . . To understand West Africa, students are encouraged to "analyze the achievements and grandeur of Mansa Musa's court, and the social customs and wealth of the Kingdom of Mali". . . . When the subject of John D. Rockefeller comes up, students are instructed to conduct a trial in which he is accused of "knowingly and willfully participat[ing] in unethical and amoral business practices designed to undermine traditions of fair and open competition for personal and private aggrandizement in direct violation of the common welfare."[24]

Nash, who argued that the standards should "bury rote learning and the emphasis on dates, facts, places, events and one damn thing after another . . .," pressed his bean counter attack:

> Every kid who went to Washington on spring break went to the Library of Congress and saw that inscription, "History is the biography of great men." Isn't that a very disabling notion in a democracy where we believe that active, knowledgeable, engaged citizens hold the fate of the republic in their hands?[25]

But Cheney stuck to her beans. "People like Daniel Webster and Thomas Edison don't appear at all. . . . The problem is they are politically incorrect white males."[26] Cheney found support in an op-ed article in the *Atlanta Constitution,* which replied to Nash's labeling of the standards as a "new American revolution in history," by observing, "This is not a revolution. American students stopped memorizing facts a long time ago; that's why they don't know when the Civil War occurred."[27]

And on and on it went. Nash called traditional teaching of American history in the schools a "mental prison." An editorial in the *Minneapolis Star Tribune* accused Cheney of employing "a nitpicking focus on whiffs of political correctness."[28] Cheney complained that the standards and accompanying material asked whether it was fair for Tip O'Neill to have characterized President Reagan, who had appointed Cheney head of the NEH in 1986, as "a cheerleader for selfishness." Nash argued for his group's version of official American history by saying, "The discussions are healthy and should go on, but we can't expect complete agreement. This is a country where I hope we have no official history." Cheney claimed that "students learning history according to these standards would have a very warped view of our past."[29] Nash argued for "open inquiry about history" and for "teachers and students to search out history for themselves." Cheney replied, "It's a very nice bunch of rhetoric. . . ."[30] Cheney and Nash appeared on the "MacNeil/Lehrer News Hour" on October 26, 1994, and by show's end were arguing with each other like a couple of schoolyard bullies vying for control of their weaker classmates.

The analogy isn't far from the truth. A letter to the editors of *Education Week* observed that "most of the debate about the content of the new history standards has to do with politics, not history." Quoting Thurman Arnold, the letter writer argued, "Men do not actually search history to avoid the mistakes of the past. They seek convenient analogies to show the dangers in failing to adopt the creed which they advocate."[31]

Cheney and Nash, the ultraconservatives and the education establishment, the Lake County School Board and the Florida Education Association—none were trying to avoid the mistakes of the past. But neither were they merely seeking convenient analogies to justify their creeds. They were instead arguing over which interpretation of America's past struggles—and what understanding of its present culture— local, state, and national governments should impose on school-age citizens. Even the thoughtful and well-informed participants in these otherwise raucous disinformation debates were caught in the spiral of incivility created whenever governments are empowered to try to control intellect and belief in the schools.

SOLID MATERIAL INTERWOVEN WITH POLITICAL BIAS
Education Week, December 7, 1994

In an article appearing in *Education Week* just a month before her book on national standards was to be published, historian Diane Ravitch gave a balanced but conservative critique of the U.S. history standards. Ravitch had been an official in the Bush administration's Department of Education and had signed a $1.6 million grant to the same UCLA group funded by Lynne Cheney's NEH. In her 1994 article Ravitch wrote that the standards "must be credited with some genuine accomplishments," including "intellectually challenging" content, a "well-conceived" set of illustrative activities, and the achievement of "successfully incorporat[ing] the experiences of African Americans, Native Americans, women, and others who used to have minimal roles in older historical accounts." But she lamented that the standards' "implicit theme seems to be the ongoing (and usually unsuccessful) struggle by the oppressed to wrest rights and power from selfish white male Protestants . . . [while] democratic ideals seem to be a hollow facade, like storefronts in a Hollywood western, [and] . . . greed, racism, and corruption appear to be the real commonalities of American history."[32]

Toward the end of her commentary on the history standards, Ravitch fell into the trap that awaits anyone who engages in the struggle over political specification of knowledge in schooling. Citing John Stuart Mill's comment that "all attempts by the State to bias the conclusions of its citizens on disputed subjects are evil," and writing herself that "historical accuracy emerges from study, inquiry, and evidence, not from voting, log-rolling, and negotiating," Ravitch nonetheless urged that the federal government—with all its voting, log-rolling, and negotiating—adopt parts of the standards but reject others.[33]

The Ravitch article contends that common ground about some topics can be achieved and argues that such current consensus ought to be certified by government agencies. Yet her argument takes no account of how easily common ground can shift in intellectual as well as political matters, and it ignores entirely the polarizing conflicts that arise, as

Mill intimated and history demonstrates, whenever politics is used to certify even some intellectual matters.

Ravitch argued for fairness in presenting different interpretations of history wherever consensus is absent. But she seemed oblivious to the fact that in any issue as perpetually political as public schooling has become, there is no agreement about where consensus ends and controversy begins. Dissent and destruction can always be manufactured—as they were in Lake County—by those whose power lies in using conflict over school content "to show the dangers of failing to adopt the creed which they advocate." Ravitch argued that government should adopt only those standards favored by the vast majority of scholars and citizens. In a conclusion that would have more appropriately capped a call for government to abandon altogether the attempt to impose standards on schools, she wrote: "As we define our history, we define ourselves. Because history matters so much, we must take care not to make some interpretations of the past 'official knowledge', while shunning conflicting views."[34]

But in *Goals 2000*, as in Lake County, Florida, politics was already moving to control knowledge.[35] If there was any doubt that government control of curriculum had become a significant means by which ideologues seek political and cultural power, it was dispelled in early January 1995. The U.S. Senate voted 99 to 1 to condemn the proposed history standards because they presented America in an unflattering light and belittled Western civilization.[36] It was a spectacle worthy of Orwell's *1984*, of Swift's *Gulliver's Travels*, or of contemporary Japan's Ministry of Education.[37]

By the end of 1994 it was becoming less clear whether the standardization of schooling that had been supported by the Bush administration, the nation's governors, and the Clinton administration could be used by conservatives as a tool to wrest control of public schooling from the education establishment or would be a means for that establishment to resist the conservative tide sweeping many local school boards. When the education establishment seemed to have temporarily gained control of curriculum standards under *Goals 2000*, conservatives attacked the idea of national standards and sought to replace them with standards created by the states and local districts—levels of government in which conservatives may have believed that they could exercise more influence.

In an article in *National Review* entitled "Local Options," two Republican former secretaries of education joined a conservative Republican senator in calling the *Goals 2000* National Education Standards and Improvement Council (NESIC) "a national school board." The authors argued that " 'the national school board' should be canned, and local control should be restored."[38] The battle over official history among national politicians in the mid-1990s became merely a contest over which level of government would be empowered to try to manipulate the work of teachers, the learning of students, and the aspirations of families. But it was becoming clear that—whether at the federal, state, or local level—government control of public schools creates the incentive to make ideological warfare a recurrent part of education policy.

The debate over historical correctness raged on during and after the time that the 103rd Congress was considering whether to adopt *Goals 2000*. But as the federal government began the process of raising local and state school conflicts to the national level, those conflicts were themselves bearing witness to the cost of intervention in school content by government at *any* level.

REMOVAL OF LITERARY WORKS FROM CALIFORNIA TEST STIRS FLAP
Education Week, March 9, 1994

CENSORSHIP FIGHT OVER SCHOOL TESTS ESCALATES
Los Angeles Times, April 3, 1994

During one of the scores of fights in 1994[39] for the ideological upper hand in California schools, a California school administrator remarked that "tests drive curriculum. By changing the test, that is one of the surest ways to change what goes on in the classroom."[40] She knew that the same politics of divisiveness and power-seeking that characterizes local, state, and national battles over curriculum is found in conflicts over testing.

The struggle referred to by the administrator began with an attack on the work of an eloquent and accomplished American author by a handful of conservative women in southern California. Initially it seemed as if the women simply wanted to pick a fight with the public schools. But as the fight developed, it involved several special interest groups, hundreds of school boards, thousands of students, the state Board of Education and the state superintendent, the state legislature, a governor running for reelection, a Los Angeles court ruling, and media attention from Los Angeles to Glasgow. By the time it ended, the new statewide student examinations had been withdrawn.

In February 1994, it was revealed that as a result of well-organized protests by the Traditional Values Coalition, the California state Board of Education had removed excerpts of two stories by Alice Walker, the Pulitzer Prize-winning author of *The Color Purple*, from the tenth grade reading comprehension section of the newly adopted "California Learning Assessment System" (CLAS).[52] One of the offending stories, "Roselily," was attacked by conservative Christians as being "anti-religious"; the other, "Am I Blue," was called "hostile to meat-eating."[41]

In "Roselily," a young Christian woman with four children reflects on her feelings, hopes, and fears as she stands at a Mississippi altar being married to a Muslim man from Chicago. The story is elegant, searching, powerfully written, inspiring of thoughtfulness and empathy in readers of any age. In the other story, "Am I Blue," a woman is physically sickened by the callous treatment of a mare whose struggles she watches from the window of her home. The story evokes a reverence and understanding of life all too rare in most humans. But critics of the story's inclusion in the CLAS test claimed to be concerned that its portrayal of reverence for all animal life would prove offensive to children whose parents raise poultry or cattle.

These objections to including two story excerpts on a test of reading comprehension seem so superficial and so literal-minded that they might have been shrugged off as an indication of nothing more than the low level of reading comprehension among the stories' critics. But they signified far deeper and more significant differences between Christian fundamentalists and the education establishment over the idea of education and the role of the public schools.

The multifaceted fundamentalist campaign to take control of the schools from the education establishment seems to rest philosophically on the idea that tolerance, rationality, and exposure to diversity threaten the survival of fundamentalist culture.[42] That culture—which provides strength and spiritual guidance for millions of deeply religious Americans—is certainly entitled to try to sustain itself through schooling its own children. But school wars, which permit only one response to many legitimate demands, usually transform such self-preservation into an attempt to control some aspect of the schooling of every child in the community. The CLAS controversy makes it clear that there are no winners in such a struggle.

The two-dimensional complaints about literature in the California examination were only the opening salvo in a campaign to discredit CLAS; and they were delivered in such an intolerant and antagonistic tone that the ensuing battle was destined to disguise the deeper issues and to prevent the public from considering them rationally. When 1.5 million students must take the same test in the service of evaluating the effectiveness of the same curriculum standards, it is predictable that sooner or later a polarizing battle will erupt over whose beliefs and worldview are to be sanctioned by the tests.

After the attack on Alice Walker's work, California's predictable and predictably divisive battle expanded immediately. In early March 1994, acclaimed author Maxine Hong Kingston withdrew permission to have her work used in California school tests. Reacting to the rapid cave-in to ultraconservatives by the state Board of Education, and reflecting on the centrality of critical thinking in her own idea of education, Kingston said, "I didn't want to be part of an exam that was organized that way. I did it in solidarity with Alice Walker. Censoring her work is censoring all our work, all our minds and our children's minds."[43]

Others who shared an open-minded, pluralistic, civil libertarian view of schooling joined the fray. People for the American Way (PFAW) accused the state's Board of Education of sending "a chilling message across the country of the threat to educational freedom and constitutional rights posed by extremist pressure groups."[44] The liberal-leaning PFAW did not mention, however, that in public schooling one group's educational freedom is sometimes another group's antireligious indoctrination.

The conservative attack broadened to include the entire CLAS set of examinations, amid claims that the test invaded family privacy, emphasized emotion instead of intellect, was too psychological, improperly sought information about "family moral virtues and practices in the family,"[45] slighted grammar and spelling, and usurped the role of parents. The challenge to the tests spread to many local school districts, where public education officials caught up in conflicting demands were confused by the vagueness in state regulation of test administration. The governor, engaged in a difficult reelection campaign, criticized censorship, but not the decision to remove the works from the test. A suit was filed in Los Angeles seeking to require parental permission for students to take the test.

The head of the Traditional Values Coalition called the chair of the state assembly's education committee a "demagogue" for objecting to the censorship.[46] As the entire conflict moved further and further from substantive debate, the accused assemblywoman claimed, "The truth is that these people are afraid of children being able to think," and suggested that her opponents in the assembly were "extremists arming for armageddon."[47] The governor offered Alice Walker an award as a "state treasure," but she refused to be so easily bought off. Feeling the growing heat, the state board of education unanimously voted in mid-March to restore the stories to the pool of literature available for future examinations.

But the brawl over CLAS went on. In late May, the governor mended fences with Alice Walker; but he also made it clear that he understood the unseverable connection between politics and public schooling. He froze the funds for the California testing system the fundamentalists had attacked.[48] In early September he promised to veto the bill reauthorizing the testing system; and in late September, with the 1994 election coming on fast, he made good on his threat to cut this "cutting-edge example of 'performance-based' testing."[49]

The censored stories had been returned to an exam that would never be used; the Traditional Values Coalition had increased its power over schooling at the expense of the education establishment; the governor was reelected with the help of the ultraconservatives; and an important, complex, and difficult issue of education policy and cultural diversity was buried in a mud slide of conflict over control of school content. An official of the Council of Chief State School Officers observed during the battle, "This is a war over what an education ought to be."[50] He was right, but like all wars, this one destroyed the possibility of discussing the issue that caused it. Whether by design or by accident, the battle left many of the combatants with a diminished sense of the legitimacy of public schooling and of its ability to accommodate differing visions of education and of life. The story was much the same in Texas, where it was textbooks rather than tests that brought on the battle.

HEALTH TEXTBOOKS IN TEXAS ATTACKED FROM BOTH SIDES
Education Week, February 23, 1996

In Texas, where conflicts over textbook content are as frequent and as boisterous as rodeos, the state board of education in 1994 ordered more than three hundred changes in the high school health texts it was reviewing for possible adoption.[51] In response to complaints of conservative Christian critics, the board required that the texts give greater emphasis to sexual abstinence, delete telephone numbers for AIDS hotlines, remove illustrations of human sexual organs, revise their discussions of homosexuality, assisted suicide, and condom use, and ensure that students know the laws against sodomy in Texas and elsewhere. After all these changes were adopted, one group of critics still was concerned that the books under review would "invite debate on issues such as children divorcing parents, needle-exchange programs, and legalizing marijuana."[52] Of the five publishers of health texts offered for approval by Texas authorities, one—Holt, Rinehart, Winston—withdrew from the political fray. When it did so, it claimed not only that "the changes weren't economically viable . . . ," but also that "We simply cannot produce a product that does not provide children with adequate instruction on life-threatening issues."[53]

These issues are as sensitive as they are important. Individual health, deeply held beliefs, the welfare of children and families, and the survival of a sane society are all at stake. Many adults have trouble discussing and resolving these issues themselves, so it is no wonder that reaching an agreement about how children should be guided through this tangled forest would be difficult and even painful. Had the disagreements been aired among teachers and parents in an individual school—even with the humility and thoughtfulness such intensely personal issues seem to require—achieving a working resolution would have been difficult.[54] But expanding the scope of the problem from a single school to an entire state transforms discourse into demagoguery and replaces emotional disagreement with ideological warfare.

Ideological warfare is exactly what Texans got in the health textbook controversy. By creating a political process to determine the content of all the textbooks that could be used by teachers, the state was virtually guaranteeing that individual freedom and community consensus would be crippled. Not satisfied with their victory over health education, ultraconservatives mounted a campaign based on textbook content in all subject areas and in 1994 took control of the Texas school board for the first time.[55]

Texas is not unique in mandating that politics determine the knowledge presented in textbooks, though its purchasing power is so great that, along with California, it has in past years exercised controlling influence over the content of textbooks around the country. There are twenty-three states that use elected or politically appointed committees to judge the content of the textbooks that teachers are permitted to use.[56] In some states there are fines of fifty to five hundred dollars for any teacher or principal who "uses or permits to be used" a text not approved by the state.[57] In one state such acts of professional judgment and intellectual freedom on the part of teachers can result in a jail term of up to six months.[58] The best that liberals and civil libertarians have been able to do is to open these textbook selection procedures to participation by all sides. This improvement has transformed the right to teach and learn into a public free-for-all instead of a closed-door exercise in negotiated censorship.

Even in states where textbook content is not subjected to political manipulation on a statewide basis, the textbook knowledge selected by school systems and teachers for presentation to students can still become politicized. And the textbook critics do not come only from the right wing of the political spectrum. In 1987 and 1988, school board meetings and social studies classes in the only junior high school in the liberal community of Amherst, Massachusetts, were nearly brought to a halt when a group of parents criticized an eighth grade history text for having a conservative bias. There were complaints of militarism in the text and of failure to portray accurately the horror of slavery and the reality of the war in Vietnam.

In spite of the fact that local teachers supplemented the text with other materials designed to show disagreements and debates over historical events, the liberal critics insisted, "Not only should children not be reading it, but it shouldn't be in the schools."[59] People for the American Way, which has labored heroically to turn back right-wing attempts to gain dominion over school texts in places like Texas, could find no censorship in the actions of the Amherst critics. After careful examination of the conflict, a PFAW spokesperson stated, "We point out incidents where people are trying to restrict curriculum. It seems. . . . this was an attempt to expand the curriculum to use more resources."[60]

The battle over textbook content is not a problem caused by the political left or right, nor is it an issue of political correctness or of family values. Any politically or ideologically oriented group can rationalize its interest in swaying the content of school texts and no group has cornered the market on truth or sincerity. Those who want children to be taught critical thinking in a marketplace of ideas express a responsibility for their children no less intense, and no more correct, than those who insist that schools give priority to spiritual life and the preservation of communities of faith.

The trouble with statewide and even districtwide textbook adoptions in a compulsory school setting is that they invite intolerance. They provide incentives and powerful rewards for people with differing visions of life to fight with each other over whose vision will be imposed on all teachers and students. As the Texas struggle demonstrates, the goal of this fight is to use the power of government to advance one worldview or ideology over another in the public schools. State textbook adoption procedures, like government control of curriculum or test content, virtually require that people of diverse beliefs engage in ideological warfare. The alternative, for most parents, is to abandon interest, commitment, and responsibility for the education of their children—to pretend it doesn't matter, to leave it to the experts alone, to disengage.

It is not only government intervention in curriculum, testing, and textbook selection, but also its built-in tendency to manipulate conscience and to monopolize the definition of community, that causes destructive conflict over public education. For individual teachers and the teaching profession, government intervention also seems to have transformed public schooling into a source of disrespect for individual conscience and hostility toward the process by which communities are sustained. Headlines:

TEACHER WHO DEFIED "MINUTE OF SILENCE" FIGHTS FOR HIS JOB
Education Week, September 7, 1994

ANTI-EVOLUTIONIST TEACHER SUES SCHOOL DISTRICT
Los Angeles Times, October 1, 1993

In a high school outside of Atlanta, a social studies teacher told his colleagues and local school administrators that he could not in good conscience participate in the "moment of quiet reflection" which Georgia state law required of students at the beginning of each school day. He felt that the law was unconstitutional, a violation of the separation of church and state, and an offense to his deeply held Christian beliefs about the place of religion in society.[61] These were issues that he had studied and thought through carefully, issues about which he was trained to teach.

Nearly three thousand miles away, in Orange County, California, another high school teacher—this one trained in biology and thoughtful about the origin of life as well as its development—told his colleagues and administrators that he could not in good conscience teach that Darwinian evolution, rather than an "intelligent creator," explained the origin of life. He felt that the California state and local district policies requiring that evolution be taught as a valid scientific theory violated his freedom to teach, frustrated his purpose "to teach my students to differentiate between philosophical belief and empirical science,"[62] and discriminated against him as a born-again Christian.

In Georgia, the teacher was first suspended, then fired for "teaching through" the moment of silence. The subject of his untimely lesson had been the Protestant Reformation. The school superintendent had forgiven the teacher his first transgression and allowed him one night in which to rethink his position and begin obeying the moment of silence requirement or lose his job. The teacher showed up for work the following day, stuck his head into the principal's office and said "the answer is no!" Then, presuming he was fired, he left school.

One student who had been in the teacher's class the previous semester spoke up for the teacher's conscience: "I don't believe he should be forced to do something he doesn't believe in."[63] Another, objecting to the interruption of her prayers caused by the teacher's civil disobedience on the previous day, spoke up for the school's power over the teacher's conscience: "When you're up there talking, I have a hard time concentrating on what I'm thinking."[64] The teacher called the superintendent a "sick, pathetic man." The superintendent recommended to the school board that the teacher be terminated for "insubordination, willful neglect of duties, and encouraging students to violate board rules."

In California, the biology teacher received a reprimand from the school district and was ordered to stop instructing his students on the theory of an intelligent creator.[80] Without further ado he filed suit for $5 million against the school board, an action that was sure to cost the board a small fortune even if they won. The superintendent, whose sympathy for the teacher's dilemma of conscience must have been dampened by the lawsuit, labeled it "outrageous," and a "travesty,"[65] and asked the court to dismiss it for being "frivolous."[65]

Whereas the Georgia social studies teacher likened himself to Martin Luther posting his concerns on the door of power, the theologically minded California biology teacher seemed haunted by the ghost of John Scopes. Said a local religion professor, "Scopes was forbidden to teach evolution and he threw down the gauntlet and taught it. Now we have somebody who is forbidden to teach what Scopes was supposed to teach, and he is throwing down his own gauntlet."[67]

In neither case was the school district inclined to accommodate the teacher's conscience. In neither case did the teacher seem even remotely interested in resolving the issue without a public fight. Dilemmas of conscience—far from being the source of learning or teaching, growth or enlightenment—were taken as gauntlets, as challenges, as preludes to combat. Colleagues became estranged from one another, lawyers were hired, banners were hoisted, and the controversy started to take on a life of its own. The Georgia incident was played out against a national backdrop of proposed school prayer amendments to the U.S. Constitution. The California conflict was acted out just a stone's throw from a district in which another school board was deciding that biblical creationism should be included in all social studies classes.[68]

The disputants, their supporters, and the media each pushed the conflict away from the possibility of pragmatic resolution and turned it into material for talk shows, special interest politics, and office-seeking politicians. Both conflicts literally became federal cases, and each side sought vindication and the vanquishing of its opponents in the name of the U.S. Constitution.

In Georgia, editorialists and private citizens chided the social studies teacher for being reckless, for being unwilling to accept the consequences of his act of civil disobedience, for undermining "the cause he has appointed himself to champion," and for "turning himself into a figure of controversy."[69] But others labeled the state's Moment of Quiet Reflection Act a mere pretext for mandating prayer in the schools. The sponsor of the challenged act was upbraided for "hypocrisy" in defending as secular a law he had originally introduced with the words "silent prayer and meditation" in its text. "Believers," said one editorialist speaking plainly about the trivialization of religion, "ought to be as outraged by this politically motivated hypocrisy as non-believers."[79]

One letter writer, who apparently thought following orders more important to a healthy society than following conscience, claimed that the teacher "epitomizes what is wrong with our society today: If one doesn't agree with a law or rule, just don't obey it. Unfortunately it's people like him who pass this attitude on to our children." A letter writer with a different philosophy of school and society wrote, "Highly competent and principled teachers should be actively sought, not terminated." Still another put a plague on both houses and expressed a weary skepticism probably bred by watching round after round of public conflict over private matters: "[The school superintendent] . . . is so incredibly inflexible that the students will certainly learn how to treat sensitive personal issues of conscience in a disrupting manner. . . . The students will learn from [the teacher] how to grandstand and play to the media for their personal agenda.[71]"

The controversies surrounding these two teachers are examples of a larger problem for public education. In all of them, individual acts of conscience were attacked for provoking too much thought and causing too much trouble for the smooth operation of bureaucratic schools. Dilemmas of conscience have become reasons for combat rather than for reflection. Religion and the spiritual plane of existence have been trivialized, secularized, and made the objects of mundane struggles over political power. And public discourse—already beleaguered by sound bites and the politics of negativism—has been stressed, strained, and contorted into a form threatening to the democratic process itself.

While the consciences of teachers, writers, students, and families were being marginalized by local control and state standards, the inability of public education to accommodate communities, or to refrain from undermining them, brought equally troubling consequences. Headlines:

HIGH COURT REJECTS N.Y. LAW CREATING DISTRICT FOR JEWISH SECT
Education Week, July 13, 1994

In late June 1994, the U.S. Supreme Court ruled that a New York State law creating a public school district for the special needs children of a small village of Hasidic Jews violated the Constitution. The Court's ruling, based on the principle of government neutrality toward religion contained in the First Amendment's establishment clause, brought tears to the eyes of the Kiryas Joel School Board president. "As parents, we have no choice but to continue our search for a suitable way to provide a quality education for the most vulnerable of our children."[72]

It would appear that the justices' eyes were clouded as well, though not with tears, for the ruling in *Board of Education of Kiryas Joel Village v. Grumet* contained six opinions kaleidoscopically conflicted about everything from First Amendment legal doctrine, to the difference between culture and religion, to the importance of geographical boundaries and the role of schooling in the preservation of human communities. All nine justices seemed frustrated with the decision that the majority's reading of the constitution compelled them to reach. The plurality opinion put it this way: "We do not disable a religiously homogenous group. . . . Nor do we impugn the motives of the New York Legislature . . . ; we simply refuse to ignore that the method it chose is one that aids a particular religious community. . . . rather than all groups similarly interested in separate schooling."[73]

Within a month of the Supreme Court's 1994 decision, the Satmar Hasidic community's search yielded a new state law seeking to accommodate the culture and religion of their disabled children. A re-created school district was then approved in its first constitutional test by a New York State trial court.[74] That decision was appealed. However this legal contest ultimately turns out for the Satmar community and their religiously motivated desire to remain whole and separate from the world, its history is testament to the difficulty of respecting communities of any kind under the present structure of public education.

The Satmar Hasidic sect was founded in the early twentieth century by Grand Rebbe Joel Teitelbaum. After the Holocaust, what was left of the Satmar community in Europe settled in Brooklyn, New York, and in 1975 they created the community of Kiryas Joel in an undeveloped subdivision in the town of Monroe, fifty miles northwest of New York City. Here is how Justice Souter saw the nature of the Satmar culture in writing the majority opinion in the *Kiryas Joel* case:

> The residents of Kiryas Joel are vigorously religious people who make few concessions to the modern world and go to great lengths to avoid assimilation into it. They interpret the Torah strictly; segregate the sexes outside the home; speak Yiddish as their primary language; eschew television, radio, and English-language publications; and dress in distinctive ways that include headcoverings and special garments for boys and modest dresses for girls. Children are educated in private religious schools, most boys at the United Talmudic Academy where they receive a thorough grounding in the Torah and limited exposure to secular subjects, and most girls at Bais Rochel, an affiliated school with a curriculum designed to prepare girls for their roles as wives and mothers.[75]

By 1984, the village of Kiryas Joel had been constructed and legally approved on 320 acres of land owned and inhabited entirely by the Satmars. Although most children attended parochial schools, the special needs children were given their schooling by the Monroe-Woodbury Central Public School District in an annex of one of the parochial schools. The atmosphere of that site was consistent with the Satmar culture, though the services provided were labeled "secular." In 1985, the U.S. Supreme Court handed down a First Amendment ruling in a Michigan case, invalidating an arrangement similar to the one by which the public school teachers and therapists of Monroe-Woodbury had been providing secular services to disabled children in a religious context.[76] Kiryas Joel's public/private arrangement for special education had to be discontinued.

There followed a ten-year struggle to find an accommodation for this cohesive community within the bounds of the constitutional wall of separation between church and state. The parents could not afford the costs required to provide private schooling to children suffering from serious mental, physical, and emotional disabilities. Like all disabled children, those of Kiryas Joel were individually entitled to an appropriate education under the requirements of the federal Individuals with Disabilities Education Act[77] and various New York State laws. And like most American families, the people of Kiryas Joel understood a strong community to be vital to the success of education, just as they knew an effective education to be vital to the survival of the community.

As the conflict developed in the mid-1980s, the members of the Satmar community were faced with a choice that no government should present to any of its citizens. If they sent their disabled children to the public school, they risked having those children poorly served— and the community's beliefs undermined—by the vastly different culture of public schools. If they did not send them to the public school, the children might remain within the fold of the community, but they would not receive the special education services that would enable them to attain their full development. If these children of the survivors of unspeakable Nazi atrocities were brought to tears by the choice with which American democracy had confronted them, it is understandable. But their suffering, compounded by anger and frustration, differed only in intensity from the hundreds of other communities of belief, heritage, language, or culture which are daily confronted with similar choices between sustaining community and securing suitable public schooling.[78]

After the 1985 Michigan ruling by the U.S. Supreme Court caused the collapse of the religious-secular compromise for the Satmar, the special needs children of Kiryas Joel were placed in the nearby Monroe-Woodbury public school. School authorities refused to provide services to the Satmar children in a secular setting outside these schools, and so the Satmar parents sued Monroe-Woodbury. The dissonance between their practices and beliefs and those of most children in the public schools led the parents to complain in their suit of "the panic, fear and trauma [the children] suffered in leaving their own community and being with people whose ways were so different. . . ."[79] The Satmar lawyers also pointed out that these deeply religious Jews had formed the community in part "to facilitate individual religious observance and maintain social, cultural and religious values. . . ."[80]

In 1988, the N.Y. Court of Appeals ruled against them. The court held that while Monroe-Woodbury *could* legally establish a separate school within Kiryas Joel if it so decided, it could not be *compelled* to do so by a court.[81] In the absence of either legal compulsion or a workable accommodation with the public schools, the community had no choice. To preserve the vital connection between community and schooling, within a year all but one of the Satmar families withdrew their disabled children from the regular public school.

At that point all local attempts at helping these children without undermining their community had failed. The New York legislature then passed Chapter 748 of the New York Laws of 1989, constituting the Village of Kiryas Joel as a "separate school district" which could, and did, erect a new public school devoted to the special needs children of the village and of Hasidic families nearby. It seemed a successful accommodation. It did require the Satmar parents to accept some secularization of schooling, such as mixed gender classes; but it also permitted the school board to be composed entirely of members of the Satmar community. But the accommodation looked to most people, including the New York State School Boards Association, which sued to overturn it, like a grant of government power to a religiously defined community. In a five-year legal battle involving four separate courts, that view was consistently confirmed. In 1994, the U.S. Supreme Court agreed that the Kiryas Joel accommodation was a clear violation of the separation of church and state.

At every level—from local school district to state legislature to state and federal courts—government officials recognized the legitimacy of the Satmar's claim to schooling that would be compatible with the deeply held beliefs of their religious community. The question was whether the special education to which their disabled children were legally entitled could constitutionally be made available without imposing an unbearable cost upon the Satmarer. That cost would include alienating the children from their community, undermining their education, and threatening the beliefs that lay at the core of Satmar life. In the end it appeared that every attempt to provide public education that respected the Satmar community without violating the Constitution failed. That failure is not traceable to the Constitution, or to the way in which the sitting justices read it. It is traceable to the structure of public education.

Considering the existing structure, and the destructive consequences that could follow a breakdown in government neutrality toward religion, the decision in *Kiryas Joel* is virtually unassailable. Justice Kennedy concurred in this judgment, but warned that "the Establishment Clause must not be construed as some sort of homogenizing solvent that forces unconventional religious groups to choose between assimilating to mainstream American culture or losing their political rights."[82] The court simply could not accommodate the legitimate claims of the Satmar and simultaneously uphold the principles of the Establishment Clause. But had it been parents instead of governments that chose where each child attends an approved school, the court's dilemma would have dissolved.

Without such a structural change in schooling, however, any accommodation acceptable to the Satmar and approved by the Court would have been so narrowly drawn that it would likely be virtually useless to other communities—including many Christian fundamentalists, who are no less entitled to respect for their community and religious values than the Satmar. The lesson of this long struggle therefore seems clear. Public schools are presently structured so that they become the enemies of private conscience and the building of communities of belief. Making it easier for schooling to be consistent with any community's most basic beliefs is a problem that can be solved by restructuring public education, not by reinterpreting the First Amendment.[83]

Perhaps nowhere in the persistent school wars is the undermining of community more starkly evident than in America's long struggle with racial discrimination. In 1994, when the *Goals 2000: Educate America Act* was adopted, the nation marked the fortieth anniversary of the Supreme Court decision declaring racial discrimination in public education unconstitutional. But, according to a Harvard University study, in that same year almost 70 percent of African American students in the United States still attended segregated schools.[84] Virtually none of these "separate" schools could be regarded as "equal" in quality to the schools attended by the children of the middle class, whatever their race.[85]

FORTY YEARS AFTER BROWN, SEGREGATION PERSISTS
New York Times, May 18, 1994

1954 TOPEKA DESEGREGATION CASE
CONTINUES ODYSSEY IN THE COURTS
New York Times, November 4, 1994

Jonathan Kozol has made it eloquently and painfully clear that the inadequacy of schooling resources that governments make available for inner-city, minority, and other poor children creates *Savage Inequalities*.[86] These inequalities, like the forced separation of the races condemned in *Brown v. Board of Education*, "may affect the hearts and minds [of children] in a way unlikely ever to be undone."[87] A majority of African American children have thus been denied the benefits of full membership in the larger community and at the same time have been deprived of a fair share of the educational resources by which any community sustains its strengths and passes them on to its children.

In the *Kiryas Joel* case, Justice Kennedy reluctantly agreed that the constitution required the court to strike down New York's 1989 attempt to accommodate the educational needs of the Satmar religious/cultural community. His opinion distinguished between the "voluntary association" which underlies strong communities, and the "forced separation" which stigmatizes them and violates the rights of their members. "Religion," he said, "flourishes in community . . ."; each is dependent on the other.[88] Kennedy might equally have noted that "education flourishes in community." For no community can sustain itself without adequate schooling; and schooling that is not nurtured by the values of the community is not likely to succeed by any measure. The victims of racial discrimination in education know this only too well.

Linda Brown was just eight years old in 1951 when her father, the Reverend Oliver Brown, became a named plaintiff on her behalf in the landmark litigation that led to the Supreme Court's 1954 *Brown v. Board of Education of Topeka* decision. Rev. Mr. Brown—like the other parents who put their children's names on the court papers that initiated America's best-known class action—was a courageous person.

He was not a leader in the antisegregation movement of Topeka, Kansas; and he reportedly agreed to participate in the litigation primarily because of "his deep conviction that God had approved it."[89] But when he performed that great act of constitutional conscience he must have understood the storm of racism that it would unleash upon his community.

More than that, he was staring into the face of three hundred years of American slavery and Jim Crow segregation, during which racially motivated hatred, exploitation, stereotyping, and brutality had systematically fragmented African American families and destroyed their culture.[90] Oliver Brown must have known from history, as well as from experience, that the health of the African American community—and the education upon which it depends—were always viewed as an enemy by the operators of a system of racism. Before the Civil War, families were broken up and African language, music, religion, education, surnames, and other aspects of culture were repressed. Myths and stereotypes were created which served to explain, even to whites of good will, why slaves could neither sustain their own communities nor participate in the white community. It was a crime in many states to teach a slave to read or write.

After the adoption of the Civil War amendments to the Constitution and after the collapse of Reconstruction, denying equal educational opportunities to African Americans was still legally permissible. Slavery was gone, but in its place was the principle of "equal but separate," a constitutional sleight-of-hand based on a premise that not even its creators believed. In the 1896 case that enshrined the infamous separate-but-equal proposition in law for fifty-eight years, the Supreme Court even went as far as to blame the victims of unequal facilities and public humiliation. In *Plessy v. Ferguson*, the majority stated the point in a way that made it clear that racism pervaded every level of American culture in the nineteenth century:

> that the enforced separation of the races stamps the colored race with a badge of inferiority. . . . is not by reason of anything found in the act [requiring separation of the races], but solely because the colored race chooses to put that construction upon it.[91]

By reinvigorating the old stereotypes of racial inferiority, the Court added the insult of stigmatization to the injury of unequal resources. Looking back at *Plessy* from the late twentieth century, one historian labeled the opinion a "permission to hate" because it demeaned African Americans and gave a legal seal of approval to racism. The Court further weakened the ability of African American communities to sustain themselves, and it would not reverse itself until the *Brown* decision of 1954.

Oliver Brown died in 1961, just seven years after the landmark reversal of school segregation that bore his daughter's name. In those seven years he witnessed the defiance of at least one southern governor standing in the schoolhouse door and swearing that court-ordered desegregation would never take place. He saw as well that only a barrage of federal court orders and a battalion of federal troops could overcome the resistance that this public hostility encouraged. He saw that some whites would rather eliminate public schooling altogether than make it equally available to African American children; and he saw that, in the name of school choice, public officials would pander to racism by providing scholarships for white children to attend segregated private schools.[92] The outward face of racism had changed since the days of slavery and Jim Crow segregation, but its substance had remained much the same.

Since Oliver Brown's death, the forms of resistance to the equal education of African American children have become even more sophisticated. They have also been entwined with economic and class discrimination. Governors no longer defy desegregation by standing in schoolhouse doors; but neither do they aggressively pursue the provision of equal educational resources for schools in minority communities. Most school boards no longer intentionally create one-race schools; but neither do they combine their districts in order to counteract the segregating effects of housing and job discrimination. Most white parents no longer support politicians who preach racial divisiveness; but neither do they oppose the tracking practices that effectively resegregate even the best schools.

In 1979, Oliver Brown's daughter Linda was thirty-six years old and the mother of two children, Charles and Kimberly. The public schools of Topeka, Kansas, were still largely segregated. The echoes of the old racial stereotypes could still be heard, and the denial of resources could still be seen in schools around the country. Linda Brown Thompson became a named plaintiff on behalf of her two children in the reopening of *Brown v. Board of Education of Topeka*. In 1994, the case that had promised to let education thrive in the African American community was still not resolved. Linda Brown Thompson looked back over her forty-three-year struggle and sighed, "It's disheartening that we are still fighting."[93]

As 1994 school segregation figures suggest, and as Jonathan Kozol's book demonstrates, the resistance to equalizing educational opportunities for African Americans still exists, and the savage inequalities persist.[94] From the point of view of the victims of racial discrimination in education, the message and the reality of public schooling remain what they always were: continued resistance to the efforts of African Americans to use schooling as a means to advance themselves, to strengthen their communities, or to gain equal access to the economic and cultural mainstream.

Both the *Kiryas Joel* case and the *Brown* case teach another message about the mutual dependence of American schooling and community. Any community—whether a community of faith or heritage or geography—needs effective schooling to sustain itself; and schools can only thrive in the context of a viable community. If a community is denied freedom or resources adequate to create effective schooling, it will be seriously weakened. And a community so undermined cannot sustain the quality education it needs to reinvigorate itself.

The conflicts sketched above are only a few of the demoralizing, frustrating, and destructive battles that every year swirl around public schooling, weakening its effectiveness and undermining the public's confidence in it. This kind of conflict is not simply the byproduct of the rough and tumble of democracy, but rather an indicator of how democracy can break down or turn against itself when it fails to respect diversity and protect dissent.

Most of these school conflicts originate when knowledge or matters of private conscience are subjected to governmental decision making, or when the definition and preservation of communities become politicized and subject to the will of the political majority. This pattern seems all the more disheartening and dangerous when one considers that constitutional democracy was designed to prevent just this kind of government involvement in matters of belief and opinion.

School wars have increased in intensity in the past decade and have drawn in more people who see no other avenue of action available to them to protect their vision of education and their independence of spirit. But they have also become a primary battleground for two self-interested and powerful combatants—the Christian Right and the education establishment. Chapter 2 focuses on these two well-organized forces and on the destruction that their combat causes. It puts the passage of *Goals 2000* in the context of this combat, and suggests that the structure of public education itself makes these otherwise avoidable conflicts inevitable.

CHAPTER TWO

School Wars:
The Education Empire
Strikes Back

At the height of World War II it was widely believed in the United States that requiring school children to pledge allegiance to the flag daily would help foster the patriotism and national unity upon which the war effort depended. It is hard to imagine a time in the twentieth century when singleness of purpose and commitment to the common good were more important to the survival of freedom.

But in 1943, with the outcome of the war still very much in doubt, the U.S. Supreme Court ruled that neither states nor local school boards have the constitutional power to require the pledge in public schools. Such a requirement, the court stated in *West Virginia v. Barnette*, "invades the sphere of intellect and spirit which it is the purpose of the First Amendment to our Constitution to reserve from all official control."[1]

The majority opinion was written by Justice Robert Jackson, who was to become chief prosecutor in the 1945 Nuremberg trials of Nazi war criminals. It remains one of the most eloquent and powerful statements ever written by an American about individual freedom of thought and belief. In that opinion, Jackson condemned the requirement of a pledge as a coerced "confession of belief" and made two prophetic statements about the consequences of school wars for both education and national unity:

Probably no deeper division of our people could proceed from any provocation than from finding it necessary to choose what doctrine and whose program public educational officials shall compel youth to unite in embracing. . . .

If it [public schooling] is to impose any ideological discipline, . . . each party or denomination must seek to control, or failing that, to weaken the influence of the educational system.[2]

The local, state, and national conflicts over schooling that increasingly afflicted America in the 1980s and 1990s bear witness to the importance of these warnings. Unfortunately, in their deepest significance Jackson's warnings have gone largely unheeded by those of good will; and they have been learned only too well by some who see in social divisiveness an opportunity to advance their own power. The regular repetition of ideological conflict over schooling has made *Barnette* into a political prophecy. Schooling conflicts have divided Americans deeply and unnecessarily. They have arisen from the need to impose one public school answer upon many individual questions of education. They have transformed matters of private conscience into battles for control of entire schools and school systems. They have pitted one community of belief against another.

Many school conflicts can be read as symptoms of the problem of ideological warfare over education that Justice Jackson described. But the cause of this problem lies deeper than mere good and ill will toward public schooling or toward national unity. It lies, as Jackson implied, with a school system that seems structurally unable to be responsive to the diverse beliefs and goals of American children, families, and communities. Because public schools are government agencies beholden ultimately to political majorities, the accommodation of any individual family or community of belief often requires that a small minority gain the approval or support of the majority from which it dissents. As well, the bureaucratic need for broad, categorical school policies covering large numbers of students, families, and schools further reduces flexibility.

This built-in resistance to diversity frustrates and diminishes many families who desire nothing more than to see their most basic personal or community beliefs reflected in their children's schooling. As this natural parental and community desire is frustrated, it is in turn transformed either into an apathetic disengagement or into a self-protective urge to impose an "ideological discipline" upon those with differing visions of life and education. When power becomes the prize, the conflict over ideology in public schools brings out the worst in good people and creates an irresistible opportunity for those who use schooling as a battleground in the culture wars.

The renewed effort to add or strengthen character education as a mission of public schools is a good example of how even the best intentions are likely to be thwarted by a school system perennially unable to accommodate diversity of conscience or to encourage the building of consensus and community.[3] Variously labeled "character education," "moral education," or "values clarification," the project seems irreproachable at first glance. Where else can William Bennett, Hillary Clinton, Marion Barry, and some of the nation's leading scholars and clergy be found on the same side of an issue? A cover story in a national news magazine labeled them "virtuecrats" because they are among the leaders responding to a "national obsession" with spiritual and moral decline and arguing that "the formation of good character [is] an urgent aim of government."[4] According to some virtuecrats, the schools should be one of the main arenas for teaching children to form and exercise their consciences, and prayer in the schools is just one of a dozen ways to do that.

The public is aware of the need. A 1994 poll found that 76 percent of adults in the United States agreed that "the United States is in moral and spiritual decline." Two years earlier, the *Wall Street Journal* reported that a wide variety of political, civic, and religious groups supported values education because "the evidence of [a] . . . moral vacuum is overwhelming." An earlier Harris poll that was quoted had found widespread approval of cheating and lying among students, but only 3 percent who would "follow conscience" if unsure of what was right or wrong in a situation. The same poll found that 64 percent of parents felt that a top educational goal should be "to develop standards of what is 'right' and 'wrong.' "[5]

It has been fashionable to find further evidence of moral decline in the allegedly amoral "generation X," or in the proliferation of gang violence, hopelessness, desperation, and ethical numbness among teenagers. Perhaps more convincing testimony that the social fabric is being shredded by a decline of individual and collective conscience can be found in the behavior of some of the nation's political, corporate, financial, and entertainment leaders and institutions. After a 1992 trip across the United States, journalist Haynes Johnson observed, "You cannot spend a day talking with Americans without hearing over and over that America's problems stem from its lack of 'values.' "[6]

Whether grounded in hard reality or fearful perception, the idea that

Americans are losing their moral compass has taken hold and given support to a multiplicity of campaigns and curricula to make the public schools into agents of morality. Even if the perceived decline were not true, Americans have always valued education that is grounded in character, produces a sense of ethics, supports the role of conscience in personal and public life, and helps build a diversity of communities. Since American compulsory public schooling got started in the 1830s and 1840s, its proponents have recognized this. They have based their support for public schooling in part on the need to make the nation's children into moral individuals and virtuous citizens. This was Plato's prescription for schooling long before it appeared in Horace Mann's campaigns and was translated into the language of democratic institutions in the United States.

The trouble now, as then, is how little agreement there is about what constitutes morality and virtue and whether government should have the power to define these matters for the schools. In almost every era in which moral education has become an issue, conflict over whose morality will be adopted by the schools has undermined the effort or made its effect destructive. In a 1995 review entitled "Can Schools Teach Character?" the *New York Times* summed up a number of such efforts by saying that educators leery of the conflict produced by character education curricula regard adopting such a curriculum as "political suicide for administrators."[7]

The backlash can indeed be daunting. For example, in the spring of 1995, the Massachusetts legislature was presented with a bill that would have required parental permission for children to participate in any discussion in a public school classroom that involved morally or religiously sensitive subjects. According to the bill's sponsor, sensitive subjects included anything about sexuality, gender, race, death, religion, emotional or psychological health, marriage, divorce, family life, or moral decision making.[8] The simultaneous demand for and rejection of character education in the public schools makes clear just how hard it is for these schools to teach anyone's idea of good character, at least under the form of governance currently in use in public education.

The effort to find broad, innocuous terms to describe the most basic virtues—such as honesty, fairness, and citizenship, or self-discipline and sympathy—does little more than sugarcoat the problem.[9] It may make the problem worse. It is not that there is anything wrong with these character strengths or with the effort to teach them effectively.

But if their adoption simply papers over the inability of schools to overcome underlying conflict about their meaning, then character education may lead to the adoption of a bland, spineless, and superficial understanding of moral education. In that case the cure will have become, not worse than the disease, but the disease itself.

When teachers become so fearful of conflict that they will not tackle the hard questions of social ethics and personal morality with their students, the character of these students is not strengthened but weakened. When those who govern the schools believe that they can mandate teaching only those values that command consensus by virtue of their vagueness, then passivity and cynicism rather than character are likely to be what students learn.

The practice of prayer in public schools presents similar problems. By the time the diversity of religious and secular beliefs in America is taken into account and the separation of church and state adhered to, a campaign to put prayer in the schools can only result in prayer that trivializes the spirituality it is meant to enhance. Passion, faith, and the internalizing of moral teaching do not arise from the imposition of the bland uniformity of the least common denominator. The lesson of all the well-intentioned, crucially important, and frustrating efforts to revitalize American character through schooling may be very much like the lesson of the *Barnette* case. Unless the right to differ in matters of conscience is protected in schooling, the building of character is likely to be a self-defeating effort.

The built-in unresponsiveness of public education to matters of conscience and the needs of community manifests itself also in the endless struggle over school reform. Virtually the entire school reform movement of the 1980s and 1990s has confirmed—albeit unintentionally—that public schools need fundamental change if public education is to survive. Yet, with few exceptions, these reform proposals fail to take account of the diversity of goals that Americans have for their children's education. Or they fail to suggest how this diversity can be accommodated without repressive policies or divisive political conflicts over matters of private conscience.

Since the 1983 federal report, *A Nation at Risk*, [10] there have been literally hundreds of major governmental and scholarly studies analyzing the shortcomings and describing the alleged ineffectiveness of public education. The sheer number of these criticisms, along with their conflicting recommendations for reform, has changed the tone of public education. An institution once confident of its place at the foundation of American democracy has been burdened with the responsibility for remedying, and sometimes accused of creating, the country's most troublesome social problems. Many teachers, principals, and superintendents have been left feeling beleaguered and defensive, uncertain of which way to move, put-upon by self-interested critics.

Virtually all school studies have recommended substantial reform. But most have avoided advocating basic structural or governance changes and have instead defined and defended changes suitable to the particular perspective of some special interest group, ideological crusade, or philosophy of education. Elements of the business community, for example, have urged changes in content and pedagogy in public schooling that would, in their judgment, better prepare American students to become productive workers in a global economy dominated by information processing and driven by technological change.[11]

That this vision of the future and definition of success might not be shared by everyone has not curtailed the corporate campaign. Nor has it made self-interested business more open to a diversity of goals and cultures. Corporate America needs trained and competent employees. And many business organizations behave as if the most appropriate and cost-effective way to train these future employees is to convert public schooling into a government-subsidized training institute for the needs of big business and the demands of technological competition. The 1996 National Education Summit—convened by the chair of the Education Commission of the States and the chair and CEO of IBM, and attended by hundreds of business leaders and all the nation's governors—signaled the growing strength of the alliance among big business, big government, and the education establishment aimed at making public schooling more effective in promoting economic and technological goals.[12]

But business is hardly the only American institution to take this self-serving, utilitarian approach to public school reform. Most school reforms have been put forward and then become passé as quickly as Paris fashions. But that has not dampened the enthusiasm of those who stand to profit from such reforms in the short run. Even when basic structural changes in public education have been called for by reformers —such as an increase in family choice among all schools, the elimination of the urban and suburban school district lines that perpetuate racial discrimination, or the equalization of resources available for schooling all children—the response has been overt negativity or covert resistance.

In effect, most modern reform campaigns have been as much a part of the problem as an effort to solve it; for either they have increased the political pressure to make public schooling over in one mold that must fit all students, or they have simply shifted the battleground of the school war from one level of government to another. Justice Jackson saw that such efforts could only lead to a chaos of conflict over which is *The One Best System*. [13] And one doesn't have to be a Supreme Court justice to see that all the good intentions brought to bear in all the reform programs in all the past twenty years have been unable to quiet the ideological wars or to eliminate the savage inequalities that victimize so many children.

In light of the continuous struggles, competing interest groups, and conflicting reform proposals that beset public schooling, it is hard to resist the conclusion that the public school system itself may be the problem. The structure of American public schooling—perhaps better called its constitution—is no longer adequate to handle the demands that are made upon it and the attitudes that are brought to it.

Fifty years ago parental and societal expectations for schooling may have been more modest, and the behavior of people seeking to have these expectations fulfilled may have been less confrontational and intolerant. The diversity of American culture and the quest for individual freedom may now have overtaken an earlier willingness to compromise, and narrow self-interest may have corroded the sense of community. Public schools, once idealized as an egalitarian escape route from poverty to self-realization and economic success, may now be so unequal that they serve primarily as a preserver of privilege for the few or as a dumping ground for those without resources or hope. Or perhaps it has simply taken a generation for people bent on dividing the nation to see how easily the weaknesses in the constitution of public schooling can be exploited for political gain.

Whatever the reason, the relationship between the structure of public schooling on the one hand and the behavior, attitudes, and expectations of the public on the other hand now seems more likely to cause destructive conflict than to enhance the quality of schooling. Alexis de Tocqueville observed after visiting the United States in 1830 that the genius of *Democracy in America* was that the character and behavior of Americans complemented the constitutional structure of their institutions—that the two enhanced each other. [14] In schooling, at least, that is no longer true.

The endless cycle of conflicts over content, the direct attacks upon public schooling and public school teachers, the dizzying array of trendy but transient reform efforts, and the pernicious persistence of inequality of educational opportunity have sapped public education of its vitality and sense of mission. Once the pride of American democracy, public education has become the object of contentious culture wars that undermine individual conscience, threaten community, and weaken the quality of teaching and learning. Even the legitimacy of the century-old agreement that one generation will provide for the education of the next has been drawn into question.[15]

The tone tells the tale. The dispirited, frustrated, and mystified are often under attack by the overzealous, the self-centered, and the divisive. Crusaders for the one-true-way do battle with hidebound defenders of the status quo. Power replaces reason and greed replaces hope in the public debate. The poor are repeatedly recycled into an underclass in spite of, and sometimes because of, school policies. Endless numbers of researchers, policy analysts, reformers, educrats, and pied pipers of pedagogy lead their followers in ever-widening circles further and further from the core of the problem.

For many families, children, teachers, and principals, the mood of public schooling has turned sour, the tone intolerant, the discourse simplistic and disingenuous. The whole institution—and its many parts—seems at times to be beleaguered, exhausted, and directionless, as it steels itself for the next blow. If he were here today, Justice Jackson might observe that the contest over the content of schooling at every level has lead public education to begin cannibalizing itself.

Crusaders and Defenders

Perhaps no one has been more successful at exploiting the constitutional weaknesses in public schooling—the interplay of structure and attitude—than the crusaders of the Christian Right. In order to protect a vision of education for their own children, supporters of the Christian Right often aggressively insist that their own beliefs be adopted by entire school districts or states. Seeing ideological programs at the heart of schooling policies controlled by the education establishment, they may try to gain control of public education or to weaken and delegitimize it.

But the Christian Right meets its match in an education establishment artful at demonizing its opponents and willing to resist virtually any attempt to change the ideology and practices of the public schooling to which it owes its existence. It is a hotly contested time; and the middle ground of the common school shrinks with almost every conflict.

So effectively do these two giants demonize each other, and so distorted has the public debate over schooling become as a result, that it is difficult to discuss the attack by the Christian Right or the defensiveness of the education establishment without seeming to insult large numbers of well-intentioned people on both sides. "Right-wing Christian" is to most Christian fundamentalists, for example, as "tax-and-spend liberal" is to many other Americans of good will: a label, a stereotype, a mischaracterization of citizens trying to improve the quality and meaningfulness of public schooling for their children and their community.

It is essential to get beyond the demonization and polarization, and to put in perspective the partisan attacks on public schooling and the hackneyed defense of the status quo there. Americans with conflicting but sincere views about schooling need to admit that some leaders on each side have been willing to misuse the legitimate concerns of their constituents. It needs to be acknowledged as well that, almost unwittingly, the parents and citizens most concerned with the quality of public education have become pawns in the pitched battles of intolerance and divisiveness that rend so many schools. Both the crusaders and the defenders in these battles have been aided and abetted by the frustrating passivity of the many bystanders who do not see themselves reflected in the nature of schooling as it is, or as it might become after the culture wars.

On the right, self-aggrandizing leaders, self-interested organizations, and unreflective individuals have been willing to exploit the weaknesses of public education in order to polarize the public and create political power to fight the culture wars. In the process, and because the education establishment has controlled the schools for so long, the leadership of the Christian Right has repeatedly shown itself to be willing to weaken public education rather than see it continue to undermine the deeply held beliefs of Christian fundamentalists.

The school wars are being fought by the Christian Right on many fronts and with a variety of weapons. At their extreme, the crusaders' goal is to make all schooling (and all other cultural institutions) consistent with the beliefs of Christian fundamentalists—to replace a secular state with a Christian theocracy. The Christian Right school strategy includes gaining a controlling interest in schools and education policy-making at every possible level, undermining public confidence in those schools and policymakers it cannot control, and picking issues and creating conflicts in a way that maximizes the Christian Right's influence and keeps the education establishment scrambling to maintain its sway.

Ralph Reed, executive director of the Christian Coalition, stated it this way in 1990: "What Christians have got to do is take back this country, one precinct at a time, one neighborhood at a time, and one state at a time."[16] Robert Simonds of Citizens for Excellence in Education, another Christian Right group, put schooling at the center of this crusade when he wrote, "There are 15,700 school districts in America. When we get an active Christian parents' committee in operation in all districts, we can take complete control of all local school boards. This would allow us to determine all local policy. . . ."[17]

In pursuit of this strategy Simonds claimed that his organization had won thirty-five hundred school board seats in fourteen states in the 1992 elections and assisted in the election of more than twelve thousand Christian conservative school board members around the country in 1993–1994.[18] The effort was deep as well as wide. Several places, such as San Diego County, California, New York City, and Pennsylvania, "experienced a virtual explosion of Religious Right activity related to the school board elections" of 1992 and 1993. The tactics included intentional disregard of the facts by data-proof ideologues, polarizing extremism that signaled the impossibility of compromise, and "stealth" candidates who concealed their right-wing agendas or their assistance from the Christian Right in order to get elected.[19]

The battle for control of local school boards is a part of a larger effort by the Christian Right to manipulate the debate over public education and to influence the content of public schooling. Before the 1994 general elections, Pat Robertson, failed presidential candidate and right-wing founder of the Christian Coalition, told a conference of his organization, "We are seeing the Christian Coalition rise to where God intends it to be in this nation—as one of the most powerful political forces in the history of America."[20] After the election, Robertson's executive director, Ralph Reed, shifted the focus from local to national government. He promised to "launch the largest single lobbying effort in our history" to eliminate the U.S. Department of Education and thereby further weaken the power of the education establishment.

With the local and national efforts of the Religious Right receiving the most resistance from the education establishment and the most attention from the media, it might appear that education policy-making at the state level would remain a depoliticized zone in the school wars. But by 1995, shifting the locus of power over schooling—among federal, state and local governments—had become another issue in the school wars.[21] With the political realignments brought about by the general elections of 1994, a majority of state legislatures jumped into the power struggle over how much and what kind of control state politicians would have over schooling.

The issues chosen to generate leverage for the Christian Right's school campaigns, whether at the state, local, or national levels, have been consistent with Christian fundamentalist beliefs. But they also have tended to be issues that, in themselves or as framed, are likely to polarize public opinion and to defy compromise. Among the most frequent targets are secular humanism, the separation of church and state, Darwinian evolution, sexuality and health education. There is little tolerance for any worldview other than that of heterosexual, white, middle-class Christians of Western European origin; little respect for freedom of expression among students and in student publications; and in general, antagonism toward teachers and students who try to explore and evaluate life's most challenging problems of personal, social, or moral conduct.

Censorship of schoolbooks has proven to be a reliable way to delegitimize public education and dispirit its personnel. While striving to maintain sincerely held Christian beliefs in their personal lives and those of their children, the Christian Right has often sought to impose its beliefs on everyone else in the schools.[22] The response of the education establishment has gone beyond a spirited defense of freedom of expression and inquiry to an insistence that a secular regime of largely liberal beliefs remain in place. By defending its own beliefs at the expense of the beliefs of Christian fundamentalists, the education establishment has exposed the weakness in the civil libertarian, marketplace-of-ideas vision of schooling. And because of the absence of meaningful choice of schooling, the Christian Right has found it necessary to exploit this weakness. One particular exchange of charges between two advocacy groups illustrates a dynamic that is repeated again and again in censorship conflicts around the country.

In 1994, People for the American Way (PFAW), a generally liberal, civil libertarian organization formed to counteract the growing intolerance of the Christian Right, reported 462 attacks on the content of books used in American public schools that year. Most of the reported book challenges came from the Christian Right. It was the highest number of such incidents in the twelve-year history of PFAW's report, "Attacks on the Freedom to Learn." The report is chilling. It describes the misleading tactics used by the Christian Right, documents the existence of a national network responsible for many of the incidents, and reveals its high success rate in undermining the freedom to teach and learn. The report's conclusions are presented carefully and supported in detail.[23]

In a preemptive strike against these conclusions, a national advocacy arm of the Christian Right, Focus on the Family, condemned the report as inaccurate a week before it was issued. The organization claimed that most of the censorship attempts did not succeed in removing books from the classroom and therefore did not really amount to censorship at all. Focus on the Family also argued that parents have the right to question what happens in the schools that their taxes support and that their children are required to attend. They appealed to the basic democratic principle of parental participation in school governance as a cornerstone of public education.[24]

PFAW countered that what the right sees as an exercise of parental rights of participation in schooling is really an attack upon the constitutionally protected freedom to learn and to teach. It pointed out that self-censorship is frequently the result of even failed attempts to remove a book from a course or from a school library. Moreover, PFAW reported that censorship efforts are almost always aimed at controlling what every student in a school district reads. Efforts by an individual student or family to avoid exposure to a book or to opt out of a course entirely were not included in PFAW's evidence of censorship.[25]

Neither side was completely honest about the nature of the struggle. The advocates for the Christian Right insisted that raising questions about the appropriateness of a text or library book was merely an exercise of a parent's right to influence a child's education. But this claim ignored the constitutional rights of those who want to teach or read the challenged book. More important, it ignored the inherent problems of an educational system in which political majorities ultimately control the general content of public schooling. A parents' group that either cannot compromise its beliefs for reasons of conscience or will not compromise them for reasons of political strategy can only advance its own cause by trying to impose itself on all parents and children in a school system. Such a group plays by majority rules because its members understand that ideology in schooling is easily made into a winner-take-all game. Either the Christian Right succeeds in determining which books everyone uses, or its members continue a struggle that demonizes the opposition and undermines public confidence in schooling. In either case, their opponents cannot win.

On the other side, the civil liberties advocates also ignored a basic fact of power in the censorship conflicts. The PFAW report did not even mention that the original selection of textbooks—by statewide, politically created government agencies in twenty-three of fifty states, for example—is as much an act of censorship as the effort to remove those materials once they have been selected. PFAW has fought to open these processes to public participation from all points on the political spectrum. But even when the process of selecting textbooks has been opened to public input and debate, it remains a political struggle over ideology and culture, and makes constitutionally protected freedoms to teach, learn, read, and publish subject to political manipulation. PFAW insists that textbook *removal* must respect these constitutional rights, but it is content to leave textbook *selection* to the political process. The education establishment knows, therefore, but does not admit, that inertia is a great source of power in school systems. It knows also that once the values of the education establishment are firmly in place, resisting the accommodation of others' values can easily be made to look like a neutral defense of freedom in the schools against a campaign of intolerance.

Up until the end of 1994, by far the most productive strategies of the Christian Right were the campaign to take over local school boards "one neighborhood at a time" and the campaign of state and local censorship as reported by PFAW. In addition to its successes in individual conflicts, these strategies polarized school communities and added to the general tone of intolerance in public discourse. The strategies that have served the Christian Right so well have weakened public regard for schooling and deflated the sense of mission in much of the education establishment.

The beleaguered education establishment, not content to rely on the inertia of its long-term control of public education, fought back on a national level. It recognized that public schooling was under coordinated attack by the Christian Right. But it also recognized that public education had become disoriented by the conflicting analyses and demands of school reformers, embarrassed by the demonstrable inadequacies and failures of schooling for children most in need, and weakened by a shortage of public confidence and a surplus of conflict. The education establishment had enormous influence and resources at stake and responded to the threat to its accustomed power.

A focus on money and jobs gives the clearest picture of what the education establishment looked like before the *Goals 2000:* Educate America Act became law in 1994.[26] The Census Bureau reported that in 1992, 55 percent of all 11,100,000 local government employees worked in education, including higher education. Among the 4,550,000 state government employees in the same year, 45 percent worked in education. Rounding off a bit, just under one half of all state and local government jobs were in education.[27] The U.S. Department of Education reported that in the 1991–92 school year, a staggering $241 billion was spent on public elementary and secondary education by local school districts. This total school expenditure figure is not very far from the amount spent on defense and the military by the world's only superpower. Of the nearly one-quarter trillion dollars collected that year for public schooling, only about 7 percent came from the federal government. The average increase in these expenditures for public schooling has been $20 billion per year, a figure that suggests that in spite of unsuccessful bond elections and successful taxpayer revolts, the education establishment has remained able to control a significant portion of state and local tax dollars.

Only about half of the reported 1991–92 schooling expenditures went for the salaries and benefits of the nation's nearly 2,500,000 public school teachers, who earned an average annual salary of under $35,000. The other half was divided among administrators and administration (nearly 76,000 administrators and 129,000 principals and vice-principals), student services (guidance counselors, librarians, aides, etc.), instructional materials, operation and maintenance, student transportation, food service, interest on school debt, and capital outlays such as construction (just under $21 billion for 1991–92). These annual expenditures do not include amounts spent for the operation of state departments of education or for the U.S. Department of Education (the figure does include funds granted by state or federal government to local school districts). Because these are national figures, they hide the enormous disparities in amounts spent from the richest to the poorest districts in each state. The budget and personnel numbers only hint at the enormous complexity of the regulatory and bureaucratic maze they support.

Other significant figures, only some of which are included in the one-quarter trillion annual figure, help describe the reach of the education establishment. The manufacture and sale of textbooks for K-12 alone is a more than $2 billion per year industry. Almost half the states have statewide textbook approval committees whose job is to select the texts that may be used by local districts.[28] Originally meant to ensure the quality of textbooks and to eliminate conflict of interest in their purchase, these committees have become political forums for the contest between the Christian Right and the education establishment.

Political conflicts and culture wars routinely develop around the selection process; and economic reality frequently causes publishers to accept the judgments of these committees even when they are at odds with the views of scholars and authors whose work is being published. What is not actually censored by government committees is self-censored by publishers fearful of the politics of textbook selection. The education establishment—and the complex legal structure that supports it—thus reaches into the publishing industry, setting the stage for more culture wars, further politicizing knowledge and scholarship, and extending the dependence of another segment of the economy on the outcome of school conflicts such as the Texas health text controversy.

The education establishment also grows as technology does. After a slow start, the use of computer software and multimedia instructional materials in the schools is growing so fast that it probably hasn't been measured. Nevertheless, access to the Internet in classrooms has already become the object of school censorship, as yet another productive part of the economy attempts to conform to the needs of public schooling controlled by the education establishment.

Testing of teachers for certification and recertification and of students for promotion, graduation, college entrance, and evaluation of the success of schooling comprise another outpost of the education establishment. In 1991–92, teachers themselves paid over $30 million for teacher exams. Students and families paid over $130 million for college entrance examinations, not counting the hundreds of preparation courses that depend on the continuation of this part of the education establishment. And all of the standardized tests and other assessments given periodically to students around the nation—touted as necessary for judging everything from the results of school reform to students' future employability—were produced by a testing industry whose share of the $250 billion, though not clearly indicated in the federal statistical summary, can only be helping to push the total higher.

Training teachers and conducting research about teaching and learning represent other significant activities of the education establishment not measured by federal statistics on annual school expenditures. There are approximately twelve hundred teacher training programs in colleges and universities around the country. Many also do research—much of it sponsored—that both stimulates and is dependent on school reform. These institutions employ forty-two thousand professors to do this research and to train nearly five hundred thousand potential school teachers each year. If every public school teacher in the United States retired at the same time, it would take only five years for this segment of the education establishment to resupply completely the public schools in the nation's more than fifteen thousand school districts. Teacher training alone is a nearly $3 billion per year industry. It has an enormous potential influence on what happens in schools and an even larger actual dependence on the survival of the education establishment.

Research and professional organizations, interest groups, and reform organizations account for billions of dollars more each year. They involve millions of people in thousands of activities that are related to public schooling but are not included in the annual expenditure reports collected by the U.S. Department of Education. Each has its own interests, constituents, resources, and, frequently, lobbying efforts at the state and federal levels. Each is in some way dependent on the continued health of the one-quarter trillion dollar annual budget of public schooling. Just a few examples of these outstations of the education establishment include the following:

- There are over eight hundred *major* professional publications and research journals devoted to schooling and education.
- There are hundreds of professional organizations for teachers, administrators, school board members, and specialists dealing with different subject matters, age groups, learning issues, management problems.
- Just two teachers' unions, the NEA and the AFT, had over three million dues paying members in 1994.[29] The National School Boards Association represented ninety-one thousand school board

members. The American Association of School Administrators had sixteen thousand members. The National PTA had 6.7 million members. They all have lobbyists, and so do the groups that oppose them. Just the energy their opponents put into trying to undermine the power and the gains made by teachers' unions creates millions of dollars worth of legal, lobbying, and public relations work.

- There are more than thirty-five different, *major* school-reform networks (excluding subject matter organizations such as the National Council of Teachers of English, Mathematics, etc.) that work with thousands and thousands of schools and districts to reform education according to their own visions of what changes are needed. The number of special interest groups seeking to change schooling is numberless and their total budgets uncountable.

- Just a glance at any education magazine or newspaper reveals the hundreds of advertisers whose teaching materials, technical assistance, training programs, assessment programs, supplies and hardware, are designed for and sold to the education establishment.

In comparison to the resources of the education establishment, all the organizations and budgets and foot soldiers of the Christian Right pale. This education establishment and its dependents, affiliates, and outstations might be called an "Education Empire" without much fear of exaggerating the reach, the resources, and the complex set of interdependent relationships that constitute the reality of public schooling in the United States. Ordinarily the term "empire" also suggests that a single person, a small group of persons, or a handful of powerful interests controls the vast resources and power of that empire. But the number and variety of organizations and persons that make up the education establishment in the United States is so great that the unifying control and narrow interests characteristic of an empire seem to be missing. Unless, of course, that unity could be created by a national reform campaign—such as *Goals 2000*—that tries to align virtually all the interrelated parts of the establishment around a single set of goals on a national and state basis.

When an industry this big, this far-reaching, and this important to the economic life of the nation and the future of its children is threatened, a vigorous response can be expected. When the education establishment seems to be losing its public support and sense of purpose, or becoming preoccupied with conflict and reform at the expense of teaching and learning, that response can be expected to be self-serving. When a $250 billion per year business becomes a prime battleground for a culture war, that response is likely to be designed to weaken the opposition permanently. It is no wonder that the comprehensive reform, reinvigorated sense of mission, and unified defense against right-wing attack promised by *Goals 2000* was so appealing to what now might be called the Education Empire.

Goals 2000 is, among other things, being used by the Education Empire in an attempt to revitalize itself and to mount a major counterattack against the Christian Right and other detractors. The two major combatants in the school wars have thus opened a new front in their attempts to impose competing visions of what schooling must be. As the early struggles over amending *Goals 2000* and over controlling national curriculum standards both show, the Christian Right and the Education Empire are pursuing their own interests without much awareness of how severely the school wars are damaging public schooling and American society. Meanwhile, individual families, teachers, students, and communities of belief seem to have little choice but to become combatants themselves in the school wars, or simply to accept the presence of occupying ideologies in their schools and classrooms.

CHAPTER THREE

Goals 2000

The *Goals 2000:* Educate America Act appears to be just another major piece of bipartisan federal legislation designed to improve the quality of public schooling. The nation has had them before: the National Defense Education Act (NDEA) of 1958, which grew out of the Cold War and was America's first response to the Soviet Sputnik success; the Elementary and Secondary Education Act (ESEA) of 1965, which grew out of the War on Poverty. But *Goals 2000*'s passage in 1994—driven by the need to revitalize the Education Empire and to resist attacks on it by the Christian Right and fueled by the desire to improve the quality of schooling and to put it in the service of national and corporate economic competitiveness—broke the mold of American public education fashioned over nearly a century and a half.[1]

Goals 2000 was amended in 1996, two years after its passage, and it may be amended again as the national political climate continues to change. But a detailed understanding of its structure—of the requirements it imposes, the mechanisms it puts in place, and the power it realigns—remains essential.

This understanding is important because *Goals 2000* has generated enormous momentum. Forty-six of fifty states have accepted the hundreds of millions of dollars already available under the Act and have begun participating in its required school reform process. The national content standards provided for in the Act have been created, and numerous professional organizations and governmental agencies are at work on implementing those standards nationally in the states.

Even if *Goals 2000* were to be repealed entirely, its ghost would still animate the school reform efforts of virtually all states. The Act provides a model of how state governments can gain control of virtually every aspect of public schooling; and the realignment of state and local education agencies required by this model is already taking place. It is therefore essential to understand the elements of the *Goals 2000* model of comprehensive school reform.

Goals 2000 is the result, as well as the cause, of a fundamental shift in thinking about the nature of public schooling in the United States. The new thinking calls for a substantial increase in the power of government—at the state as well as the federal level—over the education of individuals. This shift in power makes possible a comprehensive and standardized control of schooling imposed from the top down by education experts employed by government agencies. To understand why this way of thinking about schooling takes American education in exactly the wrong direction, it is necessary to understand how *Goals 2000*, its current manifestation, is structured.[2]

Overview of *Goals 2000*

Goals 2000 re-constitutes public education. There are five elements to this constitutional transformation of American public schooling that emerge from an analysis of the Act:

First, state governments are required to adopt content requirements —standards—for public school curriculum.[3] By using political mechanisms to create, certify, and enforce these content standards, the Act creates an official knowledge tolerated nowhere else in a constitutional democracy committed since its founding to freedom of intellect and belief.

Second, the curriculum requirements created under *Goals 2000* demand not simply student exposure to politically determined content, but also "demonstrated competency" over those subject matters as the prerequisite price for student promotion and graduation. Teachers eventually are to be judged by how successfully their students meet these competency requirements.

Third, *Goals 2000* seeks to create a systemic change in public education that literally standardizes schooling. Reforms are to be systemic in the sense that they include all elements of schooling, from curriculum content and teacher certification to student assessment and textbook publishing. Reforms are also to be systemic in the sense that they reach into every public school in every geographical community in the country.[4] The Act contains no meaningful protection for the independence of nongovernment schools or home schooling.

Fourth, *Goals 2000* dramatically changes the distribution of power in almost every aspect of schooling. From a shaky and often-conflicted compromise between families and local school districts, the locus of power in education is moved toward the more insensitive and ideologically incendiary politics of state and federal governments. The increased power over schooling granted to these governments will be felt in courts as well as in local board meetings and parent-teacher conferences. Though Goal 8 of the Act calls for increased parental participation in schooling, it is functionally irrelevant to the change in power allocation made by the Act.

Fifth, *Goals 2000* is based on a politicized and anti-individualistic concept of education inconsistent with the principles of constitutional democracy. It abandons the already weakened Enlightenment concept of education and objectifies the individual student as a commodity to be produced by schooling. Its content standards define by government action, not by individual choice, what is worth knowing, how the world ought to be understood, which questions should be asked and debated and which should not, and what educational goals are appropriate for every parent's child. In essence, *Goals 2000* envisions a standardized and comprehensive scheme of schooling imposed from the top down by experts and politicians.

Goals 2000 seeks to work these basic changes in public schooling by creating a pyramidlike structure that places the federal government— and national goals and curriculum content standards—at the top, with state governments in the middle and local education agencies at the bottom. The entire structure is brought into line by a series of planning and implementation mechanisms based on the content standards. At the state and local levels, the content standards are also to be used as the basis of student assessment (testing), teacher certification, and virtually every other part of the schooling process.

Goals 2000 is long and complex. In nearly 175 pages it defines new roles and powers for the U.S. Department of Education and for state and local governments as part of a comprehensive reorientation of all government schooling in the United States. The Act begins with sections 1–3, which include a table of contents, "Purpose," and "Definitions." The remainder of the Act is divided into titles. Title I, "National Education Goals," includes sections 101 and 102. Title II, "National Education Reform Leadership, Standards, and Assessments," is further divided into four parts: Part A ("National Education Goals Panel," sections 201–207); Part B ("National Education Standards and Improvement Council," sections 211–221); Part C ("Leadership in Educational Technology," sections 231–236), and Part D ("Authorization of Appropriations," section 241). Title III, "State and Local Education Systemic Improvement," contains sections 301–319; Title IV, "Parental Assistance," contains sections 401–408. There are three other titles not of concern in this analysis: "International Education Program," section 601; "Safe Schools," sections 701–709; and "Minority-focused Civics Education," sections 801–805.

"Section 2 of the Act, "Purpose," reads like the preamble to a constitution. It sets out the overt purposes of the legislation, including "(1) promoting coherent, nationwide, systemic education reform; (3) defining appropriate and coherent Federal, State, and local roles and responsibilities for education reform and lifelong learning; (5) supporting new initiatives at the Federal, State, local and school levels to provide equal educational opportunity for all students . . .; (6) providing a framework for the reauthorization of all Federal education programs . . .; and (7) stimulating the development and adoption of a voluntary national system of skill standards and certification to serve as a cornerstone of the national strategy to enhance workforce skills."

Titles I through III contain the core of the power shifts and structural changes that will reshape how U.S. schooling will henceforth operate. Title I of the Act adopts eight national goals for education. At the core of these goals and of the structure of the Act itself is Goal 3, "Student Achievement and Citizenship," which sets out nine subject matter areas in which American students must demonstrate competency: "By the year 2000, all students will leave grades 4, 8, and 12 having demonstrated competency over challenging subject matter including English, mathematics, science, foreign languages, civics and government, economics, arts, history, and geography, . . ."[5]

Title II, "National Education Reform Leadership, Standards, and Assessments," creates governmental mechanisms (agencies, powers, and procedures) which the federal government will use to apply national content standards and to evaluate and approve school reform plans "voluntarily" submitted by the states. Both the national standards and the state reform plans must be consistent with the goals set out in Title I.

Title III, "State and Local Education Systemic Improvement," provides a three-tiered bureaucratic mechanism for applying national standards to "fundamentally changing the entire system of public education" through the creation of state and local reform plans to be approved by the federal agencies created in Title II. Federal funds are made available to encourage the voluntary compliance of states with the systemic reform plan. Reform plans at all levels are to be consistent and each is to be based on approved content standards. No state is required by the Act to submit its content standards to the federal government for approval in order to receive the hundreds of millions of dollars available for creating and implementing state plans and standards,[6] but the practical, political reality is that virtually every state will seek the federal imprimatur eventually, especially with federal funding for reform promised by the Act for five years. The vast majority of states complied voluntarily during the first year of the Act.[7]

The overall design of the legislation, therefore, is to create and certify at the national level, curriculum content standards in nine subjects ("what students have to know and be able to do"),[8] to require the adoption of these or more rigorous standards by state and local schooling authorities, and to key all aspects of all public schooling—student performance assessments,[9] teacher training and certification,[10] textbook publishing and the use of educational technology,[11] work force skills and certification,[12] and education research and development[13]—to these content standards. Virtually every aspect of the Education Empire is to be reformed, revitalized, systematized, and standardized on the basis of a politically approved body of official knowledge.

The creation and enforcement of national curriculum content standards has been justified as a means of increasing students' performance and their preparation for competition in a global economy. It has also been justified by the need to reduce the inequalities that plague American schooling. These inequalities are most obvious in the vast differences in resources available to different school districts. But they are perhaps nowhere more destructive than in the widely varying expectations that schools and school personnel hold for their students. Such disparate expectations, which often become self-fulfilling prophecies, are especially pernicious when based on the socioeconomic status, race, or linguistic background of students, and when institutionalized in practices such as tracking and school segregation.

The national curriculum standards and so-called opportunity-to-learn standards contained in the *Goals 2000* plan are supposed to reduce these inequalities. The opportunity-to-learn standards are meant to ensure that adequate resources are available so that all students have the chance to meet the content standards applied to them. The inclusion of these opportunity-to-learn standards was insisted upon by liberal legislators and others who, while committed to alleviating the massive resource inequalities in public schooling, realized that a direct requirement of state funding equalization would never pass the Congress.[14] But in April 1996, the 104th Congress amended *Goals 2000* and, among other things, eliminated the U.S. Department of Education's authority to establish the opportunity-to-learn standards. It also ended the requirement that each state provide all schools with the resources necessary to enable every student to have the opportunity to reach the required academic standards.[15]

The second part of the equalization plan—the requirement that all students meet the national and state curriculum standards—is supposed to be direct and difficult to defeat. By requiring that all students meet the same rigorous standards of performance, the law attempts to eliminate any teaching or institutional practices that lower expectations for students historically deprived of equal educational opportunity. It is unclear whether this strategy could in fact reduce the massive inequalities that characterize American schooling nationwide. But it is clear that the intellectual and cultural uniformity advanced by *Goals 2000* is a simplistic, formal equality that ultimately could be destructive to all students and families, especially to those it is meant to help.

The *Goals 2000:* Educate America Act

To understand the nature and magnitude of the power shift created and reinforced by *Goals 2000*, a more detailed description of the Act is required, especially of the curriculum content standards which are intended to require and make consistent all education reform. The mechanisms in the Act that will lead to the political specification of knowledge in the nation's schools are the centerpiece of virtually all comprehensive reform under the Act at federal, state, and local government levels. Without them, the Act would be toothless, a paper tiger.

Section 3 of the Act, "Definitions," states that "the term 'content standards' means broad descriptions of the knowledge and skills students should acquire in a particular subject area"; the term "performance standards" is defined as "concrete examples and explicit definitions of what students have to know and be able to do to demonstrate that such students are proficient in the skills and knowledge framed by content standards"; the term " 'State assessment' means measures of student performance which include at least 1 instrument of evaluation [test], and may include other measures of student performance, for a specific purpose and use which are intended to evaluate the progress of all students in the State toward learning the material in State content standards in 1 or more subject areas."

Title I (Sections 101 and 102) establishes eight national education goals, each including a number of slightly more specific objectives. The goals are:

(1) School Readiness—By the year 2000 all children in America will start school ready to learn.

(2) School Completion—By the year 2000, the high school graduation rate will increase to at least 90 percent.

(3) Student Achievement and Citizenship—By the year 2000, all students will leave grades 4, 8, and 12 having demonstrated competency over challenging subject matter including English, mathematics, science, foreign languages, civics and government, economics, arts, history, and geography, and every school in America will ensure that all students learn to use their minds well, so they may be prepared for responsible citizenship, further learning, and productive employment in our nation's modern economy.

(4) Teacher Education and Professional Development—By the year 2000, the nation's teaching force will have access to programs for continued improvement of their professional skills and the opportunity to acquire the knowledge and skills needed to instruct and prepare all American students for the next century.

(5) Mathematics and Science—By the year 2000, U.S. students will be first in the world in mathematics and science achievement.

(6) Adult Literacy and Lifelong Learning—By the year 2000, every adult American will be literate and will possess the knowledge and skills necessary to compete in a global economy and exercise the rights and responsibilities of citizenship.

(7) Safe, Disciplined, and Alcohol-and Drug-Free Schools—By the year 2000 every school in the United States will be free of drugs, violence, and the unauthorized presence of firearms and alcohol and will offer a disciplined environment conducive to learning.

(8) Parental Participation—By the year 2000, every school will promote partnerships that will increase parental involvement and participation in promoting the social, emotional, and academic growth of children.

Title II (Sections 204–227) establishes in the executive branch of the federal government (Department of Education) a National Education Goals Panel and a National Education Standards and Improvement Council. The panel, which has eighteen government-appointed members and a staff, is charged, among other things, with reviewing the national content standards and national student performance standards presented to it by the council. The panel may disapprove of the national content and performance standards by a two-thirds vote.[16]

The Act is full of contradictory policies about whether the content standards to be approved by the goals panel are voluntary or not. The standards are repeatedly labeled "voluntary," and assurances of noncoercion appear in two sections; but the federal and state governments are given the power to approve curriculum standards. Moreover, since *Goals 2000* had its origin with Republican and Democratic members of the National Governors' Conference, and continues to rely on the power of the states to create and implement reforms consistent with the national curriculum, the assurances of voluntary participation are all but meaningless to families and individuals.[17]

Though the standards to be approved by the National Education Goals Panel are consistently labeled "voluntary," the claim is simply not believable for the following reasons: first, the entire structure of the Act rests on the application of content standards to the reform of all other aspects of schooling. Content standards are not going to be voluntary, diverse, discretionary with schools or teachers, or individualized if the result would be to weaken the Act's ability to bring about school reform; second, the desperate need by local and state school officials for resources will discourage them from dissent about national standards; third, even those state governments that do not seek federal approval of content standards must adopt their own statewide, nonvoluntary content standards and apply them to all aspects of school reform if they want to receive any federal funds under the Act.[18] The presence of required curriculum content standards on a state level is as problematic as on the national level. Fourth, one of the stated purposes of the Act is to use content standards to provide "a framework for the reauthorization of all Federal education programs," so it is likely that other federal education laws will eventually require compliance with national or state content standards created under *Goals 2000*; fifth, once assurances of voluntariness have helped make *Goals 2000* an accepted and commonplace part of the legal structure of schooling, there is nothing to prevent its being amended to remove the word "voluntary" from the content standards; sixth, substantial new powers over schooling are given to federal and state governments, but there is in *Goals 2000* no meaningful protection for the individual, family, and community educational freedoms that would provide a basis for resisting the imposition of official knowledge.

A National Education Standards and Improvement Council (NESIC) is also created under Title II of the Act. It would have nineteen politically appointed members and a staff. It is charged, among other things, with developing and certifying national content standards and national student performance standards to be sent for review to the National Education Goals Panel.[19] In adopting these standards, the council is required to consult experts and also to use "an open and public process" allowing for input from all relevant parties, specifically including advocacy groups.[20]

The council is also charged with certifying content and performance standards submitted by the states as the organizing principles of state school reform plans funded under the Act. To be certified, such state standards must be comparable to or higher in rigor than the national standards certified by the council. The reform process envisioned, therefore, is that each state will be induced by federal funds and political pressures to create a set of specific, subject matter content and student performance standards that conform to the national curriculum and that are, in turn, imposed upon local school districts through a process described in Title III.

The council's certification of national standards requires that those standards "be sufficiently general to be used by any State without restricting State and local control of curriculum and prerogatives regarding instructional methods. . . ."[21] But in giving the council the power to certify state content and performance standards as "comparable or higher in rigor and quality" to national standards,[22] as well as in empowering the council to approve state assessments aligned with the state's content standards,[23] the law removes still more power over schooling from individuals and places it in the hands of state and federal bureaucracies. Neither the council's nor the goals panel's approval of state standards is subject to any requirement that freedom of education be respected for local schools, teachers, communities, private schools, or individual students or families.

NESIC—its powers, procedures, and purposes—is a model of how government at any level can use curriculum content standards as a comprehensive means to reform schooling and place the control of individual education in the hands of the political process. But it was never put into operation. Shortly after the election of 1994, Christian Right groups that did not want to see their local victories in the school wars overturned by national content standards, and opponents of any federal involvement in schooling, began attacking NESIC. They were joined by those educrats who were frustrated that emerging national curriculum standards did not reflect the conservative agenda. The first result of this attack was that no appointments were made to NESIC, and the Clinton administration indicated a willingness to let it wither. That left the secretary of education as the focal point for approval of national standards and state reform plans.

In April 1996, a series of amendments to *Goals 2000* was included in the Omnibus Appropriations Act. One of those amendments repealed NESIC. But though one federal layer of bureaucracy was thereby eliminated, the *Goals 2000* process and the assumptions underlying it went on pretty much as before. The secretary of education still had the power and responsibility to enforce all aspects of the *Goals 2000* legislation, as he had during the time that NESIC had not functioned.[24] The National Education Goals Panel remained in place as the mechanism for final federal approval of national and state curriculum content standards. More important, the tactic of using governmentally approved official knowledge as the linchpin of systemic school reform in every state had already been legitimized and imprinted in the minds of most educators and politicians and in the practices of most state school reform plans.[25]

Title II contains another gesture toward those who believe that state control of schools is a satisfactory protection for individual educational freedom. Section 213 (h)(1) states that no state can be required to have its standards and assessments certified by the goals panel (and secretary of education) as a condition of participating in any federal education program. At the same time, however, every state that wishes to participate in the *Goals 2000* fund allocation must adopt its own curriculum content standards. The net result is likely to be fifty sets of state-mandated curriculum content standards, most but not all of which have been certified by the federal government.[26] The provision protects states from federal coercion, but not from federal inducements to conform voluntarily. It provides no protection from either coerced or induced uniformity for local school districts, private schools, home schoolers, or for those families, communities and cultures that might want to adopt different goals for the schools that sustain them.

Title III creates the political processes by which state and local public authorities are to adopt school reform plans aligned with state content standards voluntarily submitted for certification to the national panel. These reform plans are to be systemic; that is, the standards adopted under the *Goals 2000* Act are to infuse and control virtually every aspect of schooling on the state and local levels, from student performance to teacher training. The purpose of this "top-down and bottom-up education reform" is to revitalize "all local public schools" by "fundamentally changing the entire system of public education through comprehensive, coherent, and coordinated improvement. . . ."[27]

Title III authorized the allocation of $400 million for FY 1994 and promised "such sums as may be necessary" for the period through FY 1998.[28] In order to get a share of these funds after the first year, each state must submit a "State improvement plan" to the U.S. Department of Education for approval. Each state plan must be developed by a state panel described in section 306 (b).[29] To be approved, the state plan must contain curriculum content and student performance standards ("voluntarily" submitted to the national panel for approval under Title II),[30] a process for implementing state assessments (including student tests), a "process for aligning State or local curricula, instructional materials, and State assessments with the State content standards and the State student performance standards," and a process for assuring that the state's teacher and administrator preparation and licensure and continuing education are consistent with the approved content and performance standards.[31]

Section 309 requires that each state plan also provide for subgrants to local education agencies (school districts). These subgrants, which must total 90 percent of the funds received by the state from the federal government after the first year,[32] can only be received by school districts which themselves have filed a "local improvement plan" approved by the state.[33] Like the state plan required by the federal government of each participating state, the local plan that the state must require of each participating district must be developed so that it meets "the State content standards and State student performance standards." As promised by the Act, top-down control of schooling is thus made systemic, pervasive, and comprehensive by using what amounts to a performance-tested national curriculum to align federal, state, and local policies through a coordinated pyramid of bureaucratically administered reform plans.

The "bottom-up reform" encouraged by the plan is limited to requiring that each state provide flexibility to schools "to adapt and integrate State content standards into courses of study," and that the state facilitate waivers from state rules and regulations that "impede the ability . . . to carry out local improvement plans."[34] There are also waivers available for regulations of certain federal acts under section 311. But as the term "waivers," and the conditions for securing them under the *Goals 2000* Act, makes clear, relief from regulation may be refused. The underlying assumption of the Act, therefore, is that waivers are a dispensation granted by a state or federal government of nearly plenary power over schooling. There is no guarantee of educational freedom retained by the people, nor is there any recognition that governments of limited, specified powers must grant waivers where educational freedoms are at risk.

The educational powers of state and federal governments are expanded and their content standards are made consistent by the *Goals 2000* law. But there is no mention in the Act of protecting the educational freedoms of students, teachers, families, and communities—not the freedom to learn or to teach, or the right to receive an education uncompromised by racial or ethnic discrimination, or the freedom of expression and inquiry, or the freedom of intellect or spirit, or even the constitutionally based freedom to choose a nongovernment school that has not been regulated into conformity with government-controlled schools. These freedoms have received protection under the Constitution and other federal laws, of course. But the changes in power and priorities worked by *Goals 2000* are so extensive that the status of educational freedoms litigated over seventy-five years could be changed dramatically under the new regime.

There is virtually no mention of nongovernment schools in *Goals 2000*, one exception being section 1020, which prohibits the use of funds under Title III (reform planning and implementation) "to directly or indirectly benefit any school other than a public school."[35] But insulating private schools from public benefits is not the issue. For most nongovernment schools that value their independence, the problem is that they may not be insulated from the restrictions which may be imposed by the government. There is no protection from state or local attempts directly or indirectly to impose government standards on nongovernment schools as part of the mandated government reform process.

In sum, *Goals 2000*, even with the 1996 amendments, sets in motion a comprehensive reform of all public schools and every outpost of the Education Empire. The entire mechanism of the Act is made to revolve around a government-specified and performance-based curriculum. The weekly, monthly, and yearly teaching goals of every teacher are to be based on these content standards. So too are the testing, promotion, and graduation of every student; the training, certification, and continuing education of all teachers; the content of textbooks, educational technology, and teaching materials. Federally funded education research and development are intended to evaluate and enhance the effectiveness of reforms based on these same content standards. Eventually, work force skills and employability certification, and the reauthorization of all other federal education programs and aid to education, are to be made consistent with these same standards.[36] Nearly everything about schooling is to be standardized after being subjected to expert scrutiny and political struggle, while local, state, and federal school authorities are united into a single pyramid with unified goals and objectives.

Goals 2000 may initially be administered in a benevolent way by benevolent administrators dedicated to eliminating inequalities and improving the quality of learning and teaching for all. But there is nothing in the Act, or in the legal structure it creates, that would prevent benevolence from becoming despotism if the powers created by *Goals 2000* should fall into the wrong hands. Moreover, even in the right hands, the Act is so comprehensive in its design, so standardizing in its effect, and so pervasive in its application, that any dissenting family might easily experience its abstract and general benevolence as a form of individual oppression. It is the state and federal power structure created and reinforced by *Goals 2000*—and the assumptions about education that underlie this power structure—not the intentions of its administrators, supporters, or detractors that needs public debate.

The major provisions of *Goals 2000* will eventually change drastically the way in which schools are run and education policy is made in the United States. That is the intent of adopting the Act. So fundamental are the power shifts worked by *Goals 2000* that the law amounts to a re-constitution of American public schooling. This re-constitution was accomplished with very little discussion of its educational merits, without any significant public debate about its likely effects on life in a pluralistic democracy, and without consideration of any alternative means for achieving the same goals.[37] The 1996 amendments to the Act seem mostly cosmetic and not at all likely to challenge the fundamental assumption of government control of schooling that underlies *Goals 2000*.

The need to re-constitute American public education in order for it to survive in a changed and changing culture is clear. The question is whether the re-constitution provided by *Goals 2000* meets the needs of anyone other than the Education Empire; whether it enhances or inhibits the most basic intellectual and cultural freedoms; whether it moves toward real educational quality and equality, or only toward a stifling, formal uniformity; and whether it sets the nation on a practical path to preserving public education or on a short route to its destruction.

As Chapter 4 argues, *Goals 2000* is the wrong response to the problems and conflicts experienced by public schooling up until the mid-1990s. But at least its passage raises the difficult, far-reaching, and fundamental issue of how public education *ought* to be structured. An extended public consideration of how power over public education ought to be allocated for the twenty-first century has now become not only advisable, but unavoidable.

CHAPTER FOUR

Renouncing Our Constitutional Heritage

"Our whole constitutional heritage rebels at the thought of giving government the power to control men's minds."

U.S. Supreme Court Justice Thurgood Marshall

It is the essence of constitutional democracy in the United States—and a paradox which many people do not fully appreciate—that in order for the majoritarian politics of self-government to work properly, freedom of belief, intellect, and expression must be protected from majority control. This essential principle of constitutional democracy was ignored in the creation of the federal *Goals 2000: Educate America Act*, and it will be undermined by its implementation in the states.

A national school reform effort that does not respect the Constitution should not expect to be well received by those who do. Neither should it expect to succeed in reaching its own goal of educational excellence and equity. Under *Goals 2000*, the quality of public schooling and of public discourse about schooling are more likely to decline than to improve. Teachers, parents, and community members committed to improving the lives of children are likely to be displaced increasingly by politicians and ideologues, while the inequalities of educational opportunity that steal the potential of so many of these children remain largely untouched. And in a nation deeply ambivalent about its own pluralism, intellectual and cultural diversity are likely to be treated more as liabilities than as assets.

The First Amendment secures the system of individual freedoms and democratic communities upon which constitutional democracy depends. The amendment requires that government at all levels remain neutral toward the content of virtually all communication and every individual's opinions and beliefs. It anticipates that communities of belief or opinion, of interest, heritage, or worldview, will likewise remain free of government manipulation of the mind. The Constitution as a whole embodies the view that, unless the wellspring of intellectual and cultural diversity is thus protected, the "consent of the governed"[1] will be rendered hollow, democracy will become a "tyranny of the majority,"[2] and the individual mind will be at risk of becoming "the mere creature of the state."[3]

These are fundamental principles of general application. But they have been expressed most forcefully by the Supreme Court in a matter involving individual conscience in public schools. In *West Virginia v. Barnette*, the Court, foreseeing an intensification of the school wars, barred schools from requiring a daily pledge of allegiance to the U.S. flag. In so doing, it declared that state and local governments do not have the constitutional power to invade "the sphere of intellect and spirit" of children, or of the families and communities in which they live.

> The very purpose of a Bill of Rights was to withdraw certain subjects from the vicissitudes of political controversy, to place them beyond the reach of majorities and officials and to establish them as legal principles to be applied by the courts. One's right to life, liberty, and property, to free speech, a free press, freedom of worship and assembly, and other fundamental rights may not be submitted to vote; they depend on the outcome of no elections.[4]
>
> . . . We set up government by consent of the governed, and the Bill of Rights denies those in power any legal opportunity to coerce that consent. Authority here is to be controlled by public opinion, not public opinion by authority.[5]

In making its ruling, the Court overturned an earlier precedent, *Minersville v. Gobitis*, in which it approved the compulsory pledge of allegiance in public schools as "conduct required of all . . . children in the promotion of national cohesion."[6] Jehovah's Witnesses had objected to the pledge as contrary to their religious beliefs, which forbid serving or bowing down to "any graven image."[7] But Justice Frankfurter's 1939 opinion in *Gobitis* nevertheless held that government "may in self-protection utilize the educational process for inculcating those almost unconscious feelings which bind men together . . ."[8] In reaching the now-discredited decision in *Gobitis,* neither Justice Frankfurter nor the other members of the Court's majority were disparaging religious liberty or the freedom of intellect and belief. It was their view that these fundamental liberties were adequately protected as long as families had the constitutional right to attend schools not operated by government:

> Great diversity of psychological and ethical opinion exists among us concerning the best way to train children for their place in society. Because of these differences and because of reluctance to permit a single, iron-cast system of education to be imposed upon a nation compounded of so many strains, we have held that, even though public education is one of our most cherished democratic institutions, the Bill of Rights bars a state from compelling all children to attend public schools.[9]

Though the constitutional right to satisfy compulsory school laws by attending a nongovernment school was then and is now an important formal protection for intellectual and spiritual diversity, it did not relieve the Jehovah's Witnesses of the burden placed on them by the local school authorities. In response to the public school's requirement that all children salute the flag, the plaintiffs had been forced to send their children to a private school where their religious views would be respected. The result was intolerable. The Gobitis family was paying tuition to a private school and taxes for a public school that had expelled their children for refusing to abandon their religious beliefs. The Minersville, Pennsylvania, school board had in effect made the family, and all Jehovah's Witnesses, into second-class citizens who could only receive a public school education if they were willing to sacrifice their rights of conscience.

Immediately after the U.S. Supreme Court rejected the Gobitis family's freedom of conscience claim, Jehovah's Witnesses around the country were subjected to a wave of increased hostility and violence. Reacting in part to this public intolerance toward minority beliefs, the *Barnette* case overturned *Gobitis* four years later, in 1943. The case again involved Jehovah's Witnesses and the compulsory pledge; but it was freedom of intellect and belief for all persons, rather than the religious freedom of the Witnesses,[10] upon which the justices ruled. In finding even nonreligious objections to the pledge constitutionally protected, the *Barnette* Court ruled that government school authorities do not have the constitutional power to compel the pledge in the first place. The existence of the private school option did not give public school officials a power denied them by the Constitution.

Justice Jackson's majority opinion viewed the pledge as "a compulsion of students to declare a belief," and therefore different from more acceptable, state-mandated courses or instructional topics which required exposure to a vaguely defined subject but did not require an "affirmation of belief and an attitude of mind." Jackson pointed out that the Bill of Rights not only "guards the individual's right to speak his own mind," but makes it unconstitutional for "public authorities to compel him to utter what is not in his mind."[11] That confessions of belief should be used for the manipulation of young minds in their formative stages was particularly offensive to the Court:

> That they are educating the young for citizenship is reason for scrupulous protection of Constitutional freedoms of the individual, if we are not to strangle the free mind at its source and teach youth to discount important principles of our government as mere platitudes.[12]

In exploring how freedom of the mind might conflict with some aspects of public schooling, the Court also suggested that coercing confessions of belief in children trivializes and undermines individual conscience:

> It is not clear whether the regulation contemplates that pupils forego any contrary convictions of their own and become willing converts to the prescribed ceremony or whether it will be acceptable if they simulate assent by words without belief and by gesture barren of meaning.[13]

Though it did not say so explicitly, the Court seems to have understood that when government compels students to utter a confession of belief it teaches that one's conscience is irrelevant to public life, unimportant to individual integrity, and not worthy of further development—that it is something to be replaced by rules or to be manipulated by government, by politicians, and by majorities.

In overruling *Gobitis*, the court in *Barnette* not only reinforced the fundamental freedom of the individual "sphere of intellect and spirit," but it also rejected the idea that government schools can foster unity by coercive means. Aware of the lessons of history upon which the principles of the Constitution are based, the Court warned of the corrosive conflict that is created when individual conscience is ignored in the zealous pursuit of unity: "As governmental pressure toward unity becomes greater, so strife becomes more bitter as to whose unity it shall be. . . . Compulsory unification of opinion achieves only the unanimity of the graveyard."[14]

According to the Court's reading of the Constitution, achieving national unity—like building communities of any size—must be a voluntary process. Common values and commitments are the products of shared life experience, of accidents of history and moments of individual reflection, of teaching and study and the formation of conscience, all unencumbered by government coercion. Constitutional protection for freedom of the mind and for the diversity of communities that are the essence of American life does not weaken, but rather strengthens, the nation. In the Court's view, government coercion of consent to unifying values undercuts the most fundamental principles of democratic self-government. History has proven that such coercion inevitably creates a chaos of irresoluble conflict and destroys the very unity it seeks to create:

> Struggles to coerce uniformity of sentiment in support of some end thought essential to their time and country have been waged by many good as well as by evil men. Nationalism is a relatively recent phenomenon but at other times and places the ends have been racial or territorial security, support of a dynasty or regime, and particular plans for saving souls. As first and moderate methods to attain unity have failed, those bent on its accomplishment must resort to an ever-increasing severity.[15]

Justice Jackson's opinion in *Barnette* is an exploration of the constitutional connection between individual conscience and government power. It sets out the ways in which conscience and community can both be preserved and the ways in which weakening one can lead to the destruction of both. In *Barnette*, state and local governments sought to use their power over public schooling to compel a unity vital to the nation's survival. To resist this compulsion, Jehovah's Witnesses invoked rights of conscience vital to their own survival, both as individuals and as a community. In finding the balance between individual conscience and government power, Justice Jackson voiced a fundamental principle of constitutional democracy that is as important now as it was then in evaluating public schooling: "If there is any fixed star in our constitutional constellation, it is that no official, high or petty, can prescribe what shall be orthodox in politics, nationalism, religion, or other matters of opinion or force citizens to confess by word or act their faith therein."[16]

The pedigree of this principle—that rights of individual conscience ought to remain inviolate, and that government control of intellect and spirit is not only inconsistent with constitutional democracy but threatening to the construction of community—extends back to the original debate on the adoption of the Bill of Rights in 1791: "The rights of conscience are, in their nature, of peculiar delicacy, and will little bear the gentlest touch of the governmental hand. . . ."[17]

Keeping the governmental hand off the rights of conscience is central to the Bill of Rights and to the proper functioning of the whole Constitution. From that document's beginning it has been clear that if democracy is to be anything other than a political perpetual motion machine for those in power and a source of oppression for those out of power, the long arm of democratic government cannot be allowed to extend its reach to the sphere of intellect and spirit.

It is therefore nothing short of astounding that more than two hundred years later, the federal government and virtually all the state governments are cooperating in a restructuring of American public schooling that contradicts the principles upon which the nation was founded. The centerpiece of this restructuring is the *Goals 2000:* Educate America Act. But its passage in 1994 points to a larger problem than the ones it was designed to correct: whether the best efforts of American political representatives and education experts to improve the quality of public schooling will instead lead eventually to its demise and to weakening the principles of democratic self-government that have been an American birthright for more than two centuries.

Because the changes worked by *Goals 2000* amount to a reformulation of the constitution of public schooling in the United States, those changes should be evaluated in light of the constitutional principles that apply to all other government actions. This does not mean, however, that the Supreme Court should be asked whether the *Goals 2000:* Educate America Act violates the Constitution as presently interpreted. Perhaps at some point those constitutional issues will have to be decided; but the social, cultural, and educational issues—the issues of how schooling ought to be constituted and what effect that will have on the constitution of the nation—are more significant.

The re-constitution of public schooling in the United States is, in other words, a question of basic values to be decided by the people as a whole, rather than by judges, educators, politicians, and constitutional experts alone. That question begins, but does not end, with an inquiry into whether *Goals 2000* advances or hinders the values most fundamental to constitutional democracy. Because every state has a compulsory school attendance law, and because today's school children will be tomorrow's voters, the answer to this question will be felt for generations, far beyond the walls of public schools.

There are five basic elements to the *Goals 2000* legislation: the creation of an official knowledge; the use of competency testing of students to measure whether the official knowledge has been adequately mastered; a systemic mechanism for school reform that reaches into every aspect of schooling and every geographical location; a shift of power over schooling toward state and federal governments in preference to local schools, teachers, and parents; and the implicit adoption of an idea of education that makes the individual learner and teacher the least important persons in the process. Each of *Goals 2000's* elements can be evaluated in light of the principles of constitutional democracy articulated so powerfully in *Barnette,* and the road to chaos that the legislation maps out can thereby be described.

The Official Knowledge

Goals 2000 calls for the creation of national and state content and performance standards for what all public school students "have to know and be able to do" in nine subject matter areas. Even if these standards are adopted by state governments but never submitted to or certified by the U.S. secretary of education or the National Education Goals Panel, they will still amount to a body of officially approved knowledge and skills chosen by political means and forced upon individual students and teachers. No matter how much professional and community input there is in the creation of these content and performance standards, it is still government—majoritarian politics, interest group politics, the art of the practical—that ultimately determines the content of official knowledge. It is not unfair to call such politically specified knowledge a kind of orthodoxy. Certainly it has the potential to become an orthodoxy as culture wars and ideological battles increasingly erupt in politics at the state and federal level.

The adoption of an official orthodoxy for schools may be a more alarming prospect in history, economics, civics and government, and the arts than it is in mathematics, geography, or science. The former seem much more matters of interpretation, belief, and potential controversy than do the latter. But no body of knowledge exists completely independent of assumptions, beliefs, worldview, and a theory as to what constitutes evidence for the truth or falsity of its conclusions.

Science, for example, might be viewed as an objective and verifiable body of knowledge and hypotheses; but history is full of examples of politics and power seeking to control scientific conclusions. More than three centuries ago, Galileo was placed under house arrest and his astronomy was suppressed by a pope defending the then-prevailing orthodoxy that the sun revolved around the earth. Today democratic battles are fought in state legislatures and school boards over whether Genesis ought to be given equal status with Darwinian evolution in public school science classes;[18] and neither science nor spirituality receives the attention it deserves. Even mathematics can be taught in ways based on passing intellectual fads but often having lasting ideological effects.[19]

It is tempting to declare some school subjects value-neutral, or to try to make them so by avoiding controversy and pursuing only technical skills. If the attempt is not entirely futile, it is certainly undesirable and perhaps even dangerous. Virtually every subject matter and pedagogy touches important parts of personal and social life. Learning maintains its immediacy and becomes a lifelong skill as long as its connection to individual development and the problems of the human condition remain.

Teaching is often most effective when commitment and passion operate alongside discipline and critical analysis. The mythical "value-neutral schooling," looked to by some as a defense for government standards in schooling, reflects none of these. No wonder so many students and teachers are dispirited by schooling that is made bland, irrelevant, passionless, or excessively technical in order to avoid controversy. Creating an apparently neutral set of standards devoid of conflicting views and discouraging of personal engagement only makes official knowledge more destructive of deep and careful thinking.

Even where some legislators or administrators are committed to standards that require the presentation of controversial issues and competing viewpoints, the problems remain. First, experience continues to demonstrate what the *Barnette* opinion concluded a half century ago: it is extremely hard to resist the ideological pressures and polarizing tactics unleashed when government seizes the power to create official knowledge. A group devoted either to gaining control of schooling in pursuit of its own agenda or to weakening schooling so that no other agenda prevails will usually succeed in meeting one of its two goals. In the school wars, balance, moderation, and rationality are among the first casualties. How else could it be when dissenters understand that political power has gained ascendancy over the rights of conscience?

Second, if the marketplace-of-ideas version of official knowledge should prevail in some small, enlightened enclave of majoritarian politics, it is still an inadequate corrective to the dangers of politicized schooling. As every teacher knows, there is power in asking the questions that others must answer. In fact, the questions asked in science or history or economics lie at the very heart of how those subjects are defined and understood. Moreover, what is assumed today may become controversial tomorrow; and the subject of research and debate today may later be viewed as so dull, irrelevant, or misdirected that it is unworthy of intellectual inquiry. Determining which topics are to be treated as controversial and in need of balanced debate defines also what is to be assumed or go unquestioned in the classroom.[20]

For the ordinary citizen, the official knowledge will be no more easily changed or repealed than any other government regulation. Yet knowledge, learning, and even belief are dynamic. They change, often in response to dissenting, idiosyncratic, or subversive thinking. To insist that today's students be confined to questions approved by yesterday's politicians is to chill critical thought, freeze inquiry, and deprive society of one of its most creative forces. Once scholastics thought it worthwhile to debate how many angels stand on the head of a pin. Now scholars debate whether the cultural contributions of Thomas Edison were more valuable than those of Frederick Douglass, and whether space exploration is more important than feeding a hungry home planet. In fifty years, the controversy may be whether political demagogues, media moguls, or computer engineers were most responsible for fostering alienation and inhumanity in the late twentieth century.

It does not matter whether official knowledge is based on consensus or controversy, or how enlightened it may look. The devil is in the process—in the act of creating an official knowledge—not in its specific content or in its truthfulness or in whether it is consistent with the views of a majority of citizens, educators, or experts. As the *Barnette* opinion argues so eloquently, when the sphere of intellect and spirit is subjected to political regulation, freedom of thought and belief and the individual mind are shoved aside by political power. As schooling and knowledge are politicized, a pall of orthodoxy is cast not only upon the classroom, but upon both conscience and community as well.[21]

But official knowledge has its most dangerous and immediate effect in the conflict it generates. In the school conflicts described in chapter 1, almost no person or interest group could resist using the political process to try to impose its ideas of appropriate knowledge and belief on the minds of students and teachers. When the locus of these conflicts shifts from the local to the state and national governments, the effect expands exponentially. That is the nature of the culture war. Once the struggle for political specification of knowledge in schooling is engaged, the conflict over its outcome becomes sloganized, polarizing, and destructive in the extreme. That is what Justice Jackson meant when he wrote, "As governmental pressure toward unity becomes greater, so strife becomes more bitter as to whose unity it shall be."[22]

The principles of constitutional democracy and of the First Amendment especially are designed to minimize this kind of conflict. By keeping the rights of conscience, belief, and expression from majority control, the Constitution seeks to prevent conflicts over them from destroying individual liberties. By the same means, the Constitution also seeks to prevent the political process from being torn apart and rendered dysfunctional by these conflicts.[23] For over two centuries a separation of the most basic rights of personhood from the majoritarian politics by which life in the community may be regulated has been an important basis for preserving both individual liberty and the democratic governance of communities. Because the creation of official knowledge under *Goals 2000* violates this principle, it increases exactly the kind of political conflict that undermines freedom of the mind and reduces the effectiveness and legitimacy of democratic self-government.[24]

The creation of an official knowledge thus contradicts the entire idea of constitutional democracy. It corrodes the consent of the governed, and it makes the majority master of thought and belief. It makes government the arbiter of culture, and it simultaneously decreases the respect in which government is held. It threatens to turn the free mind into an object of political conflict and human communities into objects of bureaucratic regulation. It feeds the state as it starves society.

Competency Testing

At one end of the spectrum of official knowledge lie the vaguely defined course requirements imposed by many states as subjects of study or as conditions for receiving high school diplomas. To graduate, a student must take so many years of history, math, language, and other subjects, and all students must pass courses in health education, physical education, and the like. In some local school districts the content of required courses may be more specific. But whether vague or specific, all of this is knowledge to which a student must be exposed.[25] Such requirements control the "input" of schooling, but do not specify what students must learn, the "output" of schooling. Input requirements leave much of the evaluation of the substance and outcome of learning to the professional judgment of individual teachers responsive to the needs and abilities of individual students.[26]

This relatively mild form of official knowledge might seem consistent with the principles of constitutional democracy and freedom of the mind. Every voter has the opportunity to participate in the democratic process by which the requirements are adopted, teachers control most of the substance of their teaching, each child has considerable leeway to learn and develop within these requirements, and the Bill of Rights can be used to challenge requirements that do not respect fundamental liberties in the public schools. But even this form of official knowledge —the one most sensitive to individual liberty—places significant and legally questionable restraints on the right of parents to direct the education and upbringing of their children. In 1925, the Supreme Court ruled that the Constitution prevents a state from requiring that children attend public school only. Every family was declared to have the constitutional right to choose a private school, one whose curriculum requirements, no matter how loose, were not imposed by government. According to the ruling, "The fundamental theory of liberty upon which all governments in this Union repose excludes any general power of the state to standardize its children by forcing them to accept instruction from public teachers only."[27]

At the other end of the spectrum of official knowledge lie confessions of belief such as those declared unconstitutional in *Barnette*. On each school day prior to the *Barnette* decision, a student had to pledge allegiance to the flag of the United States and to the republic for which it stands. Under the watchful eye of authority—and without regard for the conscience or beliefs of the student, the family, or the teacher—a public confession of a prescribed belief and an officially approved "attitude of mind" became the fee for admission to the rest of the public school day. In the Court's view, such an invasion of "the sphere of intellect and spirit" was contrary to the very essence of constitutional democracy.

Public school requirements that invade the sphere of intellect and spirit are not offensive specifically because of the content of those requirements. The offense lies in the forcefulness of the invasion itself, in the requirement of a preordained output of the human mind. One constitutional scholar, Laurence Tribe, has described the sphere protected from government invasion as "encompassing rights to shape one's inner life and rights to control the face one presents to the world." Quoting from Justice Louis Brandeis, Tribe illuminated one concept of human individuality—of "personhood"—that underlies the Constitution:

> They [the framers] recognized the significance of man's spiritual nature, of his feelings and of his intellect. They knew that only part of the pain, pleasure, and satisfaction of life are to be found in material things. They sought to protect Americans in their beliefs, their thoughts, their emotions and their sensations. They conferred, as against government, the right to be let alone— the most comprehensive of rights and the right most valued by civilized men.[28]

Goals 2000 allows neither public school children nor their teachers and families the right to be let alone. It requires that students demonstrate proficiency "in the skills and knowledge" framed by an official knowledge that contains "explicit definitions of what students have to know and be able to do."[29] Students must not only be exposed to the official knowledge, they also must demonstrate that they have learned it. Student performance is to be evaluated not by an individual teacher applying professional judgment, but according to statewide tests based upon politically specified performance and content standards.[30] These tests and assessments constitute output requirements, such as those that might be used for quality control in assembly-line manufacturing or in the making of computer chips.

The statewide competency testing that is central to the design of *Goals 2000*, and to the national school reform it promotes, lies somewhere between the two ends of the spectrum of official knowledge. The output measures of student competency required by *Goals 2000* are an enforcement mechanism for the official knowledge. As such, they seem more restrictive of freedom of belief and intellect than are the input requirements of the old regime. But they also appear less oppressive than the humiliating and counterproductive confessions of belief declared unconstitutional by the Supreme Court in *Barnette*.

The problem is to determine whether competency testing of official knowledge, like compulsory confession of belief, so substantially inhibits freedom of intellect and belief and so effectively undermines conscience that it ought not to be the organizing principle of public schooling in a constitutional democracy.[31] There are at least three reasons why compulsory competency testing of official knowledge ought to be rejected.

First, these statewide or national mandatory tests and assessments are essentially an enforcement mechanism for the official knowledge. They vastly increase the power of government-approved knowledge to intrude upon the sphere of intellect and spirit. While input requirements are an inefficient means of judging the results of what is being done inside the classroom, they do permit substantial freedom of teaching and learning. Output requirements are more intrusive. They make up in efficiency what they sacrifice in liberty. Official knowledge becomes much more a mind-stifling orthodoxy when it is enforced by competency testing.

Competency testing of official knowledge may not be identical to the constitutionally outlawed compulsory confession of belief. But students may still deal with required performance tests in the same unfortunate way that the *Barnette* opinion saw them dealing with compulsory pledges—by forgoing "any contrary convictions" or by simulating assent "by words without belief and by gesture barren of meaning." The effects of an efficiently enforced orthodoxy are likely therefore to include the further anesthetizing of individual conscience. And as personal responses to learning become more and more peripheral to success as defined by test results, the curiosity with which every child is endowed may become subservience. This result will be devastating for young minds, as well as for democratic decision making once these minds have come of age.

Second, statewide or national competency tests, when coupled to official knowledge, are as extensive as they are intrusive. They insure that not much learning other than that required to master the official knowledge will take place in school. *Goals 2000* makes it clear that passing the tests will determine not only the success of students, but the value of teachers and schools. With public opinion and professional judgment focused on the results of competency tests, there won't be much room to move; and there won't be much time to do anything not already required. With nine subjects whose content is controlled and tested by government, virtually all other subjects—and those topics not included in the official knowledge of the nine subjects—become frills.

New ways of looking at things and the asking of unanswerable questions will wait until the required material in nine subjects is mastered. Teachers may choose the most suitable pedagogy for attaining the required objectives; but neither they nor their students will have much influence on what those objectives should be. This uniformity could become crushing, as intellectual, spiritual, and cultural diversity atrophy, and we forget the values that constitutional democracy is intended to protect. At the same time, the more extensive the required time and knowledge become, the more conflict will increase over control of the official knowledge. And as more government requirements are placed on teachers and students, more parents will discover that politics has become the primary way to control the upbringing of their children.

Third, the extensive and intrusive testing required by *Goals 2000* will further erode the professionalism of teachers and complete their conversion into agents of bureaucracy. The rights of conscience and the protection of intellectual and spiritual freedom are not restricted to students and their families. Teachers, like other professionals, try to work closely with and respect the needs of their clients.[32] In doing so, they balance their own knowledge and commitment to their craft with the aspirations, abilities, and beliefs of students, their families, and the relevant school community. These are difficult adjustments for teachers and families to make, even in independent schools. But in a public school beholden to an official knowledge and evaluated by government competency testing, these adjustments may be impossible.[33]

After *Goals 2000* has taken hold in the states, professional development for teachers will be limited further by the requirements of orthodoxy; and certificates of having mastered the official knowledge will be awarded as the false emblems of renewed professionalism. The freedom of mind and critical thinking that teachers model for their students, and that they rely on to keep the work interesting, will become an exception to the rule of politicized schooling. The joy of teaching will become the routine of training. Many teachers will find that relationships with the families of their students will become more difficult when family views about education differ from the official knowledge that teachers must impart.[34] The development and exercise of conscience will not be among the required lessons of the official knowledge; nor will there be any room for the independence of mind and the critical thinking that led Neil Postman and Charles Weingartner to refer to *Teaching as a Subversive Activity*.[35]

In *Democracy and Education,* John Dewey wrote about the educational undesirability of preconceived goals for schooling and of the effect such goals can have on teachers. Though he was not referring specifically to government-imposed goals, the view he expressed would seem even more important in a context in which politics is the teacher's "superior authority."

> The vice of externally imposed ends has deep roots. Teachers receive them from superior authorities; these authorities accept them from what is current in the community. The teachers impose them on the children. As a first consequence, the intelligence of the teacher is not free; it is confined to receiving the aims laid down from above. Too rarely is the individual teacher so free from the dictation of an authoritative supervisor, textbook on methods, prescribed course of study, etc., that he can let his mind come to close quarters with the pupil's mind and the subject matter. This distrust of the teacher's experience is then reflected in lack of confidence in the responses of pupils. The latter receive their aims through a double or treble imposition, and are constantly confused by the conflict between the aims which are natural to their own experience at the time and those in which they are taught to acquiesce.[36]

The problem, of course, is not created by the use of competency tests or output measures in themselves. Most teachers have goals for teaching and many employ tests or other performance assessments to find out if their goals are being met. They use these same measures to assess what students already know, what teaching techniques work best for particular students and subjects, and what work should be pursued in next month's lessons. These tests can be more or less intrusive, touch appropriately or inappropriately the inner life of the student, be part of meaningful learning or a prelude to pointless memorization. But contrary to the requirements of *Goals 2000,* these are judgments that teachers responsive to students and families, not governments responsive to interest groups and majoritarian politics, are best equipped to make.

Output measures are useful and constructive tools when used by teachers who have an ongoing professional relationship with their subject matter and their students' families. If adopted by governments and required of all students and teachers, however, competency testing becomes a means by which politics determines the learning goals and the developmental progress of all children regardless of their individual, family, or community values. The problem is not with the use of competency testing and performance standards for judging what a student has learned, but with the political prescription of that testing and those standards.

Systemic Reform

The systemic nature of school reform under *Goals 2000* completes the conditions for creating a three-headed orthodoxy in American education. There is first the politicized official knowledge—the curriculum content standards being created in each state and for the entire nation. Second is the enforcement of this official knowledge by state or national competency testing. And third is the requirement not only that content standards and competency testing extend into every classroom in every public school in every state, but also that the standards be reflected in all approved textbooks, teacher training, teacher certification, federal school aid programs and regulations, federally funded research and development, and certificates of employability for students not going on to college.[37] This control of virtually all aspects of schooling through the enforcement of content standards brings American education perilously close to the dictionary definition of a totalitarian system.[38]

There are, of course, pragmatic and seemingly innocuous grounds for preferring a system of purposeful and efficient uniformity to a hodgepodge of diverse, decentralized, unsynchronized schools. The president of the American Federation of Teachers, for example, has argued that parents who move in midyear from one state to another because of their employment should not have to worry about a school whose curriculum is unfamiliar or leaves their child either hopelessly behind or horribly bored. This consideration may be relevant to a highly mobile society. But it hardly rises to the level of a concern powerful enough to override the most fundamental principles of constitutional democracy.

Having learned during this century that in education there is no *One Best System*[39] capable of serving adequately the diverse needs, beliefs, and abilities of all American children, the nation has nevertheless adopted in *Goals 2000* a comprehensive school reform plan that attempts to bring every aspect and location of schooling into a single, "coherent, nationwide" system.[40] Such uniformity will be stultifying for nearly everyone; and will likely prove to be an ineffective substitute for the real equality of educational opportunity so conspicuous by its absence in many public school districts.

Having learned during this century that large, centralized, coercive schooling practices disengage students and families from education, breed resentment and resistance, and reduce both the joy and effectiveness of teaching,[41] the nation has nevertheless adopted in *Goals 2000* a school reform plan so thorough that it makes centralization[42] and unresponsiveness the rule from which only government can grant exceptions.[43] The Act's supporters have emphasized statutory provisions under which standards are voluntary, parental participation is encouraged, and waivers from government regulations are available. But in view of the sweeping changes created by the Act, the protective provisions are ineffective and the reassuring claims therefore seem disingenuous.

Having learned during this century that America's cultural diversity remains a significant source of its social and economic creativity[44] and is essential to democratic discourse and sound political decision making,[45] the nation has nevertheless adopted in *Goals 2000* a comprehensive school reform plan that imposes a single set of content standards upon a diverse student population. Though the intent may be to create a common culture and to enhance the economic and civic capability of all citizens, the effect is likely to be just the opposite. Cultural diversity will not be respected and the benefits it creates will not be enhanced by schools that are required to subject a significant portion of the transmission of culture to systematic political regulation.

Having learned during this century that the attempt to use compulsion in the schools to create unity in the nation inevitably promotes conflict and creates "only the unanimity of the graveyard,"[46] the nation has nevertheless adopted in *Goals 2000* a school reform plan that seeks to create a unity of educational goals by defining "what every child should know and be able to do."[47] The educational goals set out in *Goals 2000* and the content requirements used to effectuate those goals may be attractive to a majority of Americans.[48] But imposing them by government fiat, rather than letting them rise or fall on their own merits, can only turn Americans against each other and ultimately transform potential unity into virtual repression.

Having learned during this century that achieving a just "consent of the governed" requires that authority "be controlled by public opinion, not public opinion by authority,"[49] the nation has nevertheless adopted in *Goals 2000* a school reform plan in which political authority systematically imposes official knowledge upon young minds. When Justice Jackson wrote of the danger of strangling "the free mind at its source," he referred not only to the importance of intellectual freedom in itself, but to its role in assuring the open debate by which community consent is generated and government authority is legitimized.

Having learned during this century that the U.S. Constitution forbids making the child "the mere creature of the state" and prevents government from so regulating schools that families have no choice but to accept government-approved instruction,[50] the nation has nevertheless adopted in *Goals 2000* a school reform plan so systematic and comprehensive that it leaves the vast majority of Americans with no alternative but to accept official knowledge and politically approved goals as their own.[51] Under such a regime, school choice becomes a mockery.

The creation of an official knowledge and its imposition by competency testing are bad enough. The systemic nature of these reforms is worse still, for together they become a school orthodoxy from which there is virtually no escape. Nearly 90 percent of children in the United States attend public schools, and most families cannot afford an alternative. Within the public system the possibility of getting waivers of federal or state regulations only accentuates the problem of orthodoxy, for it is government that determines where the freedom to teach and learn may be exercised. Systemic reform in effect imposes a uniform authority upon the vast personal and cultural diversity of the nation and submits its most fundamental educational freedoms to the vagaries of politics.

To add insult to injury, the far-reaching and comprehensive systematizing of American public schools indicates a haughty, know-it-all attitude on the part of government and its school reform legislation. It indicates as well a presumption that many parents are educationally incompetent. There is no humility in *Goals 2000* generally, least of all in its commitment to systemwide reform. Even the most responsive and enlightened governments and policy planners—like parents, teachers, and communities—make mistakes; but *Goals 2000* casts these inevitable mistakes in $250 billion per year of concrete. Democratic self-government is based in part on the principle that no person or organization is infallible. *Goals 2000*'s emphasis on systemic imposition of the current politics of education is an arrogant reversal of this principle.

The Question of Power

When the Jehovah's Witness children refused to recite the pledge of allegiance and to salute the flag in a daily public school ceremony, they were guided by their community's sincerely held religious belief that a flag is a graven image before which God commands "thou shalt not bow down thyself." When the U.S. Supreme Court upheld the Witnesses' refusal, it based its decision not on the rights of religion, but on the constitutional liberty of every citizen to be free of government invasions of the sphere of intellect and spirit. Indeed, the Court went further. It found that the Constitution denies any agency of the state the *power* to require such a confession of belief or otherwise to coerce the beliefs, ideas, opinions, or expressions of the human mind.

The question of government power was central to the constitutional decision in the flag salute case and it is central to the constitutional effect of the *Goals 2000:* Educate America Act. That law allocates most of the power over the content of public schooling to government at the federal and state levels. Politicians, administrators, and the experts in their employ draw up, certify, and implement the content standards that will be used to align and enforce all aspects of *Goals 2000* school reform. By a combination of financial inducements, government regulations, and political processes, the enforcement of these content standards moves from federal government to state government to local government to individual teachers and their students.

By the same mechanisms, the power to control the content of learning and teaching will be moved steadily upward to higher and higher levels of government. The legislation requires that each participating state submit a plan to the federal government for creating and imposing content standards on school reform efforts and, in turn, that each local school district submit to the state a reform plan that is based upon the same content standards. This hierarchic scheme makes even more destructive the conflict-ridden past practice under which significant power to control individual education resided in local governments.

Under the old regime, local curriculum determinations often led to school wars based upon differences in beliefs, aspirations, goals, and preferences in education. But they were generally overridden only by state and federal requirements based on specific programs or justified by particular constitutional needs such as equal educational opportunity or the education of disabled children.[52]

Under the *Goals 2000* regime, higher levels of government virtually occupy the field. They have the power to determine what all children will learn, while local districts and individual schools are left to determine the details of how these requirements will be enforced or to petition for exceptions to the rule of higher authority. The freedoms of conscience and community thus become the victims of greater power at higher levels of government. Though many Americans may agree with the standards adopted for schools by state and federal government, it would be a mistake to judge the acceptability of this top-down exercise of curriculum power on the basis of the apparent popularity or acceptability of the content standards currently imposed. The question asked about *Goals 2000* should be, not what children should learn in public schools, but whether government and politics should be empowered to answer such questions.[53]

As the power to regulate public school content is allocated to higher levels of government, curriculum issues will become more susceptible to overly simplified public debate, divisive interest-group politics, and ideological posturing. Curriculum conflict will be dominated by abstract issues more important to politicians and groups with aspirations for state and national power than to educators or parents seeking improvement in the quality of schooling. More parents, students, and teachers will put aside their private consciences for the sake of their public schooling. As state power and national power become the currency of schooling, sensitivity to the individual needs, learning styles, and educational goals of students and their families will fade still further and be replaced by unnecessary and unmanageable conflict over matters best left to individuals and communities.

An increased politicization of schooling will be one result of shifting the balance of power to state and federal governments. And power once granted is not easily taken away. Educators, government administrators, and politicians who—in the judgment of current majorities—make good use of their increased power over education, might later be replaced by people with less enlightened purposes. But by then it will be difficult to abandon the commitment to centralized and standardized schooling except with a Herculean effort. Once a shift of power over schooling becomes an accepted fact of life, even its opponents should be viewed with a jaundiced eye. American history is littered with examples of dissenters who railed against government regulation when they were out of power, but forgot the merits of individual freedom once they gained control of the levers of power.[54] The only reliable protection against such misuses of power over fundamental freedoms is not to grant the power in the first place. That is the lesson learned by the founders of the nation, who crafted a federal constitution of limited, enumerated powers and further secured individual liberty with a Bill of Rights that put freedom of the mind beyond the reach of government.

The effects of centralizing power under *Goals 2000*—especially the power to create national and state curriculum content standards—may also be felt in the courts. Some of *Goals 2000*'s supporters saw in the creation of content standards a means to end the widely varying and often discriminatory expectations and institutional practices that some schools and teachers offer to poor and minority children. These supporters believed that a uniform set of achievement standards would provide an effective basis for litigation seeking equal educational opportunities. By giving courts a concrete basis for judging whether all students were being offered the curriculum and resources necessary to attain the required standard of competence, *Goals 2000* was intended to hasten legal enforcement of equal expectations and opportunities for all students. But even if this litigation strategy is available under the Act—and it may not be[55]—its benefits may be overshadowed by the shift of power to state and federal governments.

Goals 2000 will have a more negative and significant effect on the use of courts to protect the rights of conscience and community already found in the Bill of Rights. Under the old regime there were many cases in which dissenting individuals and communities invoked the Bill of Rights to protect these rights against infringements by school authorities. In most of these cases involving freedom of belief and intellect, the courts placed a heavy burden upon those accused of denying or infringing fundamental freedoms. A government agency, for example, usually had to justify the contested policy by demonstrating its overwhelming importance to the well-being of society. In the absence of such a compelling government interest, those asserting their fundamental freedoms usually prevailed.[56]

The problem with a national and state curriculum established pursuant to an act of Congress is that it is likely to be all-too-convincing to the courts as a compelling justification for infringing upon individual and cultural freedoms. When the federal government and most of the states adopt curriculum standards and pronounce them essential to individual and American competitiveness in the global economy—or vital to the survival of civic virtue in a democracy—most courts are likely to listen carefully. The power granted to state and federal governments under *Goals 2000* thus not only makes possible the creation of an official knowledge, but it also helps defend that official knowledge against claims that it violates freedom of belief and intellect under the Constitution.

Once accepted by the public, *Goals 2000* will change the balance of power in schoolhouses and courtrooms in a way unlikely ever to be undone. That change in schooling will very likely undermine the freedom of intellect and spirit that has been so essential to the American experience. At its core, *Goals 2000* alters the relationship between individual conscience and government power. By vastly increasing the latter, it marginalizes the former. Justice Jackson called a similar imposition of power upon the rights of conscience an attempt to "strangle the free mind at its source," and suggested that it would "teach youth to discount important principles of our government as mere platitudes."

Jackson observed that in schooling, as elsewhere, the question of power over the mind has already been answered by the principles of constitutional democracy. The Constitution in general, and the First Amendment in particular, denies to governments any significant power over the expression and formation of intellect and belief.[57] The whole purpose of the Bill of Rights, according to *Barnette*, "was to withdraw certain subjects from the vicissitudes of political controversy." "Fundamental rights may not be submitted to vote. . . . [They] depend on the outcome of no elections." In a constitutional democracy the political manipulation of the mind—whether in school, in the press, at worship, or on the street—invalidates the just consent of the governed and the legitimacy of the government. The Bill of Rights "denies those in power any legal opportunity to coerce that consent."

Goals 2000's curriculum content provisions may or may not violate specific provisions of the U.S. Constitution as presently written and interpreted. This book makes no argument on that point. The issue before the American public is much larger. Does the nation want a massive reform of public schooling that—even if technically legal— contradicts the most fundamental principles upon which the Constitution is based? Justice Thurgood Marshall implicitly answered by stating eloquently these constitutional principles: "Our whole constitutional heritage rebels at the thought of giving government the power to control men's minds."

The Mis-Conception of Schooling

In addition to all its other flaws, the *Goals 2000:* Educate America Act is based on an anti-individualistic concept of education. No matter how much the explicit content of required government standards and tests may seem to support the principles of constitutional democracy (for example, in civics and government), the existence of such substantive requirements for all schools remains authoritarian and unjustifiable except when necessary to achieve compelling government interests. The real lesson taught by adoption and implementation of government-specified knowledge is that, as Justice Jackson put it in *Barnette,* "important principles of our government [are] mere platitudes." To the extent that this lesson is learned by students and accepted by the general public, it will push public consciousness about schooling in a direction neither desired nor anticipated by most advocates of national and state standards.

Public schools that are standardized on the basis of official knowledge, subjected to top-down control of curriculum, and thoroughly systematized, are at odds with the principles of constitutional democracy. They substitute the elitism of Plato's Republic[58] for the democracy of Franklin's.[59] Such a system will accelerate the breakdown of the assumptions that most Americans have traditionally brought to schooling—that education is primarily an individual journey whose goals arise from each individual's family and community life, rather than from the needs of government or the pressures of political majorities and vested interests.

Though critical thinking, independence of mind, creativity, and respect for diversity may survive this regime-of-the-system, it will hardly provide the kind of atmosphere in which they are likely to flourish. Neither will systematized and standardized schools nurture curiosity, foster respect for the self and for the life of the mind, or develop and promote the exercise of individual conscience. As philosopher Maxine Greene put it in questioning the appropriateness of national, state, or other external goals for education in the arts, "Extrinsic standards do not infuse a life. They are not chosen; they are enacted or imposed."[60]

In the society at large, the conception of schooling underlying *Goals 2000* will also weaken the rational, unconstrained exchange of ideas and knowledge essential to democratic self-government, the intellectual and cultural liberty that are the wellsprings of social progress, and the voluntary formation of community in which individual education thrives.[61] Securing equal educational opportunity—which ought to be among the nation's highest priorities—cannot realistically be expected from public education reforms based on imposing uniformity upon a pluralistic culture.

Shifting the balance of power over learning and teaching to the federal and state governments is likely to transform the idea of education in the public mind for the worse, making the net effect of the legislation on constitutional principles still more negative and far-reaching. Eventually schooling may be viewed as nothing more than centrally planned technical training. The goals of such training will be to produce in students only that knowledge and those attitudes of mind which the government in power has decided are necessary for global economic and technological competitiveness.[62] Educational goals generated by individual families, communities, and the great traditions of intellectual disciplines will be cast aside if they contradict government plans.

This change in public consciousness will affect the expectations of citizens and, in turn, the thinking of legislators and judges as they make decisions about the educational freedoms claimed by dissenters. With virtually no public debate, the federal government under *Goals 2000* will change the public's perception of the nature and expansive possibilities of schooling and further erode the complex connection between democracy and education.[63]

In sum, the five changes adopted by *Goals 2000* are so fundamental that the legislation resembles an amendment to the U.S. Constitution more than a federal statute for school reform.[64] Yet the long and careful process constitutionally prescribed for such changes has not been followed, and the public has not had a chance properly to consider the appropriateness of these changes to the fabric of American life. It is clear that the issues of power raised by *Goals 2000* are basic to a constitutional democracy and vital to the health of public schools. When local government had partial power over conscience and community in the schools, school wars erupted and proliferated. *Goals 2000* will increase the number and intensity of these conflicts and further erode the rights of conscience and the building of community.

The question raised by these events, but not answered by public debate, remains. What would be the best allocation of power and accountability for public schooling in the twenty-first century? To answer this question the nation needs an extended public discussion of whether and in what way the constitution of public schooling *should* be amended. A court ruling about whether the *Goals 2000* statute violates the Constitution as presently written would be no substitute for such a public debate. Neither would a return to local control, which, as chapter 5 suggests, has shown itself in the past fifteen years to be an unworkable compromise between conscience and power in public education.

CHAPTER FIVE

The Legacy of
Local Control

The re-constitution of American education by *Goals 2000* opened yet another front in the school wars. On this new front the Christian Right, among others, has sought to gain some ground on the Education Empire by attacking the federal government's role in making education policy. Claiming that federal programs, federal aid, and federal regulations necessarily disempower families and communities, the leadership of the right has been able to obscure the historical effect of programs, aid, and regulations created by state and local school authorities.

By that same tactic the right has indulged its passion for persuading the public that a vaguely remembered local past is preferable to a fearfully imagined national future. One result was a call for a return to local control, by which advocates meant control of schooling content and resources by local and state political majorities. But it is local control that has given the nation its current moribund public schools and brought upon them the increasing conflicts of conscience and community that so undermine the effectiveness of public education.

As a response to *Goals 2000*, the attempt to resurrect local control is not much more than a convenient political tactic, for it holds virtually no promise of reducing the politicization of public schooling or of restoring the respect for conscience and community that *Goals 2000* so thoroughly undermines. To appreciate fully why returning to the failed compromise between conscience and power under local control would be such an ineffective response to the new power allocation under *Goals 2000*, one needs to examine the legacy of local control as well as the similarities between the effects of government control of education at the federal, state, and local levels.

Such an examination suggests that, like *Goals 2000*, local control can secure neither freedom of intellect and belief nor equal educational opportunity in public schools. It can advance neither the empowerment of parents and communities nor the professionalism of teachers. It can neither reduce unnecessary conflict over matters of conscience nor increase the overall quality of education available to American children.

The Rights of Conscience and the Building of Community under Local Control

Freedom of intellect and belief and the rights of conscience in education have always been treated with ambivalence by American culture. The very design of public schooling—in which local political majorities, bound by the Constitution to respect the rights of dissenters, were nevertheless given broad latitude to determine the content of compulsory schooling—reflects this ambivalence. It is basic as well to what Charles Glenn, Jr., called the *Myth of the Common School*.[1] From the mid-nineteenth century, the nation seems to have believed that it could preserve a democracy based on individual freedom by subjecting virtually all children to a single value-inculcating process in a common public school. This contradiction is acted out in many school conflicts, undermining conscience and community and reducing the effectiveness of public schooling already pressed by a surge in public expectations and political demands.

Under the regime of local control, federal courts, applying the principles of constitutional democracy to school conflicts, carried the ambivalence about government power and private conscience into the present. Sometimes the courts upheld the rights of families to determine the content of schooling for their own children. Sometimes they affirmed the power of local school districts or states to inculcate in all children the beliefs of a political majority temporarily in control of the public schools. In many cases the courts did both. This ambivalence

about conscience and power in education is exemplified by three landmark cases: *Pierce v. Society of Sisters,* decided by the Supreme Court
in 1925, *Wisconsin v. Yoder,* decided in 1972, and *Island Trees v. Pico,*
decided in 1982.[2]

Pierce challenged an Oregon statute that required that each child of
school age attend a public school. In the early 1920s, with the nation
awash in fear of immigrants and hostility to the culture, beliefs, and
political ideas they might bring with them, the intent of the statute
was to "Americanize" a diverse population by controlling the education
of their children. Public schools were to inculcate in all children the
beliefs regarded by the government as necessary and appropriate to a
politically formulated vision of the future. The effect of the legislation,
which the Ku Klux Klan supported, was to prohibit parents from choosing nongovernment schools and to drive those schools out of business.
But the Supreme Court unanimously held the Oregon statute to be
unconstitutional, ruling that it "unreasonably interferes with the liberty of parents and guardians to direct the upbringing and education of
children under their control."[3]

In a ringing opinion that has come to be regarded as the charter of
educational freedom in America and the constitutional foundation of
the right to choose a nongovernment school, the Court ruled, "The
fundamental theory of liberty upon which all governments in this
Union repose excludes any general power of the state to standardize its
children by forcing them to accept instruction from public teachers
only."[4]

Though the Court stated that "the child is not the mere creature of
the state," its ambivalence about the conflict between parental rights
of conscience and government interests in ideological self-perpetuation
was plain. "No question is raised," Justice James McReynolds wrote,
"concerning the power of the state reasonably to regulate all schools, to
inspect, supervise and examine them, their teachers and pupils." The
Court went still further, noting that the state was not prevented by the
ruling from requiring "that certain studies plainly essential to good
citizenship must be taught, and that nothing be taught which is mani-
festly inimical to the public welfare."[5] The Court did not indicate
whose beliefs would define either good citizenship or the public welfare, though clearly the legislation and the case itself arose because of
widely diverging views on these matters among the citizens of Oregon.

In enunciating a constitutional right for families to satisfy a compulsory attendance law by choosing nongovernment schools, the Court left ambiguous how much that right could be curtailed by government regulation of private schools. That ambiguity is now as deeply ingrained in law as in culture. Since 1925, the *Pierce* ruling has been affirmed and used countless times as the ground for new decisions. During that time two developments have deepened the ambivalence found in the original ruling.

On the one hand, the courts have provided further protection for the family's right to choose by invalidating government regulations of private schools when they were so detailed and comprehensive that they rendered the private school virtually identical to the public school. The state could not impose, with so-called minimum standards, a uniformity that it was prohibited from creating by banning school choice outright.[6] In one case the Supreme Court of Ohio, ruling on a conflict involving private religious schools, quoted with approval the testimony of educational experts that "unequivocally demonstrates the absolute suffocation of independent thought and educational policy . . . engendered by application of these 'minimum standards' to non-public institutions."[7] Still, private schools and home education gained the protection of the Constitution only in the most extreme cases, leaving insecurity and the threat of government regulation as the constant companion of nongovernment schooling.

On the other hand, economic changes have steadily eroded the value of the constitutional right to choose an alternative to public schooling. Because the cost of all schooling has risen so steeply since 1925, school choice has been transformed from a right of conscience into a privilege of wealth. Within fifty years of the *Pierce* decision, the freedom it guaranteed had become available only to the relatively few families who receive scholarships or whose wealth make them able to afford private school tuition on top of state and local school taxes.[8] Thus, while the independence of the nongovernment schools that parents may choose has increased marginally, the practical ability to choose those schools has decreased significantly.

Pierce found in favor of a parental right to choose private schooling because plenary government power over the inculcating of belief violates a liberty fundamental to constitutional democracy. But *Pierce* also acknowledged that the government could regulate important aspects of that liberty. This continuing and deepening ambivalence about the clash of conscience and power in schooling has generated increased conflict and resentment over belief inculcation in public schools. However, nearly every chronicle of the school wars over the past fifty years suggests that such conflict and resentment are largely the products of local control, not the results of federal legislation or regulation.[9]

It has been argued that the ambivalence expressed in *Pierce* was actually a timely compromise between individual liberty and the need for social cohesiveness in a diverse democracy. According to this argument, times have changed since 1925, and the compromise has become outdated, distorted, and nearly unworkable. To reduce conflict and resentment, this argument continues, the compromise is in need of adjustment. But its basic outlines are sound.[10]

In contrast, others have observed that there is no valid reason to have the burden of a failed compromise fall almost exclusively on the shoulders of the middle class and working poor. According to this alternative argument, the Court's ambivalence is the product of its refusal to confront the central contradiction of American public schooling: majority control of individual education. The principles upholding freedom of conscience against the power of the state—articulated most clearly in the First Amendment—already establish the outline of the only acceptable constitutional compromise between liberty and cohesiveness. Taking these principles seriously, the argument continues, would require a restructuring of public schooling to create a "separation of school and state" under which government would be deprived of the power to control or regulate educational content in all schools.[11]

Neither argument has been influential enough to bring about a change in the structure of schooling, though both arguments understand that the old regime of local control has weakened public schooling and undermined the exercise of the rights of conscience. Nearly seventy-five years of school wars have demonstrated this to be a chronic problem reflected not simply in legal decisions but in the everyday reality of public education. The last two decades have turned this chronic problem into an acute crisis. *Wisconsin v. Yoder* provides an example of how the ambivalence ingrained in American law and culture about rights of conscience in education has perpetuated this crisis. In *Yoder* the crisis of conscience becomes the crisis of community.

In 1968, Jonas Yoder and two other Amish residents of Wisconsin refused to send their fourteen-and fifteen-year-old children to public or private school after the eighth grade. The Amish claimed that informal education in the close-knit Amish community was all these children needed for a good life now and salvation later. But the local public school administration—and later the state of Wisconsin—did not see life or education in this way. The Amish act of conscience—based on sincere and deeply held religious beliefs—was characterized by the state as a threat to public education and a challenge to the future of mainstream culture. Yoder and the other parents were convicted by a state court of violating Wisconsin's compulsory attendance law. In its 1971–72 term, the U.S. Supreme Court heard their appeal and considered whether the Amish desire to preserve their culture and transmit its values to their children was outweighed by the authority of the state to maintain a system of compulsory schooling that did not accommodate Amish conscience.

For three centuries the Old Order Amish have been dissenters from the culture of social and technological progress, seeking to live as much like early Christians as possible. As a simple religious community, they view formal schooling of adolescents as a worldly threat to their values; and consistent with this belief, they practice a separation from the modern world that helps preserve a coherent and self-sufficient community.

The Amish use no modern conveniences and therefore contribute to none of the world's modern plagues. They use no electricity, drive no cars, watch no television, and cause no pollution. They are, in a way that touches the cultural memory of Americans, hard-working, God-fearing plain people. Their religious beliefs hold that a child should be baptized as a teenager upon deciding to take the religious community as his or her own. This view is held by a community in which religious values pervade everyday life and in which the church is not a building but a characteristic of everyday life. The Amish claim before the Supreme Court was that enforcement of the compulsory attendance law would compel them to violate these religious beliefs and would destroy the system of values underlying their community.

In considering the Amish claim of conscience and community against the state's power, the Supreme Court recognized—as it had implied in *Pierce*—that inculcating values is an inevitable part of every form of schooling and touches upon the most fundamental individual liberties:

> They [the Amish] object to the high school and higher education generally because the values it teaches are in marked variance with Amish values and the Amish way of life; they view secondary school education as an impermissible exposure of their children to a "worldly" influence in conflict with

their beliefs. The high school tends to emphasize intellectual and scientific accomplishment, self-distinction, competitiveness, worldly success, and social life with other students. Amish society emphasizes informal learning-through-doing, a life of "goodness" rather than a life of intellect, wisdom rather than technical knowledge, community welfare rather than competition, and separation rather than integration with contemporary worldly society.[12]

Basing its decision in part on *Pierce,* the Court ruled that the First Amendment right of free exercise of religion protected the Amish community from the threat posed to it by compulsory school attendance beyond the eighth grade. To the Court, the Wisconsin claim of authority to inculcate the Amish children with values that offended their religious community was no more valid constitutionally than Oregon's attempt to ignore the consciences of dissenting families by requiring public school attendance of all children.[13] Neither local nor state school authorities in Wisconsin had justified their actions by a compelling government interest,[14] and the Amish were therefore being unjustifiably subjected to "requirements of contemporary society exerting a hydraulic insistence on conformity to majoritarian standards."[15] The state's compulsory attendance law was held unconstitutional as applied to the Amish.

In the *Yoder* decision the right of a dissenting community of belief to be free of government-mandated schooling that undermined those beliefs was elevated to constitutional status. But the old ambivalence about the rights of conscience in schooling remained. At the same time that the Court gave a substantial victory to Amish educational freedom, it specified that no other group or individual making a similar claim of conscience would necessarily be granted such an exemption.[16] Only this community and its beliefs would be entitled to protection under the U.S. Constitution. The Court stressed, almost in apology for its decision, that "It cannot be overemphasized that we are not dealing with a way of life and mode of education by a group claiming recently to have discovered some 'progressive' or more enlightened process for rearing children for modern life."[17]

In fact the Court went still further, gratuitously calling into question the sincerity and worth of other beliefs that might be subjected to the majority's "hydraulic insistence on conformity." By indicating that it would apply to later school conflicts the nearly useless distinction between religious and other forms of belief protected under the First

Amendment, the *Yoder* decision trivialized conscience, undermined the growth of community through education, degraded dissent, and exaggerated the ambivalence that has bedeviled the Court for decades:

> If the Amish asserted their claims because of their subjective evaluation and rejection of the contemporary secular values accepted by the majority, much as Thoreau rejected the social values of his time and isolated himself at Walden Pond, their claims would not rest on a religious basis. Thoreau's choice was philosophical and personal rather than religious, and such belief does not rise to the demands of the Religion Clauses.[18]

But it is not simply the centrality of religious principles that distinguishes the Amish from hundreds of other communities that might be equally offended by the beliefs inculcated in schools. What mattered to the Court in *Yoder* was the nature of Amish religious principles and whether they are attractive to the mainstream culture. The ambiguous message thus sent by the Court to the supporters of local control was, "Don't violate the educational and religious freedoms of a historically nonthreatening and religiously attractive community like the Old Order Amish; but you have the constitutional power to require that majority beliefs be the basis of value inculcation for others who have no real choice but to attend public schools."

Yoder's expression of ambivalence, like that of *Pierce*, leaves educational freedom in a tenuous position under the regime of local control. Some constitutional protection for the rights of conscience and community in schooling may be expected. But most of the power lies with local and state education authorities to determine whether dissenting individuals and communities will be accommodated by the public schools that serve to inculcate majority values in the rising generation. Since tolerance, as Justice Jackson pointed out in the *Barnette* case, is often reserved for those things that don't matter much and withheld from things that "cut to the heart of the existing order,"[19] the prospects for educational freedom under a return to local control are not good. The history of local and state actions in this area—and the conflicts these actions have caused—demonstrate that the cost of ambivalence about freedom of intellect and belief in the schools has always been high.[20]

The members of the school board of the Island Trees Union Free School District apparently felt none of this ambivalence. In 1976 they banned from the public school libraries and curriculum of Levittown,

New York, nine books, by including those authors Kurt Vonnegut, Langston Hughes, Richard Wright, Bernard Malamud, and Piri Thomas. Among the reasons given for this act of wholesale censorship were claims that Malamud's *The Fixer* was "anti-Semitic" and that *Best Short Stories of Negro Writers,* edited by Langston Hughes, was "anti-Negro." The School board reached its bizarre decision by ignoring the recommendations of the committee it had appointed to review the books; and, by doing so, it insured that the courts would eventually judge the whole episode to have defied not only reason but the Constitution as well.

The board's actions set off an unpleasant and sometimes irrational conflict among the residents of Levittown, a post-World War II housing development just east of New York on Long Island. The conflict was political, personal, intellectual, emotional, and, eventually, legal. There were arguments over whether the board members had removed educationally unsuitable materials from the schools or were simply acting on an ultraconservative ideology acceptable to a majority of the predominantly white, middle-class town that had elected them. There were other arguments about whether a leading African American author could possibly be "anti-Negro" and a leading Jewish author "anti-Semitic." Some wondered whether the board had created in these accusations and misjudgments a plausible pretext for the suppression of First Amendment freedoms. To this public debate came a high school student named Steven Pico, who thought that as a matter of conscience he should be able to read these books in the school library if he pleased, study them if assigned by his teachers, and make up his own mind about their place in his educational development.

After six years the matter came before the U.S. Supreme Court, where *Board of Education, Island Trees Union Free School District No. 26 v. Steven Pico* became the leading legal example of American ambivalence about conscience and schooling. In this 1982 case, the conflict between a constitutional commitment to freedom of intellect and belief, and the politicized desire to use public schooling to mold the minds and spirit of the next generation, reached its peak. In sending the case back to the federal district court for further consideration, the Supreme Court made it clear that the board's actions were constitutionally impermissible.[21] Relying in part on *Pierce, Barnette,* and a long line of First Amendment cases dealing with freedom of intellect and belief, the Court stated that a school board's "discretion to determine the content of their school libraries . . . may not be exercised in a narrowly partisan or political manner," because "our Constitution does not permit the official suppression of ideas."[22] The Court ruled:

> If petitioners [the school board] *intended* by their removal decision to deny respondents access to ideas with which petitioners disagreed, and if this intent was the decisive factor in petitioner's decision, then petitioners have exercised their discretion in violation of the Constitution. To permit such intentions to control official actions would be to encourage the precise sort of officially prescribed orthodoxy unequivocally condemned in *Barnette*.[23]

As in *Pierce* and *Yoder*, the Court's forceful condemnation of officially approved orthodoxy was fatally compromised by ambivalence. First, the *Pico* decision deals only with the *intention* of school boards that remove books already purchased for their schools. If the intention is an apparently neutral, educational one, but nevertheless has the *effect* of suppressing ideas or of establishing an official orthodoxy, the Court would approve a school board's action. Second, the Court ruled only on the *removal* of books from school libraries. It avoided the question of whether in *selecting* books for a school library, authorities doing the bidding of the political majorities that elected them may create an official ideology. It avoided as well the question of whether a board with the same prohibited intentions could remove the same books, not from the library, but from the school curriculum, which the Island Trees board had also done.

Last and most important, the Court expressed its ambivalence directly, by saying that it was in "full agreement" with the Island Trees school board, "that local school boards must be permitted to establish and apply their curriculum in such a way as to transmit community values, and that there is a legitimate and substantial community interest in promoting respect for authority and traditional values be they social, moral, or political."[24]

In making this statement about the power of school boards to inculcate community values in the minds of students, the Court did not mention what should be done constitutionally to account for the views of a community's dissenters. Nor did it take account of the political conflict in Island Trees over whose values were to be considered "traditional." What the Court gave with one hand—the constitutional right of students to be free of an officially approved orthodoxy—it took away with the other hand.[25]

In performing this intellectual sleight-of-hand, the Court hid its refusal—or inability—to confront the central contradiction built into the structure of American public schooling. Every school and teacher must, in deciding upon teaching materials and curriculum and standards, make choices that affect the values, beliefs, information, and ideas to be presented, studied, and inculcated in students. There is no value-neutral education that is worthy of the name. But when these inevitable choices are the subject of majoritarian decision making by governments —even local governments—and are given force by compulsory attendance and school finance laws that in effect permit only a relative handful of families to choose their schools, the rights of conscience in public schools are distorted beyond recognition. The extraordinary number of challenges to books and curriculum around the country are testimony to the fact that the High Court's ambivalence about power and conscience in public education remains a powerful and unsettling influence on American public education.

The Constitution has been read in *Pierce, Yoder, Pico,* and a hundred related cases and conflicts to protect against only the most blatant violations of the freedom of belief and intellect in schooling. In the process, the ability of political majorities to use the everyday events of schooling to impose their beliefs upon dissenting families and communities has been strengthened. This imposition contradicts the most fundamental principles of constitutional democracy, which deny government the power to manipulate the human mind.

Discriminatory Schooling under Local Control

During nearly two hundred years of American slavery it was a crime in many locations to teach a slave to read or write. The reason was simple. To maintain this brutal and inhuman system of exploitation, it was necessary to dehumanize thoroughly its victims, both in their own minds and in the minds of those who profited from their exploitation. Slaves could not be permitted to gain the basic education that might have opened the New World to them, made them aware of the struggle for freedom elsewhere, dismantled the myths and stereotypes that bolstered their oppression, and given them the intellectual tools to strengthen a community of resistance to that oppression.[26] Being deprived of all education not useful to the master was an injustice that paled, of course, in comparison to the terror, dismemberment, destruction of family and culture, deprivation of liberty, and denial of human rights suffered by slaves. But illiteracy was an important part of a system meant to reduce its victims to the status of things.[27]

Even where slavery had been abolished, discrimination in the provision of education was a common practice. Though the form of this discrimination changed in response to challenges against it, the fact of discrimination remained a resilient feature of local control of public schooling. In late eighteenth-century Massachusetts, for example, Boston public schools were racially integrated. But mistreatment of black students caused most of them to leave the integrated schools and petition the local school board and the state legislature for a separate African school that would treat its students with more dignity and educate them more effectively. When the petitions were rejected, private actions were taken, and in 1806 a racially separate school was established by African Americans in Boston. Within a few years the Boston school committee began to subsidize this school and to take increasing control over its administration and teaching. By the 1830s this control was so complete, and its effect on the quality of African American education so negative, that Boston had in effect created racially segregated public schools providing inferior education to blacks.

The African American community then filed suit in state court seeking integrated schools as a means of remedying the racism experienced in a school run by whites for blacks. In 1850, the Massachusetts Supreme Judicial Court rejected the integrationist claim, ruling in *Roberts v. Boston* that racial prejudice was not created by law and could not be changed by it. Frustrated at every turn in their efforts to find nondiscriminatory schooling for their children, the African American community turned to the state legislature, which in 1855 passed legislation outlawing race-based exclusion in all public schools. But the integration was accomplished by the Boston school committee in a way that continued to deprive African American students of equal educational opportunity.[28] After sixty years of struggling with both separate and integrated schooling, the African American community had discovered that racial discrimination can change its form far more easily than its substance. Both form and substance were the products of local control of schooling.

After the Civil War and the end of Reconstruction, slavery in the South was replaced by Jim Crow segregation nationwide. In this era of separate-but-unequal, local control was again primarily responsible for racial discrimination in the provision of public schooling. Though *Plessy v. Ferguson* was a federal case dealing with racial segregation in Louisiana's public transportation, its effect was to legitimize legally the racism promoted by all forms of local control in the Jim Crow era. Defying both logic and fact, the Court even went as far as to blame the victims of segregation for the suffering imposed on them by law:

> We consider the underlying fallacy of the [black] plaintiff's argument to consist in the assumption that the enforced separation of the two races stamps the colored race with a badge of inferiority. If this be so, it is not by reason of anything found in the act, but solely because the colored race chooses to put that construction upon it.[29]

In the 1896 ruling on the segregation of railroad cars in Louisiana, the U.S. Supreme Court made the infamous lie of "separate but equal" available to jurisprudence and public consciousness everywhere. In doing so, *Plessy* issued what one noted historian has called a "permission to hate,"[30] a permission that—as far as local control of schooling was concerned—would not be revoked until 1954.

Racial segregation in schooling meant enormous disparities in the physical and financial resources devoted to black as compared to white education. It meant tangibly inferior schooling for African American children. It also meant that state and local governments were systematically exercising their prerogative of local control to stigmatize, insult, and demean the entire African American community.

In Florida, for example, a state law required that the separate textbooks used in teaching black and white students separately be stored in separate warehouses during the summer recess, an act completely devoid of rationality. But the maintenance of irrational hostility and racial stereotypes has been as important to school segregation as it was to slavery. Also important is the role that racial discrimination in schooling has played in demoralizing African American students and interfering with their learning. Racial segregation deprives them of the knowledge and skills that would help them be effective participants in the social, economic, and political life of their communities and of the nation; and it undermines for everyone the culture and consciousness necessary for racial equality.

The sorry legacy of local control in discriminatory schooling was recognized constitutionally in *Brown v. Board of Education of Topeka*, when the High Court ruled that "in the field of public education the doctrine of 'separate but equal' has no place. Separate educational facilities are inherently unequal."[31] Though the Court did not acknowledge the negative effects that segregation had on white students who gained from it a false sense of superiority, it did recognize some of the harms done to black students: "To separate them from others of similar age and qualifications solely because of their race generates a feeling of inferiority as to their status in the community that may affect their hearts and minds in a way unlikely ever to be undone."[32]

Though *Brown* was a major constitutional and moral victory in the struggle for equal educational opportunity, resistance in the name of local control has over shadowed this victory.[33] It was the principle of local control that prompted Orville Faubus, governor of Arkansas, to stand in the door of Central High School in Little Rock in 1957, surrounded by the Arkansas National Guard troops he had called out, and declare that he would defy the desegregation orders of the federal courts.[34] It was local control that accounted for the decision of Prince Edward County, Virginia, school officials to close the public schools entirely in the early 1960's and contribute to the support of private segregated academies rather than comply with constitutionally mandated school desegregation.[35] It was local control that created a "freedom of choice" plan in New Kent County, Virginia, as a means of continuing to deprive African American children of equal education until that plan was invalidated by the Supreme Court in 1968.[36] It was local control that formed the core of resistance by Charlotte-Mecklenburg, North Carolina, school authorities—backed by the Nixon Justice Department—to every school segregation remedy available to federal courts in 1971.[37] And it was local control that underlay the attempt by the school board of Washington Parish, Louisiana, to resegregate its public schools by establishing a rigid system of ability grouping and tracking in formerly segregated schools.[38] In the North and the West the story was the same. Local control was the source of, or argument for, resistance to equal educational opportunities in Denver, Boston, Dayton, Austin, Indianapolis, and on and on.

But no conflict in the long struggle over discriminatory schooling paints a clearer picture of the unfortunate role of local control than that involving Detroit and its surrounding, predominantly white, suburbs. By the early 1970s, a growing majority of Detroit's public school students were black, and the vast majority of them attended segregated city schools. These segregated schools were created partly because white families were moving to the surrounding suburbs in increasing numbers, and partly because the Detroit school board had engaged in practices that created, maintained, and significantly increased racial segregation within the city's school system.

The result in Detroit was a pattern of segregation seen then and now in virtually every metropolitan area in the nation—a ring of overwhelmingly white and relatively well-to-do suburbs surrounding a major city populated largely by racial minorities historically and currently denied access to equal or even adequate public schools. To put the matter in more sinister tones, white families found it possible to escape integrated schooling by "running from blacks in the inner cities, and hiding in the suburbs behind an impressive array of economic, social, and legal barriers."[39]

Whatever the motives of Detroit's school board, its citizens, and the surrounding suburban communities, the effects were painfully obvious and obviously painful. Almost every child in the entire metropolitan area, whether black or white, attended a racially segregated school in a system that provided far fewer resources for identifiably black schools and that came about almost exclusively because of the choices made by white families, white school boards, and other agencies of local control.

A class action challenged this pattern of segregated schooling; and by the time *Milliken v. Bradley* reached the U.S. Supreme Court in 1974, a trial court had concluded that in spite of a voluntary desegregation plan adopted by Detroit in 1970, a pattern of "government action and inaction at all levels" had created and maintained both segregated schooling and the segregated residential patterns that make local control so important to some people. As a remedy for the discriminatory schooling documented by the plaintiffs, the trial court ordered implementation of a metropolitan desegregation plan involving Detroit and fifty-three suburban school districts.

On appeal, the Supreme Court acknowledged the facts and effects of segregated schooling in the case, but rejected the metropolitan remedy even though it was the only effective means of desegregating the school systems involved. It was the first time in twenty years that the Supreme Court had rolled back a desegregation plan adopted by a federal district court; and the Court's reasoning virtually guaranteed that inner city blacks would be confined to the segregated schools created by white flight to the suburbs.[40]

The Court reached its conclusion by a series of constitutional contortions that one dissenting justice called a "talismanic invocation" of local control.[41] School district boundaries became "sacrosanct" in spite of twenty years of constitutional precedent in which the Court had turned back every other form of resistance to equal educational opportunity offered by segregationists.[42] The constitutional test of whether minority children had been subjected to the pains and privations of segregated schooling was not whether they had to attend segregated schools, but whether direct evidence of the racial motives of suburban school boards could be presented.[43] Sending a message heard in school boards, state agencies, and federal trial courts across the country, the High Court reassured whites opposed to school desegregation that their suburban enclaves would remain secure from the constitutional command of equal protection of the laws: "No single tradition in public education is more deeply rooted than local control over the operation of the schools; local autonomy has long been thought essential both to the maintenance of community concern and support for public schools and to quality of the educational process."[44]

Local control thus became, after years of struggle, the talisman that could be invoked reliably to curtail the desegregation of schooling required by the principles of constitutional democracy.[45] Minority children could be subjected to all the harms and insults, all the deprivations and degradations, that had been so painfully documented in a generation of desegregation cases and so endlessly suffered in nearly a century of Jim Crow segregation. The only justification was the preservation of local control.

The effects of discriminatory schooling become grimmer still when the savage inequalities wrought by unconscionable school finance policies are taken into account. In some state legislatures and federal courts, wealth has become an acceptable basis for depriving children of equal educational opportunity. The dream that public schooling could be a universal means to freedom and self-development has thereby been put aside; and for some it has turned into the nightmare of a permanent underclass. The school finance policies responsible for these inequalities are routinely defended as necessary to the preservation of local control.

School finance mechanisms in the fifty states are extraordinarily complex and difficult to understand. But the technical complexity often hides some very simple and outrageous inequalities, as John Coons, Stephen Sugarman, and William Clune demonstrated in 1970—and as more recent studies of resource inequalities have confirmed.⁴⁶ The effects of these inequalities are given an extraordinarily compelling human face in Jonathan Kozol's *Savage Inequalities.*

More frequently than not the key factor in school finance mechanisms is that no matter how much the voters of a school district may be willing to levy in property taxes to support their public schools, they are severely limited by the value of the property they can tax in their district. There are countless examples of school districts with low property values taxing themselves at maximum allowable rates but still raising a half or a quarter or even a tenth of what a district with high property values can raise by taxing itself only minimally. Most state governments try to ameliorate this situation. If one district, for example, can raise only two thousand dollars per pupil while another raises eight thousand dollars per pupil with the same or lower tax rate, the state will, through a complex series of formulas adopted legislatively, provide more state aid to the poor district than to the wealthier district.

In considering the adequacy of such attempts at equalization, it must be remembered that state governments created, and have full power to change, the entire mechanism by which local and statewide school taxes are raised and expended. Under the finance schemes adopted by most legislatures, state aid does not come close to equalizing the per pupil funds available in all local districts.⁴⁷ For a particularly striking example, consider that in New York State in 1989–90, New York City had available $7299 per pupil for public schools while the Long Island suburb of Manhasset had $15,084 per pupil.⁴⁸ The difference translates into teacher salaries, the physical condition of schools, the quality and age of teaching materials, student-teacher ratios, and all the other elements of public schooling that lead those who are able to move to wealthier school districts to do so.⁴⁹

But many families are not able to move, or are prevented from moving by residential or other forms of discrimination. The result is that under finance schemes designed by the state—a form of local control—the accident of where a family happens to live determines how much money will be spent on the schooling of its children. The substantial inequalities, which Jonathan Kozol has rightly labeled "savage," warp the education available to many children. It is no wonder that the possibility of metropolitan school desegregation, which would have broken down school district lines and equalized per pupil funds for city students, met such resistance from wealthy suburbs. The Supreme

Court put an end to this route to equal educational opportunity in *Milliken v. Bradley.*

This form of wealth-based discriminatory schooling has been challenged in court. The first major case came in 1973, when the Supreme Court reversed a federal district court in Texas and ruled that even a wide disparity in the level of funding for public schools does not constitute a violation of the Equal Protection Clause of the Fourteenth Amendment.[50] Among the Court's overt reasons for turning a blind constitutional eye to this arbitrary discrimination against large numbers of children was the importance of local control:

> [The Texas financing system] permits and encourages a large measure of participation in and control of each district's schools at the local level. . . . In part, local control means . . . the freedom to devote more money to the education of one's children. Equally important, however, is the opportunity it offers for participation in the decision making process that determines how those local tax dollars will be spent. Each locality is free to tailor local programs to local needs.[51]

Thus the law "in its majestic equality, forbids the rich as well as the poor to sleep under bridges, to beg in the streets; and to steal bread."[52] In invoking the talisman of local control, the Court conveniently ignored the fact that if a state chose to provide all school funds from statewide taxes and to distribute them equally regardless of the relative wealth of local districts, local control of the use of those funds would be more meaningful than under the Texas financing scheme. In this case local control really meant the freedom to maintain discriminatory schooling, under a school finance system that discriminates in favor of some children at the expense of other children.

Since *Rodriguez* was decided, the focus of legal action trying to remedy vast inequalities in school funding has shifted to state legislatures and to state courts acting under state constitutions. A substantial number of states are or have been the scenes for protracted struggles over these issues. There have been few complete successes, some partial successes, and many unresolved problems generated by the resistance of privileged school districts.[53] In sum, however, as *Savage Inequalities* so eloquently demonstrates, the extremes of wealth and poverty continue, and the destruction of schooling for millions of American children remains a persistent fact of American public education. The regime of local control continues to be the primary force behind this destruction, a fact that will not be ameliorated one whit by repealing *Goals 2000.*[54]

The Legacy

During seventy years of local control, the constitutional compromise between conscience and power in education has worn thin—if it ever had any useful substance. The ambivalence embedded in this failing compromise has deepened of late, and school conflict has increased accordingly. The willingness of the courts to place local control above the rights of individual conscience and the welfare of diverse communities has revealed that the structure of schooling under the regime of local control is itself deeply inconsistent with the principles of constitutional democracy.

The legal reality has simply reflected and reinforced the realities of public schooling. Beyond the courtrooms and into the schoolrooms, the chilling of the freedom of intellect and spirit and the undermining of community have become regular fare for teachers, families, students, and communities of every description. In conflict after conflict in the school wars, the exercise of conscience has been restricted when it should have been rewarded, discouraged where it ought to have been developed, trivialized where it ought to been the subject of thoughtful inquiry.

Ironically, community is also stigmatized more often than it is supported under the regime of local control. Trying to preserve or create a school community based on heritage or belief is seen as a move toward balkanizing America. And as local and state governments become hostile to any school community they do not control, the very idea of community cohesion becomes a threat to those in power, an act of social separatism, and a sign of intolerance.

The repeating conflicts over conscience and community that characterize schooling under local control are just the tip of the iceberg. Self-censorship by teachers, timidity and fearfulness in principals and superintendents, lessons of obedience for students, the reluctant disengagement of many parents from the schooling of their children, hostility to all but geographically defined and government-approved school communities, and the absence of spiritual commitment and intellectual passion in public education are all signs that, under local control, schooling is increasingly at odds with conscience and community.

Discriminatory schooling—itself an attack upon community and a violation of conscience—has been another part of the negative legacy of local control. Until 1954, local control was the bulwark of slavery and Jim Crow segregation in schools. For over forty years thereafter the talisman of local control formed the basis for resisting the desegregation of public schools. It became also the primary justification for defending vast inequalities in school resources and the doctrine that legitimized neglecting the education of the children most dependent on public schooling. The continuing effects of discriminatory schooling have made conscience and community, already disfavored by public schooling, nearly inaccessible to racial minorities and the poor. No African American community has received the protection of community that the Amish received in *Yoder,* and few poor people have benefited from the rights of conscience and school choice awarded by the Court in *Pierce.*

The call by opponents of *Goals 2000* for a return to local control of schooling has thus been largely a political tactic that obscures an important truth about American education—that there is little to choose from between *Goals 2000* and local control. The legacy of local control of schooling has been hostility toward pluralism and racial equality, partial blindness toward the principles of constitutional democracy, ambivalence toward freedom of intellect and spirit, endless political conflict over matters best left to voluntary private decisions, and an inability—even an unwillingness—to deliver public education capable of strengthening the development of conscience and the building of community. *Goals 2000* will take the nation to the same self-destructive destination, only by a shorter route.

CHAPTER SIX

Conscience and Community

No theory of freedom in our age will be either effective or relevant that does not recognize the present centrality of the quest for community.

Robert Nisbet [1]

Public schools in the United States continue to fail at educating too many of their pupils. They continue to deny too many children any semblance of equal educational opportunity. And they continue to ignore or disparage too many individuals, families, teachers, and communities with strongly held dissenting values. From the point of view of conscience and community, these destructive effects of public schooling under local control are similar to those that will result—in intensified and less manageable form—from the institutional and intellectual entrenchment of *Goals 2000*. *Goals 2000*, in other words, will make a bad situation worse; it will accelerate the decline of conscience and community in schooling and society.

Under the regime of local control, neither freedom of conscience nor the growth of community has been adequately protected from the encroachment of state power. The courts, and the ambivalent way they have applied the Constitution, have been only partially responsible for this problem, whose main cause is a structure of public schooling incapable of accommodating the vast diversity of American society. Some combatants in the school wars have exploited these weaknesses in the constitution of American schooling, trying again and again to dislodge the hidebound Education Empire and to seize education power as a means either to protect dissenting beliefs or to advance the ideological ends of some special interest group. Other combatants, using the same tactics or clinging tenaciously to the vestiges of discriminatory schooling, have so polarized and politicized the common school that it has lost its effectiveness as a means of creating unity out of diversity.[2]

The historical result has been a series of battles for control of government schools that threaten the quality of education, poison the public discourse, and undermine the nation's support for public education. Intimidated by these power struggles, the bureaucratic culture of education has become hostile to the rights of conscience and to the growth of community, behaving as if each were a threat to successful schooling. Conscience—its exercise by teachers, its development in children, and its place in our primary institution for transmitting culture—has been rendered nearly irrelevant. Community—its maintenance within schools as a necessary context for learning, and its support by schooling as an essential part of a free and meaningful life—has been subverted.[3]

Under the regime of *Goals 2000*, many of the problems created by local control of schooling are likely to get worse. For fifty years the nation has in practice ignored Justice Jackson's warning that majoritarian control of intellect and spirit in public schooling would eventually divide the nation and weaken its schools. In the past two decades this division and weakness have increased enormously. Now, as if unaware that in locally controlled schooling we have nearly discarded the principles of constitutional democracy, supporters of *Goals 2000* seem willing to expand the problem by raising it to the state and national levels.

In matters of conscience and community, the future of public education looks grim indeed. How else can the standardizing effects of creating a systemically enforced, performance-tested official knowledge be understood? What other result can be expected from a centralizing shift of power over schooling that is based on an anti-individualistic, even anti-intellectual concept of education?

There is little to choose from in the contest between *Goals 2000* and local control as presently practiced. Both local control and *Goals 2000* marginalize conscience, and both undermine community. And as long as any level of government is permitted to control the content of schooling, the destructive cycle of culture wars fought on school grounds will continue. As an institution deeply involved in child rearing, schools should be one of society's most significant promoters of conscience and community. Instead, they have become an obstacle to the development of both. The resulting problems extend far beyond children, families, and schools.

Democracy in America: Then and Now

When the sense of community and the exercise of conscience become impoverished in the society at large, state power is increased to the detriment of individuals and the pluralistic nation they inhabit. History makes the case. In the 1830s, when universal, compulsory, and publicly supported schooling was just a twinkle in Horace Mann's eye, the relationship among community, conscience, and the potential for tyranny in a democratic society had already been seen clearly and analyzed prophetically by Alexis de Tocqueville in *Democracy in America.*

For more than 150 years *Democracy in America* has been widely regarded as the most perceptive analysis ever made of the character and institutions of the American people.[4] Its author, a French aristocrat and lawyer who traveled to the United States in 1830 with the intention of studying its prisons, was a great admirer of the American democratic experiment. He had foreseen that democracy was the irresistible wave of the future in the old world as well as in the new. But his knowledge of the French Revolution of 1789 made him aware of the excesses to which democracy might go.[5] His analysis of democracy in America was characterized, therefore, neither by cynical criticism nor by overly enthusiastic praise. The book contains instead an analysis of how the constitution of American character interacts with the constitution of its political and social institutions to strike a dynamic balance of forces capable of sustaining a healthy democracy.[6]

Among the many vital balances Tocqueville saw in the constitution of American culture was the tension between individualism and majoritarianism. His analysis of how the tendencies toward excessive individualism and a "tyranny of the majority" were kept in check in 1830 illuminates the problem of conscience and community in American public schooling today. Tocqueville feared the rise of tyranny even in a democracy based on the consent of the governed, and he saw one potential cause of this tyranny in an unexpected place, the unchecked individualism which equality made possible:

> Despotism, which by its nature is suspicious, sees in the separation among men the surest guarantee of its continuance, and it usually makes every effort

to keep them separate. No vice of the human heart is so acceptable to it as selfishness: a despot easily forgives his subjects for not loving him, provided they do not love one another. He does not ask them to assist him in governing the state; it is enough that they do not aspire to govern it themselves. He stigmatizes as turbulent and unruly spirits those who would combine their exertions to promote the prosperity of the community; and, perverting the natural meaning of words, he applauds as good citizens those who have no sympathy for any but themselves.[7]

Tocqueville thus put forward the idea that individual freedom and the maintenance of a diversity of communities are inseparable. They are dependent upon one another; and if either is weakened, both will be destroyed. Tocqueville's analysis of American democracy led him to conclude that freedom cannot depend only on the legal protection of individual rights it requires a multiplicity of functioning communities that bind together individuals and create local allegiances that are independent of the state. As long as citizens are voluntary participants in such communities and associations, he observed, they have a basis for continually regenerating the common values and shared beliefs, the empathy and trust, that protect them from isolation, alienation, and the excessive individualism that "saps the virtues of public life."[8]

Tocqueville feared an atmosphere of alienation, lack of perceived common interest among citizens, and centralized state power; for democratic governments, practicing the ultimate form of divide-and-rule politics, could then become tyrannical. Participation in the "free institutions" of democratic governance was one form of community involvement that would counterbalance the alienating effects of excessive individualism:

> As soon as a man begins to treat of public affairs in public, he begins to perceive that he is not so independent of his fellow men as he first imagined, and that in order to obtain their support he must often lend them his co-operation. . . . [Local freedom] perpetually brings men together and forces them to help one another in spite of the propensities that sever them. . . . Free institutions which the inhabitants of the United States possess, . . . remind every citizen and in a thousand ways that he lives in society. They every instant impress upon his mind the notion that it is the duty as well as the interest of men to make themselves useful to their fellow creatures. . . .[9]

Even more important in building communities for holding tyranny at bay was the tendency that Tocqueville observed among Americans, and the constitutional right they had,[10] to form voluntary civil associations

based on religious, moral, cultural, economic, educational, or other
common purposes:

> Thus the most democratic country on the face of the earth is that in which
> men have, in our time, carried to the highest perfection the art of pursuing in
> common the object of their common desires. . . .
> Feelings and opinions are recruited, the heart is enlarged, and the human
> mind is developed only by the reciprocal influence of men upon one another.
> I have shown that these influences are almost null in democratic countries;
> they must therefore be artificially created, and this can only be accomplished
> by associations.[11]

The existence of free institutions of governance guaranteed by the
United States Constitution and the natural tendency of Americans to
form voluntary civil associations also provided multiple sources of authority in the life of a pluralistic society. In a multiplicity of such
authorities, as well as in the building of the communities of shared
values that support those authorities, Tocqueville saw a vital protection
against the erosion of individual freedom and the rise of a tyrannical
government.

Individualism is inseparable from community in another way as well.
As Robert Nisbet, who has probably thought more deeply than anyone
since Tocqueville about the importance of community, put it, "neither
personal freedom nor personal achievement can ever be separated from
the contexts of community."[12] The very definition of individualism
therefore involves the existence of community.[13] Though Nisbet does
not deny the value of the individual who, like Thoreau, stands aside
critically from all community, he defines individual freedom partly in
terms of the multiple communities with which individuals associate.
"Freedom to" is as important as "freedom from":

> Genuine freedom is not based upon the negative psychology of release. Its
> roots are in positive acts of dedication to ends and values. Freedom presup-
> poses the autonomous existence of values that men wish to be free to follow
> and live up to. Such values are social in the precise sense that they arise out
> of, and are nurtured by, the voluntary associations which men form.[14]

Contrary to the popular and polarizing misconception, individual
freedom and the development of community are not mutually exclusive; they are mutually dependent. Tocqueville, like Nisbet, saw this
clearly, and neither of them disparaged individualism or suggested that
individual rights be curtailed in deference to the importance of commu-

nity. Both men viewed as essential the formation and continuance of uncoerced intermediate associations among individuals. *Democracy in America* refers frequently to the spirit of "voluntary association" and to the "unlimited freedom of association" that Americans can claim, and sees both as basic to the preservation of individual freedoms.[15] These perceptions about the relationship of freedom and community hold an important lesson for public education in America.

In exploring the deep cultural connections between individual freedom and the creation of community so urgently needed in an era of individual isolation, Nisbet put the matter directly in terms of individual conscience:

> moral conscience, the sense of civilized decency, will not long survive separation from the associative ties that normally reinforce and give means of expression to the imperatives of conscience. Separate man from the primary contexts of normative association, . . . and you separate him not only from the basic values of a culture but from the sources of individuality itself.[16]

But the importance of community to the life of society goes beyond its role in sustaining individuality and individual freedom. The loss of the spirit of community undermines the quality of daily life in a hundred other ways; and it has been a central fact of modern history, as scholars, journalists, and personal experience have made clear to most Americans.[17] Isolation, alienation, the lack of faith in a better future, and the search for shared values are more than just popular laments. They are the conditions of life—or the feared conditions of life—for many people who believe that they see around them signs of a collapsing culture. They may also be conditions of schooling in America.

The loss of community feeds the fear that shared beliefs have so disintegrated that they are no longer adequate to explain the past or to predict the future; no longer capable of establishing identifications among diverse people; no longer available to create the networks of mutual respect, support, and responsibility needed to sustain social and psychological security. One communitarian leader, viewing "the community as a moral voice," has seen in the silencing of that voice the cause of much of the antisocial behavior, selfishness, and inhumanity that bedevil American life.[18] Nisbet too saw that the replacement of a sense of community by "amorphous suspicion in a group," can "lead to a wholesale dissolution of moral trust."[19]

Community, like a school, might be based not only upon geography, but upon heritage, language, tradition, life experience, or any other source of shared beliefs, common values, and agreed meanings.[20] In the extreme, a society whose members are deprived of the communities that give life to shared beliefs will experience an erosion of them and will be on the road to chaos. Such a society can depend neither on individual conscience nor on a sense of community to preserve its moral fabric. Its idea of order is imposed, mechanical, devoid of meaning.[21] Such a managerial society may become one "in which the capacity to do is developed beyond any historical example but in which no one knows what is worth doing."[22]

Focusing on power, Tocqueville saw that the extreme consequence of loss of community is tyranny, the end of individual freedom. What made democracy successful in the America of 1830 was that the forces that pushed in the direction of extreme individualism were checked by equally powerful forces that drew Americans into numberless civil and political associations and voluntary communities. Without these communities the individual would stand naked before the power of the state.

At the same time, Tocqueville saw that the inevitably centralizing and monopolizing tendencies of government in a majoritarian democracy were also restrained by the unwavering commitment of Americans and their constitution to individual autonomy as a fundamental part of human dignity. A reduction in either individualism or community could distort and eventually destroy constitutional democracy. Nisbet summed up this inevitable interdependence of freedom and community with appropriate forcefulness: "The liberal values of autonomy and freedom of personal choice are indispensable to a genuinely free society, but we shall achieve and maintain these only by vesting them in the conditions in which liberal democracy will thrive—diversity of culture, plurality of association, and division of authority."[23]

Justice Jackson saw a similar mutual dependence of freedom and community in the *Barnette* flag salute case, especially where freedom of the mind and communities of belief are concerned. The similarity between Tocqueville and Jackson on this subject conveys a powerful lesson of American history. Freedom of conscience and the vitality of multiple communities are essential to the survival of the American democratic experiment and of American public education; and neither conscience nor community can thrive without the other.

According to the principles of constitutional democracy articulated by Jackson, the "sphere of intellect and spirit" must remain unrestricted by all government. Without protection for individual freedom of mind, the process of majoritarian self-rule would produce not a legitimate consent of the governed but a repressive and self-justifying order. And as individuals associate to build the communities essential to civil society, the beliefs around which these communities form must likewise remain unregulated by government. Otherwise, community becomes a mere code word for totalitarianism. The survival of legitimate and functional communities at all levels requires a guarantee of the individual's rights of conscience. Individual freedom is a condition necessary for community.

According to Tocqueville and Nisbet, distorting the mutual dependence of community and freedom—including freedom of the mind—would defeat democratic government. Any substantial weakening of the ability to form and sustain community would turn healthy individualism into the debilitating alienation that "saps the virtues of public life." This alienation and loss of community would in turn deprive society of the "diversity of culture, plurality of association, and division of authority" that constitute a primary defense against tyranny. The maintenance of individual freedom requires a multiplicity of communities standing between the state and the individual. Community is a condition necessary for individual freedom.

Conscience and Community in Public Education

The historical experience of the United States makes it clear that neither individual freedom of intellect and spirit nor the cohesion provided by viable communities can survive without the other. A constitutional democracy must have both or it can have neither. The same is true for public education, which has long been regarded as a vital part of American culture and democracy.[24] It will not be possible to sustain a sense of community in public schools, or to enhance the survival of communities outside the schools, without vigorously protecting the rights of conscience as they relate to public education. At the same time, it will not be possible to maintain individual freedom and the rights of conscience, either in or out of school, unless public education can reinforce rather than undermine the multiple communities of a pluralistic society.

Schooling is one of the most important face-to-face institutions in modern culture. It is capable of being used as a forum in which adults can explore, define, preserve, and pass on to children a sense of community and a respect for the importance of individual conscience as a compass to help guide daily life.[25] Because, along with knowledge and skills, culture is inevitably transmited through education, schools are a vital part of every family's ability to sustain itself, to honor its heritage, and to secure its future. If, as this book has tried to show, public schooling under local control is structured in such a way that it cannot perform these functions well—and if school reforms under *Goals 2000* make this problem worse instead of better—then the nation is at risk of losing an institution central to its survival. The inability of public schools in the United States to advance the mutually dependent goals of conscience and community has been one of its most troubling failures, a failure that sends both school and society into a downward spiral.

Evidence for this failure of public schooling has been found in the conflicts taking place while the 103rd Congress debated and adopted *Goals 2000*, in the cases and controversies that make up the legacy of local control, in the history of the school wars, in the analysis of the official knowledge and the standardization of schooling made possible by *Goals 2000*, and in the continuing struggles for power over the minds of children and the ideology of their parents. The evidence continues to be found in the personal experiences of the generation of Americans whose children are now in school, have recently completed school, or are about to enter school.

With the adoption of *Goals 2000*, public schooling has embarked upon a short route to chaos. Even before 1994, schooling had become a politicized institution that simultaneously discourages the compromises necessary to build communities and penalizes the exercise of individual conscience necessary to express and sustain those communities. Somehow the institution that virtually everyone has regarded as a bulwark of democracy in America has become a threat to its continued vitality and to some of the fundamental values that make life in a democracy worthwhile.

But just as the principles of constitutional democracy and the insights of Tocqueville expose a basic problem with public education, they also suggest the direction that a possible solution should take. The basic structure of public schooling could be changed, not to enhance the power of federal and state government as *Goals 2000* has done, and not to return to the bankrupt legacy of local control, but to make it easier for families, students, educators, and society at large to build communities and to respect conscience.

The focus of this change must be on creating conditions capable of enhancing *both* conscience and community, or neither will benefit. By pursuing this path the nation also might defuse much of the ideological conflict that plagues the schools and might reverse the declining fortunes of public education in America. Three conditions, drawn from the evolving experience of schooling and democracy in America, are necessary to make public schooling more hospitable to conscience and community.[26]

Defining Community

The first condition would require recognizing the changing nature of communities at the end of the twentieth century. Just as there are many communities, there are many kinds of communities. Historically, communities have been defined geographically for purposes of organizing local control of schools as well as for recognizing neighborhoods, towns, cities, and states.[27] Geographical communities may have been—and may still be—the strongest, deepest, and most satisfying communities for their members, and they may still be the most practical way to organize the units of democratic government.[28] But times have changed, and geography is no longer the only—or even the primary—way that many of us define the communities that sustain us. Schooling, more than most institutions, can be strengthened by recognizing and incorporating these changes.

The culturally diverse people of the United States, especially the large majority who live in metropolitan areas, often define their communities by reference to their shared beliefs, heritage, religious conviction, language and culture, or even their personal philosophy or goals for schooling their children. Sometimes these communities coincide with geographical units. Increasingly, they do not. To refuse to recognize this reality would be to promote either continued conflict or a coercive homogenization that undermines the multiplicity of communities upon which freedom depends. These are the very effects which the restructuring of schooling is meant to reduce.

In a culturally diverse society in which the definition of community is continuously changing, geography may be anachronistic and self-defeating as the only basis on which to organize school communities. The fear that a school system that is based on strengthening a diversity of communities will "balkanize" American society seems self-defeating as well. Compulsory assimilation may seem an effective route to community cohesion, but history makes it clear that "compulsory unification of opinion achieves only the unanimity of the graveyard."[29]

Schooling can provide focal points for a multiplicity of communities, helping them to develop and in turn taking strength from them. Or schooling can thwart the development of communities by insisting on a geographical definition of community that in effect encourages polarizing ideological battles among diverse people over whose beliefs will be upheld by the local school district.[30] Recognizing nongeographical as well as geographical definitions of community for school purposes reduces destructive conflicts over conscience in schooling and allows more leeway for the exercise of conscience and for the development of diverse communities. By recognizing nongeographical as well as geographical communities, local control of schooling would be redefined as a principle of governance applied to each individual school and to those families with children enrolled in it. The citizens of a vast, pluralistic nation would thus be encouraged—or, at least, permitted—to define community for themselves and to use schooling in ways that reflect the diversity of their daily lives and the variety of their most important goals.[31]

Securing the Independence of Schools and Teachers

The second condition requires a recognition that communities that are forged by government coercion of belief are just that, forgeries. They are repressive. They convert community from something to be desired into something to be feared. A school community created by government coercion is self-destructive; it makes compromise seem like character weakness, and conscience seem like mere defiance of authority. And it breeds unnecessary conflict. As Justice Jackson put it, "As governmental pressure toward unity becomes greater, so strife becomes more bitter as to whose unity it shall be."[32] As long as government at any level—local, state, or federal—has the power to impose content requirements or performance standards on schools and students, the bitter and destructive strife over issues of conscience and community in public education will continue.

Securing the independence of every school and of every school teacher at every level from content coercion by government is the practical remedy.[33] Education, like religion, thrives in community, and must have the same independence from government as religious institutions have. School independence is a clear condition not only for sustaining community and strengthening conscience, but also for reinforcing their mutual dependence as functions of effective schooling. Independence is a condition for reinvigorating schools as intermediate institutions standing between citizen and state. It is a condition for sustaining the multiple cultural authorities that keep a diverse and decentralized democracy from becoming a tyrannical monolith. It is a condition for the professionalism that reinvigorates teaching and its relationship to families. And it is the central condition for preserving freedom of conscience for all participants in the schooling process.

If a diversity of communities is to be encouraged, and if schooling is to realize its potential as a shared experience growing out of and enhancing community, schools and school teachers—whatever their relationship to each other—must be free of government-imposed content regulation except in the most compelling cases. If students and teachers are to be encouraged to explore and express the individual conscience that is so often grounded in community, then the schools in which they work together must be made independent of government power over those explorations and expressions. The same freedom of the mind and spirit that has been essential to the vitality and success of nongovernment schools and teachers and to home education[34] must be accorded irrevocably to their "public" counterparts.

This independence—the freedom from government coercion of the content of curriculum—must not be restricted to those teachers, schools, or communities that happen to be centered upon religious beliefs. If schooling as a wellspring of community and conscience is not to be poisoned by government regulation, all schools and their teachers must be equally entitled to a guarantee of independence. Recall the shortcomings of a case like *Yoder.* In that now-you-see-it-now-you-don't statement of constitutional principles, one religious community was allowed its educational independence under the First Amendment only because virtually all other communities, secular or religious, were to be denied theirs.[35] Yet in a very real sense, the tenuous community-information trying to take shape according to its own beliefs is as much in need of school and teacher independence as is an established and well-defined community such as the Amish. Recognizing the variety of communities and their equal value to their members requires that all kinds of communities, and the schools they create or depend upon, be granted equal independence from government content requirements. In this matter, at least, a separation of school and state is required.[36]

Establishing an Equality of School Choice

The third condition necessary to enhance conscience and community through schooling is based on the importance of freedom of intellect and belief. Unless all individuals are equally entitled to freedom of intellect and belief, every individual's humanity will be diminished, political consent will lack legitimacy, and the communities on which individuals rely will be weakened by repeated conflict over matters of conscience.

To secure this freedom of the mind in society at large, each individual must retain the freedom to choose from among a diversity of communities and the freedom to leave any community that undermines that individual's basic beliefs or is in any other way unsatisfactory. Each individual must also, like Thoreau, retain the freedom to choose independence without any community.

Some communities may construct themselves on the basis of strict rules, unbending tenets of belief, or an authoritarianism offensive to many who value democracy. But no person can be prevented by government from joining such a community or be forced by law to remain in it. A democratic society full of diverse communities and respectful of individual dignity must guarantee not only the freedom of expression and belief, but the right of the individual to join or leave any community for any reason. A constitutional democracy built upon individual freedom, and committed to the proposition that "the very purpose of a Bill of Rights [is] to withdraw certain subjects from the vicissitudes of political controversy, to place them beyond the reach of majorities and officials . . . ,"[37] must make individual liberty in matters of belief and intellect in schooling a central condition of its existence.

The importance of individual choice in schooling, as in the society at large, rests as much on the realities of community building as on the preservation of human dignity and the effective functioning of political democracy. Participation in community building and decision making brings each individual face to face with the need for compromise and cooperation. The formation, ongoing redefinition, and continuing vitality of most communities depends on the voluntariness of this participation. Within such a community, the willingness of individuals to find common ground, to fashion conscious compromises and implicit agreements, and to reorient themselves in ways that make conflict constructive are all crucial. But without secure rights of conscience—including the right to choose another community or to form one in which one's belief's may be more easily accommodated—this willingness to compromise for a common good may disappear.

A person who has no choice but to accept the beliefs that others have prescribed, especially where education is concerned, is likely to regard participation in community building as a sham. An individual put in this position may withdraw from all community, with the consequences for alienation and tyranny that Tocqueville described. Or such an individual may, out of sheer self-defense, work either to weaken the community or to take it over and impose their own beliefs on others. That is what Justice Jackson meant when he warned that if public schooling "is to impose any ideological discipline, . . . each party or denomination must seek to control, or failing that, to weaken the influence of the educational system."[38]

Anybody who is forced to participate in a community—who does not have a reasonable way out—will find that private negotiating power is diminished, personal integrity is devalued, and individual conscience is trivialized. Like any monopoly, an involuntary school community can easily ignore the views or needs of dissenting individuals who either cannot realistically go elsewhere or who, if they do leave, cannot take with them the resources they need to participate in another community.[39] An involuntary community formed by such pressures does not last; and it does not provide a spirit of community because it is held together by fear and coercion rather than by genuine agreement.[40]

To put the matter more directly, freedom of intellect and spirit in schooling must be guaranteed to every family if schooling is once again to become a primary institution for building and sustaining conscience and community. Since the content of schooling cannot justifiably be controlled by government, the practical way to guarantee this essential freedom is to assure that every family with a school-age child has an equal right and adequate resources to choose the school that child will attend. If the right of school choice is not made equally available to all regardless of wealth, the guidance of conscience and the support of community will continue to be undermined by public schooling, and the savage inequalities of schooling will simply be extended down the generations.

The conditions that need to be established in order for public education to enhance conscience and community are three: the adoption of a flexible way of understanding and defining community for purposes of schooling; the securing of the independence of all schools and teachers from government regulation of content except in the most compelling circumstances; and the vigorous protection of the freedom of intellect and belief by establishing an equality of school choice for all families regardless of wealth.

In the 1925 *Pierce* case it appeared that the Constitution guaranteed the right of school choice to all as a matter of fundamental liberty. But economic changes virtually repealed this right, rendering the *Pierce* compromise unworkable and making the schooling of most children a matter of political struggle. In the 1943 *Barnette* case it appeared that the Constitution could prevent public schools from imposing an orthodoxy of belief on any child or family. But legal, cultural, and economic changes virtually eliminated this protection against the politicization of schooling and left the weaknesses in the constitution of public schooling easy and profitable to exploit.

In 1994, the adoption of the *Goals 2000:* Educate America Act further undermined these rights and protections, increased the intensity of the perennial ideological battles over schooling, and fundamentally changed the allocation of power within the nation's schools. As a result, it will take a re-constitution of public education to establish the conditions necessary for conscience and community to prevail over power and politics in the public schools.

CHAPTER SEVEN

The Re-Constitution of American Schooling

Public education has never been more important to the future of the United States or to the quality of life of its individual citizens than it is today. Yet the structure of public schooling adopted over a century ago has outlived whatever usefulness it may have once had as a forum for balancing individualism and community. Under the regime of local control, public schooling has in many ways become self-defeating. Changing times, changing needs, and changing demands have been transforming one of the nation's greatest assets into one of its most costly liabilities. The signs of decay and dissatisfaction can be seen everywhere.

The corrosive conflicts over curriculum, textbooks, libraries, and tests that have made public schooling a prime battleground for the culture wars have repeated themselves again and again. The weaknesses in the structure of public education increasingly have been exploited by those who seek ideological power through engaging in the school wars. The Education Empire has resisted attacks on public schools but seems to prefer clinging to its accustomed domination to examining critically the structural weaknesses that lead to school wars.

As a result, the public discourse about public education has turned sour and unproductive. Diverse Americans have ignored their commonalities and turned against each other needlessly, as if motivated by the belief that a single vision of good education must be defined by a political majority and uniformly applied by a school bureaucracy to every child. Hundreds of thoughtful school-reform proposals have been turned into blunt weapons for power struggles and school wars.

The ineffectiveness of public schooling has been most evident in the inability of the quarter-trillion-dollar a year Education Empire to provide a large number of children with even the minimal literacy necessary to prepare for their future and to understand their past. This ineffectiveness has knocked the bottom out of public support for public schools. Probing beneath the surface satisfaction with schooling that sometimes emerges from public opinion polls, a 1995 survey found that more than 60 percent of families with children in public schools would send their children to private schools if the funds were available. Few parents seem to believe that the public schools that worked so well for them are capable of working as well for their children.

The conflict-ridden ineffectiveness of schooling seems more tragic in view of the increasing unwillingness of older generations to make the sacrifices necessary to provide for the education of the youngest generation. Some younger families in turn seem so pressed by economic conditions that they are willing to protect their own children at the expense of the needs of other people's children and even of the elderly. As intergenerational ties weaken, school taxes needed for the most basic services—and the hundreds of billions of dollars needed to rebuild or replace decaying school buildings—have been routinely rejected by voters turned selfish in the face of dwindling resources, persistent school conflict, and perpetually unfulfilled promises of educational improvement.

Most dangerous, from the perspective of this book, has been the public schools' devastating disrespect for freedom of intellect and belief and their inability to accommodate individual conscience and to encourage communities of belief, heritage, interest, or locality. This suppression of conscience and community has been a result of the structure of schooling under local control, rather than the intentions of its personnel or the actions of most families involved in school conflicts. Because the problem is structural in origin, it has not been solved by individual programs designed to foster the spirit of community or the education of character. The polarization and suspicion generated by most school conflicts have served the interests of power more than the interests of children. And because political majorities must be moved in order to make any significant change in schooling, even those who begin by trying to improve school quality often end by undermining some of the nation's most fundamental liberties.

Through all of this, the nation's courts have been unable to apply the Bill of Rights to the problems of public schooling with anything but the most ambiguous results. Especially where the "sphere of intellect and spirit" has been at issue, the courts have provided protection only at the margin; and even there, many courts have taken away almost as much freedom as they have secured. The courts' failure adequately to preserve and defend America's most fundamental freedoms in the schools, and to make them equally available to all, has been a consequence of maintaining a school system in which political majorities can exercise significant power over curriculum. It has not resulted from any flaw in the ability of the nation's judges or in the general principles of constitutional democracy that they interpret. The suppression of conscience and community in public schooling has been especially devastating for those children, families, and communities most in need of good public schools.

Matters have been made still worse under the regime of local control by the persistent inequalities of educational opportunity that characterize public schooling in America and the inability of society to remedy discriminatory schooling. For large numbers of children who happen to have been born to poor families or who attend schools in tax-poor school districts—and for the racial and ethnic minorities disproportionately represented in these districts—discriminatory schooling has often perpetuated the savage inequalities that diminish so many young lives. And under both federal and state constitutions the courts have been unable to correct much of the inequality of educational opportunity that makes schooling society's economic sorting machine.

Beneath and running through all these problems of conscience and community in public schooling has been the inability of public schools to give effect to the common understanding that education is about more than learning basic skills and acquiring the knowledge upon which modern culture is based. Virtually every parent and every teacher know that schooling inevitably touches emotional intelligence as well as intellectual ability, passionate beliefs as well as provable facts, individual conscience as well as political power, personal goals as well as national needs, and ultimate meanings as well as economic well-being.

Yet the politicization of schooling—which puts the most important aspects of education out of reach in many classrooms—threatens to reduce education to technical training. In one opinion poll, three-quarters of American families were reported to feel suspicious of learning for its own sake or hostile to well-educated individuals.

Everywhere there have been signs that the structure of public schooling under local control has undermined the purposes of public education. As the 1980s and 1990s wore on and public schooling in America became a prime battleground in the culture wars, the government of the United States attempted to come to the rescue. Motivated in part by the desire to improve the quality of education for all children in an age dominated by technological values, and mindful of the need to reinvigorate a moribund school system under attack from all sides, two presidents and a bipartisan legislative effort brought forth the *Goals 2000:* Educate America Act. But the effort was a miscalculation of gigantic proportions and is likely to exaggerate many of the problems that characterize the regime of local control. By reinforcing the worst aspects of politicized schooling, and by ignoring or disparaging the principles of constitutional democracy, *Goals 2000* has hastened the demise of public education at the hands of public schooling.

Goals 2000 is at bottom a reallocation of power over schooling. It increases the power of the federal and state governments to control the content of schooling and creates governmental mechanisms by which that power becomes the basis for controlling every aspect and every outpost of the Education Empire. From curriculum requirements to textbook content, from student testing to teacher certification, from the granting of federal and state education funds to the development of individual education goals, *Goals 2000* lets majority politics rule the public school.

To many Americans, those who control the levers of power under *Goals 2000* may seem benevolent in their intentions and actions. But there is nothing in this standardized, systematized, and government-centered reallocation of power that could prevent the most autocratic and intolerant forces from gaining the upper hand. Nothing, that is, except majority politics. But when majority politics is empowered to determine the content of schooling, that schooling becomes part of a tyranny of the majority, and it makes a mockery of freedom of the mind. The culture wars that are visited upon schooling by majority politics will be intensified by *Goals 2000*; and the suppression of conscience and community that has bedeviled public education for years will increase as well.

The assumption that accompanies the reallocation of power under *Goals 2000* is a kind of Platonic belief that the state has the right to determine what every child will be required to know and value. Eventually this assumption is bound to filter into the well of public opinion and poison still further the public conception of the relation of schooling to democracy. This change will in turn erode the nation's intellectual and cultural diversity and weaken the effectiveness of every call for freedom of belief and intellect in the schools. In the end, *Goals 2000* will undermine the principles of constitutional democracy which for two centuries have been the basis for protecting conscience and community from being overwhelmed by government power.

The increased politicization of schooling is acceptable to some scholars and interest groups just as long as their own beliefs—whether in democratic education or in religious fundamentalism—are victorious. But history teaches us in all such struggles over the imposition of belief that these victories are short-lived and self-destructive. They always end by undermining the principles upon which democratic self-government and individual liberty are based. By ignoring the rights of conscience and subverting the communities that are necessary to preserve liberty, *Goals 2000* has set the nation's schools on a short route to chaos.

A repeal of *Goals 2000* and a return to local control of schooling will not help. The legacy of local control, built up over most of this century, is evidence enough that control of school content by government at *any* level breeds more conflict than compromise. Substantial changes in the expectations that Americans have for public schooling, and in the lengths to which many will go to have those expectations met, have rendered inadequate the old compromise between local power and individual rights of conscience. Changes in the way that the quest for community is pursued have made the exclusively geographical base of local control unworkable and increasingly destructive. Decades of discriminatory schooling carried out under the banner of local control have victimized generations of children. There is ample evidence that the campaign for a return to local control is not in the interests of freedom, or of equal educational opportunity, or of respect for a diversity of conscience and community.

The problems of *Goals 2000* are the failures of local control made more intense and systematically unavoidable. Neither allows individual liberty and cultural pluralism their necessary and proper role in the maintenance of democracy. Neither is structured in away that is likely to nurture conscience and support the growth of community. Both place dissenting families and communities in a position of seeking to control the schooling of others in order to gain any influence over their own. Both rely primarily on government coercion where individual autonomy and voluntary compromise should prevail. It seems that the proponents of local control of schooling differ from the proponents of state and national control mostly in their judgment about where the thirst for political and cultural power can most easily be satisfied.

Constitutional Moment

The distribution of power *is* at the core of many of the problems of public education; and it underlies many of the frustrations, disappointments, and unproductive conflicts experienced by parents, teachers, and communities. When the concern is whether conscience and community will yield to power, its distribution and concentration are of the greatest importance. But neither *Goals 2000* nor local control succeeds in offering a workable solution, for both empower governments to control the content of schooling. This failure raises a constitutional issue, though not in the narrow sense of questioning whether *Goals 2000* or local control might be held to violate the U.S. Constitution.

The constitutional issue concerns instead how public education *should* be constituted and which principles of governance should be reflected in that constitution. By legitimizing a massive shift in the power over public schooling—away from individuals and toward state and national governments—the passage of *Goals 2000* has opened fundamental questions about public education that have not been adequately addressed in public debate during this century. For all the problems created or exaggerated by *Goals 2000,* this statute and the political reaction to it have presented the American public with an opportunity to reconstitute public schooling in order to save public education.

The issue of how public education ought to be re-constituted, like the constitutional issues that confronted the nation at the close of the American Revolution and the Civil War, can only be resolved by "We the People." But unlike the dilemmas of those two constitutional moments, this one can be successfully handled only to the extent that *all* the people participate in its resolution and find their common interests and their common sense reflected in it. For all the considerable genius and revolutionary insight of the Framers in 1787, it was property, race, and gender that determined whose interests would be reflected in the new Constitution. After the Civil War, though the results were more enlightened in some ways, the failures were again attributable to the initial decision about who would sit at the constitutional table.

The task of re-constituting public education is simply too important to be left to self-interested political leaders, power-hungry culture warriors, one-issue interest groups, and educrats more in touch with the needs of the Education Empire than with the lives of children, teachers, and families. Events have brought America to another constitutional moment. It is time to turn the deadening struggle over school reform into an extended public discussion among ordinary citizens—We the People—about the re-constitution of American schooling.

More than half a century ago, in a case involving the quest for community, the rights of conscience, and an education conflict bred of mindless intolerance, Justice Robert Jackson made clear the constitutional principles that have sustained democracy in America:

> The very purpose of a Bill of Rights was to withdraw certain subjects from the vicissitudes of political controversy, to place them beyond the reach of majorities and officials. . . . One's right to life, liberty, and property, to free speech, a free press, freedom of worship and assembly, and other fundamental rights may not be submitted to vote; they depend on the outcome of no elections.

Now it is time to add the freedom of education to the list of fundamental rights explicitly protected by the U. S. Constitution from political manipulation at all levels of government. It is time for ordinary citizens, asserting what Washington called the right "to make and alter their constitutions of government," to reclaim public education from political majorities, bureaucratized school officials, and the corrosiveness of discriminatory schooling. It is time to put public schooling beyond the reach of those who seek to use the power of government to manipulate the freedom of the mind and spirit.

The ways in which *Goals 2000* and local control continue to undermine public education, and the constitutional lessons drawn from the continuing erosion of conscience and community during the school wars, suggest a starting point for a re-constitution of American schooling. By taking seriously the principles of constitutional democracy, four interlocking ideas can be sketched about how to limit government power and protect the sphere of intellect and spirit in public education.

Equal School Choice: Every family with a school-age child, and every school-age child fifteen years old or older, should have the right to choose the school (including home school) that child will attend *and* to have public funding for such school attendance paid to that school. No section of the U.S. Constitution or law, or of any state constitution or law, should be interpreted to prevent such choices or to deny such funding. Nor should the exercise of the right of choice or the provision of public funding for such choices be conditioned on the sacrifice of the rights of conscience.

School and Teacher Independence: Every school serving school-age children, by whomever operated, and every school teacher, by whomever employed, should be entitled to independence from federal, state, and local government regulation of the content of the education they provide. Except as justified by a compelling government interest based on the U.S. or state constitutions, there should be no regulation applied to any school or teacher, by any agency of government, of the substance of curriculum, teaching, instructional materials, libraries, tests and assessments, educational goals or practices, or other matters substantially touching the content of schooling.

Right to Publicly Funded Education: Every school-age child should be equally entitled to an education, and to public funding for such education from the state in which that child resides. No school-age child should be denied the right to education, or the right to state funding of that education, nor should any school, school practice, or teacher diminish the education of any school-age child on the basis of race, ethnic or linguistic background, gender or sexual orientation, religion, mental or physical disability, or any matter of conscience.

Equal Funding: Every state should provide public funding for the education of all school-age children. Regardless of any state law or constitutional provision to the contrary, such state funding should be provided as equal schooling grants for all school-age children on a per capita basis, without regard to a child's area of residence, family economic status or wealth, or local tax base or tax effort. Such per capita state funding should follow the child yearly to any school he or she attends; and there should be no other form of state or local aid to schooling. Any state or federal agency wishing to provide additional funds to meet special educational needs should be allowed to do so, but only by increasing the per capita funding equally for all children in a specified category.

These suggested ideas are derived from the discussion of conscience and community contained in this book. They are not the only imaginable principles for the re-constitution of education. Nor are conscience and community the only important issues facing schooling in America, though this book has tried to raise these issues to a greater level of public concern. These four suggested ideas are not even sufficient. But school reform campaigns and school wars in the 1980s and 1990s make clear how necessary they are. There are other ways to change the distribution of power, liberty, and resources in schooling that will be advanced by other people with differing perspectives. One hopes that out of an extended and open public discussion of these differences, and of the possible compromises among them, a satisfactory re-constitution of schooling may emerge.

It falls to ordinary citizens to seize the constitutional moment and depoliticize public education. In order to succeed in securing the fundamental freedoms of education and in adopting basic changes in the distribution of power where the Education Empire now rules, an extended dialogue among the people must eventually produce an education amendment to the U. S. Constitution. This must be the long-term goal for a number of reasons inherent in past and current conflicts over schooling.

First, what can be granted by the ordinary operation of government politics can be taken away by the ordinary operation of government politics. But a constitutional democracy withdraws from politics those rights that are fundamental to individual dignity, to the maintenance of self-government, and to arriving at a just consent of the governed. To rely on politics-as-usual to solve the school problems created in large part by politics-as-usual would be as fruitless as it would be foolish. Only a change in the U.S. Constitution can restrict government power over schooling and thereby reduce the incentive for political factions to turn public schools into cultural battlegrounds.

Second, a long history of attempts to apply to public schools the

First Amendment's freedom of intellect and spirit and the Fourteenth Amendment's equal protection of the laws has largely failed. Though there have been important victories, the net result of the relevant constitutional rulings has been as much to reaffirm the power of political majorities in public schooling as to protect the rights secured by the twin pillars of liberty and equality. Even the victories that have been won have been eroded by changing economic and cultural conditions and by the unwillingness or inability of the courts to use the principles of constitutional democracy to force a change in the structure of public schooling. Only an education amendment to the Constitution can make explicit the necessary definition and limitations of government power over schooling.

Third, it is a well-known fact of life that he who pays the piper calls the tune. It is as iron a law of politics as it is of business. Any merely legislative proposal calling for public funds to be used to support a right to education for all school-age children, but forbidding government from regulating the content of that education, must therefore be judged to be naive at best. Many advocates of freedom of education and most independent schools have been reluctant to support any form of government aid for fear that accepting it would mean a sacrifice of the independence that is at the core of their being. Only the adoption of an education amendment to the Constitution can secure the revolutionary demand that all children's schooling be publicly and equally financed, but that its content not be governmentally regulated.

Unfortunately, the process for amending the U.S. Constitution, though more difficult, thoughtful, and time consuming than politics-as-usual, seems as much in the hands of established interests and insurgent culture-warriors as is public schooling itself. The public discourse about fundamental constitutional issues has often been distorted, polarized, and taken away from ordinary citizens as a result. Issues that could significantly affect the future of the nation or the liberties of individuals have been lost in the rush for power or trivialized by talk show attacks and sound bite political campaigns.

It is therefore predictable that under current conditions, politicians and interest groups bent on elevating their own interests above those of the people as a whole will quickly attempt to manipulate any public discussion of fundamental changes in the structure of schooling. It is sad and paradoxical that it should be so; but it is nevertheless true that in order to amend the Constitution to remove schooling from politics, the nation must first create a public dialogue that circumvents governmental bodies and politics-as-usual. The dangers of proposing an education amendment at the outset of a sorely needed public discussion about the re-constitution of schooling are therefore considerable. But the dangers of remaining silent or inactive are greater still.

These facts of political life impose a dilemma upon the effort to re-constitute schooling—how to foster a genuinely open, extended, public discourse about conscience, community, and the distribution of power in American schooling without having that discourse taken over by the dominant powers or by politics-as-usual.

A dilemma of greater magnitude, one involving the re-constitution of society rather than of schooling, arose early in American history. In the early 1770s, as colonists in America grew weary of arguing unsuccessfully for their rights under the English constitution, committees of correspondence were established among revolutionary colonial leaders. The task of these committees, which were located throughout the colonies, was two-fold. They discussed the revolutionary ideas that would soon find their way into the Declaration of Independence, and they communicated with local citizens in order to spread these ideas throughout the countryside and involve the common person in the movement for independence.

The committees of correspondence were a kind of "Internet" of ideas, news, protest, education, and dialogue that helped create the unity necessary to resist the British Empire, whose officials, troops, and colonial governors intimidated colonial assemblies. These committees were necessary in part because politics-as-usual was not conducted in the interest of the people. They were uniquely effective in an economic, legal, and political atmosphere that made many newspapers and other forms of communication hostile to almost any sentiment that opposed British control of the colonies. The committees of correspondence worked outside the legal and institutional structures controlled by the empire; and, by mobilizing revolutionary opinion, they eventually helped bring about a new constitution for America. Perhaps this early experience suggests that today's citizens, concerned with the demise of public schooling and threatened by the deterioration of conscience and community, can find a similar way to seize the current constitutional moment and re-constitute public education.

Getting around or beyond politics-as-usual is always a revolutionary task. In view of the on-going school wars and the hostility, defensiveness, and distorted public discourse that have accompanied them, the late twentieth century may seem an unproductive time to begin such a task. But it is precisely because the old constitution of schooling has had such negative effects, and because *Goals 2000* will almost certainly continue to exaggerate them, that this is the time to consider a re-constitution of schooling. In any case, the adoption of *Goals 2000* has already radically re-constituted schooling. The fact that this program was adopted without serious public debate and without following the formal process for amending the Constitution leaves the American people with a usurpation of power than no democracy can safely ignore.

One key to a discussion of re-constituting schooling in such an atmosphere is this: if there is nothing to be won by fighting over government regulation of the content of schooling—that is, if the government has no power to make such regulations—there will be little incentive to engage in such fights. And if Americans with diverse backgrounds and beliefs and goals do not find it necessary to struggle politically over their children's education, individual conscience and the development of community will have more room to grow. Though preserving freedom of conscience may involve the risk of developing some schools that are abhorrent to mainstream values, everyone will benefit in the long run from less conflict over the content of schooling.

The present time may also seem unfavorable for the re-constituting of schooling because there is so much difficult debate about privatizing almost all functions of government. But the "sphere of intellect and spirit"—where freedom of belief, intellect, opinion, conscience, and voluntary community reign—is by definition unlike almost any other sphere of life. The justifications for privatizing these matters in schooling is virtually the same as for protecting religion, speech, press, or assembly from the hand of government. And these justifications do not apply to most other functions of government, from national defense to environmental protection, and from accessible health care programs for social security and the enhancement of the public welfare. There is nothing in the commitment to preserving the privacy of conscience and community in schooling that would require its supporters to advocate the privatization of any other government program that helps to form a more perfect union.

The present may also seem an unfavorable time because the Education Empire and the Christian Right continue to be locked in battle over ideology, power, and self-interest in the schools. One usually claims it is fighting for the creation of a democratic community, the other for the rights of individual conscience. Neither side shows signs of weakening, and neither seems concerned about the destructiveness of their conflict. Under the current structure of schooling, this conflict is likely to go on forever.

But in education as elsewhere in a constitutional democracy, freedom of individual conscience and the growth of community are mutually dependent, not mutually exclusive. In fact, the understanding that we cannot have one *without* the other ought to form the intellectual basis for a compromise between the two most powerful combatants in the school wars. But intellectual solutions, though necessary, are not sufficient. Only the actions of ordinary citizens can re-constitute public education so that it is consistent with the principles of constitutional democracy.

Among the scores of school reform programs advanced over the past twenty-five years, finding any common ground may seem difficult. The sheer number of such proposals is overwhelming. In addition to *Goals 2000* and the call for a return to the failed regime of local control, the country has been bombarded by proposals for the following: charter schools, free-market vouchers, controlled vouchers, public school choice, democratic education, separation of school and state, national testing, homeschooling, vocational education, back to basics, holistic education, performance testing, school-to-work linkages, teacher re-training, school decentralization, site-based management, school tax limitation, multiculturalism, administrative accountability, distance learning, family values, technological literacy, religious training, official knowledge, parental involvement, bureaucratic reorganization. These and dozens of other programmatic proposals have been advanced in the name of more effective schooling.

But a constitutional amendment for education cannot spell out a particular program for schools. It must, like the Bill of Rights, be based upon a few broad principles which specify government powers, secure fundamental freedoms, and establish the ground rules under which particular programs may be created, put into service, and judged for their constitutionality. Perhaps the abundance of reform programs available ought simply to suggest that once the people agree on the fundamental principles for re-constituting schooling, there is sufficient technical expertise available to design mechanisms consistent with those principles.

Finally, the present may seem to be a bad time for a widespread public discourse about re-constituting schooling because of the great weight of constitutional law that has been created in matters of education over the past seventy-five years. The issues of freedom of expression, freedom of belief, privacy, invidious discrimination, due process, parents' rights, students' rights, and resource discrimination have already been thought through. But they have been passed upon by courts applying the Constitution to an institution not in existence at the founding. Moreover, it is the states, not the federal government, which have the power to regulate schooling, and state constitutions interpreted by state courts have governed most of the conditions of public schooling.

Imagining how schooling would change if this vast constitutional structure were radically altered might therefore involve venturing into risky and unfamiliar territory. Americans might have become so habituated to the current structure of public schooling that we cannot even imagine how a structure truly consistent with democratic principles would operate. So why put at risk all of this wisdom, and the institutions that have grown up accepting it, by pursuing the lengthy discourse among ordinary citizens that could ultimately lead to an education amendment to the U.S. Constitution?

Because state and federal constitutional rulings about education are ambiguous at best. Because discriminatory schooling, corrosive conflict, the marginalization of conscience, and the undermining of community have continued in spite of these rulings. Because just as citizens two hundred years ago needed a Bill of Rights to secure freedom under a federal constitution of limited powers, so do citizens today need constitutional protection against governments that, with *Goals 2000*, have gained nearly unlimited power over schooling. Because both state and federal courts have nearly exhausted the possibilities for applying the principles of constitutional democracy to a school system structured in contradiction to those principles. Because, in the area of schooling at least, the wisdom of the ages is fast becoming the dead hand of the past.

This book has suggested that by marginalizing individual conscience and undermining the growth of community, *Goals 2000* has put American public schooling on a short route to chaos. It has suggested that a return to the regime of local control will not change the ultimate destination, even if it extends the journey.

It has urged the creation of widespread public and private conversations, outside of politics-as-usual, as a prelude to a proper re-constitution of American schooling. It has argued that such a dialogue ought to be based on securing the principles of constitutional democracy in public education; and that ordinary citizens should in time insist on a federal education amendment that guarantees equal educational resources for the exercise of equal educational liberty.

It has claimed that it is possible to reduce the incessant and debilitating conflict over conscience and community in public schools by removing, through a constitutional amendment, the power over school content from all levels of government. It has claimed that although the nation cannot create the one best system of schooling for all children by seizing this constitutional moment, it can make it possible for each child, family, teacher, and community to pursue their own vision of good education.

And finally, it has hoped that because these are among the worst of times for American public schooling, they may be the best of times for re-constituting American public education on a foundation of common ground and common sense.

Epilogue

Robert Bolt's play, *A Man for All Seasons*, begins and ends with a character he calls "the common man." The play was published more than thirty years ago, and had Bolt written his play today he would no doubt have called his creation "the common person," for the presence of this character is meant to help us all gain access to the heroic proportion of Sir Thomas More's life. The common man's basic costume is plain, black tights "from head to foot," and his face is "crafty and loosely benevolent." Using a series of different costumes, the common man plays six different characters in the play: More's steward Matthew, a boatman, a publican or pub keeper; and, after Sir Thomas resigns as chancellor, More's jailer, jury foreman, and executioner.

After beheading More at the end of the play, the common man sheds his executioner's garb and has the last word directly with the audience.

> I'm breathing . . . Are you breathing too? . . . It's nice, isn't it? It isn't difficult to keep alive, friends—just don't make trouble—or if you must make trouble, make the sort of trouble that's expected. Well, I don't need to tell you that. Good night. If we should bump into one another, recognize me.

The common man is a survivor. He goes with the flow, plays the roles society offers to those bent on survival, fights no one else's battles, takes few risks of his own, comments good-naturedly on the strengths and weaknesses of others, rocks no boats, and has a bemused respect for the contradictions and sufferings of the human condition. He neither has nor wants a conscience.

In the middle of the play More resigns as chancellor of England in an effort to avoid further conflict with King Henry over the divorce of his first wife, Catherine. More informs his servants that he is no longer a great man and can therefore no longer afford a great household. Everyone will have to find employment elsewhere. But Matthew, the common man, is asked to stay, albeit at reduced wages. He refuses, and More tells him that he understands but will miss him. Matthew's response, alone on the stage, captures the dilemma of mere survivors caught between uncompromising conscience and overwhelming power:

> Miss me? . . . What's in me for him to miss? . . . I nearly fell for it. "Matthew, will you kindly take a cut in your wages?" "No, Sir Thomas, I will not." That's it and that's all of it! All right, so he's down on his luck! I'm sorry. I don't mind saying that: I'm sorry! Bad luck! If I'd any good luck to spare he could have some. I wish we could all have good luck, all the time! I wish we had wings! I wish rain water was beer! But it isn't! . . . And what with not having wings, but walking—on two flat feet; and good luck and bad luck being just exactly even stevens; and rain being water—don't you complicate the job by putting things in me for me to miss! . . .

The common man understands that in order to survive in a world whose common currency is power—power to which he has no access, and from which he can expect to be given no quarter—he must avoid having a conscience. He must avoid making the kind of trouble that's not expected. But though he survives physically, in part by taking roles antagonistic to his former employer and friend Sir Thomas, the common man has ultimately let himself and the community of common persons down. He has the opportunity to stand for something, but is held back by the knowledge that the operation of power in society depends upon the marginalization of conscience in individuals.

The common man helps us to get close enough to More to understand the courage that sustains his conscience and exposes him to betrayal. But the common man—as attractive and crafty as he is—is denied a transcendent sense of self and must therefore accept tyranny over the mind and spirit as a condition of survival of the body. Thus does Bolt suggest that if we would make society a saner place, and one less dominated by unprincipled and ultimately corrupting power, common persons must accept and sustain the existence of conscience. A community that is worth defending leaves room for the exercise of conscience and for its development in the individual mind. And the exercise of conscience is what keeps a community from embarking on the short route to chaos that More declined to take.

Perhaps "We the People," the ordinary persons who by democratic birthright are entitled "to make and alter our own constitutions of government," should seize the opportunity to exercise and preserve conscience wherever possible. Perhaps in providing for the education of our children we should, as the common man says, put things in them for them to miss, and for us to miss. Perhaps ordinary persons should make trouble that is not expected, should act outside of politics-as-usual, should re-constitute American education by removing the power of government to manipulate the freedom of the mind and spirit. By doing these things as a community, and by respecting each other's right to differ about the goals of schooling, we might even discover, when it is finally done, that we are all still breathing.

Notes

Introduction

1. For years the Gallup and Phi Delta Kappa polls have shown public education to enjoy a favorable rating of just under 50 percent. In 1995, Public Agenda Foundation, a New York City-based research organization, issued a report, "Assignment Incomplete: The Unfinished Business of School Reform," which asked more probing questions than the pollsters had about the nature of public and parental reactions to public schooling. The results were dramatically worse than the other, more superficial polls had been indicating. Some of the figures are reported in chapter 7 of this book. The report is available from The Public Agenda Foundation, 6 East 39th St. New York, N.Y. 10016. It was reported on in *Education Week*, October 18, 1995, p. 1. In May 1996, David Matthews of the Charles Kettering Foundation published *Is There a Public for Public Schools?* in which he demonstrated with the aid of a decade's research that "there are disturbing indications that the compact between the public and public education is close to null and void" (comment from Matthews's press conference). The book is available from Kettering Foundation Press, Dayton, Ohio.

2. Myron Lieberman, *Public Education: An Autopsy* (Cambridge: Harvard University Press, 1993).

3. Hillary Rodham Clinton, *It Takes a Village: And Other Lessons Children Teach Us* (New York: Simon and Schuster, 1996). Clinton explained: "I chose that old African proverb to title this book because it offers a timeless reminder that children will thrive only if their families thrive and if the whole society cares enough to provide for them" (12).

4. *A Nation at Risk* was the first and most powerful of the modern school reform reports. (National Commission on Excellence in Education, *A Nation At Risk: The Imperative for Educational Reform* [Washington, D.C.: U.S. Government Printing Office, 1983].) Since then there have been at least 150 major reports calling for nearly 150 different reforms and based on almost as many diagnoses of the real problems of public schooling. Reading and analyzing the patterns in these reports can become a terminal preoccupation. Those who are so inclined may wish to begin with the ERIC index available in most libraries and on-line.

5. *West Virginia State Board of Education v. Barnette,* 319 U.S. 624, 637 (1943), is discussed at length in chapter 4.

6. The judgment about the success or failure of schooling depends on how one defines success. This book suggests that the level of conflict over public schooling is so high that it not only undermines conscience and community, but also leaves very little energy and goodwill for improving other aspects of schooling.

One of the areas in which most people recognize that public schooling has serious problems concerns the abilities of its students and graduates as measured by various standardized assessments. Even there, there is disagreement; and some of it is based on ideology. A few liberal researchers have argued that the school quality crisis has been manufactured by conservatives seeking to undermine the public's confidence in public schooling. See "Have Schools Failed? Revisionists Use Army of Statistics to Argue No," *New York Times,* Dec. 13, 1995, B6. See also David Berliner and Bruce J. Biddle, *The Manufactured Crisis: Myths, Fraud, and the Attack on America's Public Schools* (Reading, Mass.: Addison Wesley, 1995). The debate is extended in "Education Policy Analysis Archives," an electronic scholarly journal that can be found at ⟨Info. asu.edu⟩. In vol. 4, no. 1 (Jan. 1996) L. Stedman reviews *Manufactured Crisis* under the title "The Achievement Crisis is Real," and in the next number (Feb. 1996) Berliner and Biddle reply.

7. The importance of community to education—and its relationship to the structure of schooling—is well articulated in Clifford Cobb's excellent analysis of vouchers and deregulation, *Responsive Schools, Renewed Communities* (San Francisco: Institute for Contemporary Studies Press, 1992).

In an introductory section headed "Rekindling Community," Cobb suggests that the changing ways Americans define community are now hampered rather than helped by a school system that restricts choice.

> In a community, people take responsibility for collective activity and are loyal to each other beyond immediate self-interest. They work together on the basis of shared values. They hold each other accountable for commitments. In earlier centuries, a person was born into a community and a set of reciprocal obligations. Now, those who seek an identity as part of a larger whole must invent community by voluntarily committing themselves to institutions or groups." (2)

8. Emphasis added. Benjamin Barber, *An Aristocracy of Everyone: The Politics of Education and the Future of America* (New York: Ballantine, 1992).

9. Though the power of conscience has been uniformly recognized, its benefit to the human condition has not. In *The Moon and Sixpence,* the British writer Somerset Maugham expressed a jaundiced view of conscience as it functions in most people, seeing it as society's policeman, "a spy seated in the central stronghold of the ego," a servant of social conformity, "the guardian in the individual of the rules which the community has evolved for its own preservation" (W. Somerset Maugham, *The Moon and Sixpence* [New York: Grosset and Dunlap, 1919], 81).

Writing just before the outbreak of World War I and reflecting on the excesses of industrial capitalism in the late nineteenth century, Walter Lippmann was more cynical still. "Our conscience," he wrote, "is not the vessel of eternal verities." It is instead a tyranny "bound up with the very evil it is supposed to eradicate," for "all innovators have been at war with the public conscience of their time" (Walter Lippmann, *A Preface To Politics* [New York: Mitchell Kennerle, 1914], 193). Lippmann was very specific about the corruption of politics and business that fueled the Progressive Era. "Capitalists did not violate the public conscience of America; they expressed it" (148).

This was not at all the view of conscience held by the founders of the American experiment in democracy. Speaking less than a month after the signing of the Declaration of Independence, Samuel Adams saw conscience as a source of individual resistance to tyranny: "freedom of thought and the right of private judgment, in matters of conscience driven from every other corner of the earth, direct their course to this happy country as their last asylum." The quotation is from a speech given at Philadelphia in August 1776, and is reprinted in Louie Heller, ed., *Early American Orations* [Freeport, N.Y.: Books for Libraries, 1970], 81). Adams was one of the more radical of the American revolutionaries.

The nation's first president saw the matter similarly, exhorting his fellow Americans to "labor to keep alive in your breast that little celestial fire called conscience" (George Washington, *Rules of Civility and Decent Behavior* [Chester, Conn.: Applewood Books, 1988], Moral Maxims, # 110, 30). Nearly two centuries later, dramatist Lillian Hellman followed Washington's maxim when she refused to betray innocent acquaintances during the anticommunist witch-hunt of the 1950s: "I cannot and will not cut my conscience to fit this year's fashions." (The statement was in a letter to the House Committee on Un-American Activities [HUAC] on May 19, 1952. Hellman was willing to testify about herself but not about anyone else, an arrangement HUAC spurned.)

Discussions of conscience have moved from the sublime to the ridiculous and everywhere in between. Calling conscience "the holy and inviolable law of humanity," Immanuel Kant argued that "conscience is the representative within us of divine justice" (Immanuel Kant, *Lectures on Ethics* [New York: Harper and Row, 1963], 133). But in approaching the matter from an ocean and a century away, Mark Twain saw it differently: "It is by the goodness of God that in our country we have those three unspeakably precious things: freedom of speech, freedom of conscience, and the prudence never to practice either of them" (Mark Twain, *Following the Equator: A Journey Around the World* [New York: AMS Press, 1971], 198).

The relationships among individual conscience, transcendent morality, and the norms of society are hard to decipher in theory. But in practice no one has made them clearer than Martin Luther King, Jr. For King and the civil rights movement he led, the witness for individual conscience had the capacity to call forth and bring into action a universal conscience that would condemn racism and advance social justice. That was the power of nonviolent civil disobedience. King inspired a whole generation with examples of how the gap between individual conscience and community norms might be bridged.

10. The idea that we Americans are constantly in the process of "constituting" and re-constituting the society and that we have not only a written Constitution but also a constitution of character and society, is borrowed from Charles Lawrence III's article "Promises to Keep: We Are the Constitution's Framers," 30 *Howard Law Journal* 937 (1987).

In the article, Lawrence quotes professor Hanna Pitkin's "The Idea of the Constitution," 37 *Journal of Legal Education* 167 (1987):

> Professor Hanna Pitkin has written that there are two uses of the word constitution that do not refer to the Constitution of the United States but that are worth attending to in considering how we may give meaning to that document.
>
> "The first of these uses is constitution in the sense of composition or fundamental make-up, the constituent parts of something and how they are put together, its characteristic frame or nature." When we speak of a person's constitution we refer to her physical makeup (we say she has a robust or a delicate constitution) or of her temperament or character. "With respect to a community this use of the word constitution suggests a characteristic way of life, the national character of a people, a product of a particular history and social conditions." A constitution is SOMETHING WE ARE, a mode of self-articulation.
>
> "The second use of constitution which deserves our attention is its function as a verbal noun pointing to the action or activity of constituting—that is, of founding, framing, shaping something anew." Constitution describes the human capacity to make a new beginning. A constitution is SOMETHING WE DO. . . . This effort to express our true selves is the subject of constitutional discourse, a discourse which should not be restricted to lawyers, judges and scholars, but should be engaged in by us all. (942–43)

In this book I have used the term re-constitution in all of the above senses; that is, to suggest a process for changing how public education is put together. Re-constituting American schooling is something we should do based on something we are, and should ultimately be expressed in a change in the U.S. Constitution.

11. The full quotation reads: "Education in its fullest sense is inescapably a moral enterprise—a continuous and conscious effort to guide students to know and pursue what is good and what is worthwhile." Many of the continuing school conflicts concern the definition of "what is good and what is worthwhile." See the "Character Education Manifesto" available from the Boston University Center for the Advancement of Ethics and Character.

Chapter One. Education Headline News

1. Larry Rohter, "Battle over Patriotism Curriculum," New York Times, Sunday, May 15, 1994. sec. 1, p. 22.

2. *Lake County Education Association, FEA/United v. Lake County School Board,* Petition for Declaratory and Injunctive Relief, Cir. Ct. of 5th Circuit, Lake County Fla., filed June 20, 1994.

3. Letter of Florida state commissioner of education, Doug Jamerson, to Patricia Hart, chair of Lake County School Board, June 21, 1994 (quoted from Florida Statutes 1992 Regular Session, Chapter 92–100).

4. Peter West, "Fla. Union Vows to Fight District's 'Americanism' Policy," *Education Week,* May 25, 1994, 3.

5. The term is drawn from Michael Apple's excellent book, *Official Knowledge: Democratic Education in a Conservative Age* (New York: Routledge, 1993), which makes clear how conservative forces have used the struggle over defining legitimate knowledge to their own advantage. Apple makes an important argument from the left that public education ought to remain subject to democratic struggle rather than being privatized; but his argument takes insufficient account of the principles of constitutional democracy discussed in chapter 4.

6. Quoted in Rother, "Battle over Patriotism Curriculum," sec. 1, p. 22.

7. All three students were quoted in Rick Badie, "Love It or Hate It, School Policy Commands Attention," *Orlando Sentinel,* Sunday, May 22, 1994, p.1, Lake Sentinel section.

8. Sally Gertz, FEA/United Counsel, telephone conversation with author, Jan. 2, 1995.

9. This and the following quotations are drawn from Florida Education Commissioner Doug Jamerson's letter to the Lake County School Board's chairperson, dated June 21, 1994.

10. The commissioner failed to point out that a similar state statute passed in West Virginia had been declared unconstitutional by the U.S. Supreme Court in 1943. The case, *West Virginia v. Barnette,* is discussed in chapter 4.

11. *New York Times,* May 15, 1994, 22.

12. *Lake County Ed. Assoc. v. School Board,* Defendants Motion to Dismiss, p. 5. Filed June 20, 1994. Case # 94–1129-CA01.

13. Telephone conversation with Sally Gertz.

14. Christopher Cross, president of the Council for Basic Education, an "advocate of the liberal arts for all elementary and secondary students," wrote in defense of the proposed history standards that the impetus for the standards had come in 1989 from "a collaborative effort of business leaders, the nation's governors . . ., and President Bush and the entire Bush Cabinet" (Public letter of Christopher Cross, dated November 15, 1994).

15. Guy Gugliotta, "Up in Arms about 'The American Experience,' " *Washington Post,* Oct. 28, 1994, p. A-3.

16. Additional funds for the development of American standards came from the Department of Education, for a total of more than two million dollars. See

"Panel Unveils Standards for US History," *Education Week,* Nov. 2, 1994, pp. 1, 10.

17. Lynne V. Cheney, "The End of History," *Wall Street Journal,* Oct. 20, 1994. NESIC, the National Education Standards and Improvement Council, was created and empowered by the *Goals 2000:* Educate America Act.

18. As if the national history standards panel saw Cheney's competing panel as a threat to their own primacy, Gary Nash announced early in 1995 that Cheney's criticisms were prompting a serious reexamination of the proposed standards and possible revisions. *Washington Post,* Jan 14, 1994, quoted in *Daily Reportcard* [an electronic newsletter on the internet], Jan. 18, 1995.

19. For chilling descriptions of how McCarthyism of the 1950s brought fear and intolerance to Hollywood and television, see Victor Navasky's *Naming Names* (New York: Viking Press, 1988) and Walter Bernstein's film *The Front.*

20. Cheney, "The End of History."

21. Transcript, "MacNeil/Lehrer NewsHour," Oct. 26, 1994, p. 13.

22. Reported by Reuters and quoted in Gugliotta, "Up in Arms," A-3.

23. Gugliotta, "Up in Arms."

24. Cheney, "The End of History."

25. Gary Nash quoted in " 'Politically Incorrect' White Males Ousted from History Guidelines," by Associated Press, *Chicago Tribune,* Oct. 26, 1994, p. 2.

26. Ibid.

27. Joanne Jacobs, "Failures of Western Civilization Are Stressed," *Atlanta Constitution,* Nov. 30, 1994, Op-ed p. A-12,.

28. Editorial, *Minneapolis Star Tribune,* Nov. 14, 1994, Metro edition, p. 8 A.

29. *Education Week,* Nov. 2, 1994, p. 10.

30. "MacNeil/Lehrer Newshour," Oct. 26, 1994.

31. Charles Breinin, "History Learned Is More Important than History Taught," letter to the editor, *Education Week,* Dec. 14, 1994, p. 45.

32. Diane Ravitch, "Standards in U.S. History: An Assessment," *Education Week,* December 7, 1994, pp. 48, 40. Diane Ravitch has written a thoughtful book on standards, *National Standards in American Education: A Citizen's Guide* (Washington, D.C.: Brookings Institution, 1995).

33. Ravitch, "Standards in U.S. History," p. 40.

34. Ibid.

35. Chester Finn, director of the Hudson Institute's New Promise of American Life project and a former official of the Department of Education appointed by President Reagan, has criticized some of the groups who worked on the standards. In a letter responding to Christopher Cross's defense of national standards he described some standards advocates as "major carriers of the plague of political correctness that is subverting American education and weakening the culture." Finn renounced the standards project he had once supported:

> In my view, the new Congress should abolish the apparatus created to give official sanction to these standards. Insofar as they can make their way in the "marketplace of ideas" and get themselves adopted, on their merits, by states, communities, schools or individual educators, so be it. (Chester E. Finn, Jr., letter to author, Nov. 15, 1994)

Finn was an early supporter of school choice; but he also embraced the creation of national and state standards, at first as a government enterprise, and later as a private effort whose work product might be adopted by local or state school authorities (Charles E. Finn, Jr., telephone conversation with author, Jan. 1995).

36. AP story in *New York Newsday*, Jan. 19, 1995, quoted in *Daily Reportcard*, Jan 24, 1995.

37. Japan's Ministry of Education has a national textbook screening process and has established national standards of school curricula. For years the ministry has played down the country's role in World War II and the atrocities for which it was responsible, presumably because they cast Japan in an unflattering light. In 1994 Japan's justice minister declared that Japanese atrocities in China were "a fiction" and set off an international controversy. Several years earlier, a survey of high school graduates indicated that only one-half had been taught about World War II. One teacher warned that this miseducation might lead the next generation to accept passively the remilitarization of Japan.

After the education ministry revised its standards in 1989 to stress modern history, critics still worried that the official version of history would claim that Japan was not totally responsible for its actions in the war. Japanese history as it is taught in the schools has become politicized, meant to influence what the next generation will know and therefore how it will react to government policy. The Japanese experience bears a remarkable resemblance to the constitutional trap into which U.S. school policy is falling. See, "Regrets and Resistance in Japan, Some Lessons of WWII are Still Hard to Learn," *Washington Post*, Aug. 28, 1994, p. C-2. and "What Japan Doesn't Know: Nation Debates What Teens Should Learn about World War II," *Christian Science Monitor*, May 18, 1990, p. 14.

38. Lamar Alexander, William J. Bennett, and Dan Coats, "Local Options," *National Review*, Dec. 9, 1994, pp. 42–44.

39. People for the American Way, "Attacks on the Freedom to Learn," 1993–94 report, 41.

40. Florence Webb quoted in "New Achievement Test Brings Sharp Questions," *New York Times*, May 4, 1994, late edition, p. B 8.

41. Also removed from the pool of stories available for reading comprehension exams was a story by Annie Dillard about a snowball fight. It was claimed that the story was too violent. See "Removal of Literary Works from California Test Stirs Flap," *Education Week*, March, 9, 1994.

42. See Nomi Stolzenberg, " 'He Drew a Circle that Shut Me Out': Assimilation, Indoctrination, and the Paradox of a Liberal Education" 106 *Harvard Law Rev.* 581 (1993).

Enlightenment values—to the extent that they remain at all in public schooling—have also been seen as threatening by the Old Order Amish, who in 1972 successfully used the clash of cultures and a claim of free exercise of religion to avoid compulsory schooling in Wisconsin for their children above the eighth grade. See *Wisconsin v. Yoder* 406 U.S. 205 (1972).

43. "Maxine Hong Kingston Withdraws Story in Protest over Test Censorship," *Asian Weekly*, March 11, 1994, p. 1.

44. *Education Week,* March 9, 1994.

45. Nanette Asimov, "Conservatives Fight in Court on State Tests," *San Francisco Chronicle,* April 27, 1994.

46. Jean Merl, "State Yanks Academic Test Question," *Los Angeles Times,* Feb. 26, 1994, p. A-1.

47. "Censorship Fight over School Tests Escalate," *Los Angeles Times,* April 3, 1994.

48. "Gov. Wilson Freezes Funds for Calif. Testing System," *Education Week,* June 1, 1994.

49. *Daily Reportcard,* Sept. 29, 1994.

50. Ramsay Selden, director of the state education-assessment center of the council, quoted in Karen Diegmueller, "Model Exam in Calif. is Target of New Attacks," *Education Week,* May 4, 1994, p. 12.

51. The number of changes ordered varies from 300 to 400 to 1000, depending on which report is read. See Debra Viadero, "Health Textbooks in Texas Attacked from Both Sides," *Education Week,* Feb. 23, 1994, and Sam Dillon, "Publisher Pulls a Textbook in Furor on Sexual Content," *New York Times,* March 17, 1994, p. B-10.

52. *Education Week,* Feb. 23, 1994, p. 15.

53. "HRW Textbook Pulled in Texas," *Publishers Weekly,* March 21, 1994.

54. In Hatfield, Massachusetts, a 1994 controversy over the distribution of condoms in the public high school resulted in "an ugly confrontation" in which "parents who used to sit next to each other at their children's sporting events now made a point of finding distant seats," and in which "an ancient, long-unquestioned social contract—that a town should pay for its children's free public education—is now . . . up for grabs." See Anthony Giardina, "Fighting in the Schoolyard," *Harpers Magazine,* April 1994. The article makes clear that a structure of schooling that virtually requires people to do battle over matters of conscience is risking self-destruction.

55. Millicent Lawton, "G.O.P. Gains Control of Texas School Board for the First Time Ever," *Education Week,* Nov. 16, 1994, p. 20.

56. See Stephen Arons, "Lessons in Law and Conscience: Legal Aspects of Textbook Adoption and Censorship," in *Language, Authority, and Criticism: Readings on the School Textbook,* ed. Suzanne de Castell, Allan Luke, and Carmen Luke (New York: Falmer 1989).

57. Tennessee Statutes Chap. 20, Section 49–2020.

58. Louisiana Revised Statutes sec. 352D.

59. "Parents Upset about Textbook," *Daily Hampshire Gazette,* Sept. 25, 1987, p. 9.

60. "Controversial Textbook Draws National Attention," *Daily Hampshire Gazette,* July 13, 1988, p. 9.

61. The teacher lost the initial round of his constitutional battle against the state's "Moment of Quiet Reflection" statute.

62. "Anti-Evolutionist Teacher Sues School District," *Los Angeles Times,* Oct. 1. 1993, p. A-3

63. *Atlanta Constitution,* Aug. 24, 1994, p. C-1.

64. *Atlanta Constitution,* Aug. 23, 1994, p. F-6.

65. "Anti-Evolutionist Teacher," *Los Angeles Times.*

66. On July 25, 1994, the Ninth Circuit Court of Appeals remanded the biology teacher's suit, *Peloza v. Capistrano,* to the federal district court, denying the defendant's motion to dismiss the suit for failure to state a claim and for being frivolous. Docket # 92–55644.

67. "Anti-Evolutionist Teacher," *Los Angeles Times.*

68. The battle between Genesis and Darwinian evolution seems destined to continue forever under the present structure of public schooling. See "Creationism Fight Returns to Nation's Classrooms," *New York Times,* March 10, 1996, and "70 Years After Scopes, Evolution Hot Topic Again," *Education Week,* March 13, 1996, pp. 16, 21.

69. Kris Jensen, "Brian Bown's Moment in the Limelight," *Atlanta Constitution,* Sept. 6, 1994, p. A-6.

70. Editorial, "Controversy of Moment," *Atlanta Constitution,* Aug. 24, 1994, p. A-15.

71. Letters to the editor, *Atlanta Journal,* Aug. 27, 1994, p. A-12.

72. "Ruling Leaves Anxiety among Parents," *New York Times,* June 28, 1994, p. D-21.

73. *Board of Education of Kiryas Joel Village School District v. Grumet* 62 U.S. Law Week 4665, 4671.

74. *Grumet & Hawk v. Cuomo,* 617 NYS2d 620 (1994). On appeal, the statute was declared unconstitutional in August 1996, leaving the New York statute constitutional.

75. 62 USLW 4665, 4666.

76. *Aguilar v. Felton,* 473 U.S. 402 (1985) and *School District of Grand Rapids v. Ball,* 473 U.S. 373 (1985).

77. 20 U.S.C. sec. 1400 et. seq. The law entitles special needs children who meet certain requirements to an appropriate education in public schools or in private settings if their individual evaluations show that they cannot get an appropriate education in the programs offered by public schools. Though some families pursued administrative remedies that might have placed their children individually in a suitable private school, most did not. Apparently they sought a single solution applicable to all the children so that the community could maintain its responsibility for them and their integration in the community. See *Kiryas Joel v. Grumet,* 62 USLW 4665, 4670.

78. Christian fundamentalists may easily identify with the Satmars' choice. The issue is put in bolder relief, however, by examining its parallel to the Amish experience. In fact, the Kiryas Joel dilemma is remarkably similar in the issues it raises about the preservation of community and the structure of public education to that of the Old Order Amish of Wisconsin.

The Amish sought to have their children released from all compulsory school attendance laws after the eighth grade in order to be educated within their community. The Satmars wish to secure, within their community, the publicly funded schooling to which their disabled children are legally entitled. The Amish succeeded at law because the First Amendment's Free Exercise Clause was read as protecting them from the dissonance between their community and public schooling (*Wisconsin v. Yoder*, 406 U.S. 205 [1972]). The Satmars appear to have failed at law because the First Amendment's Establishment Clause has been read as denying them protection from a similar dissonance. As will appear later in the book, the problem is not with the Court's reading of the First Amendment, but with a monopolistic structure of public education that denies the constitutional right of school choice to most Americans.

79. 62 USLW 4665, 4666.

80. Id. at 4670, fn. 9. In the earlier case in which the N.Y. Court of Appeals ruled that the Monroe-Woodbury school authorities could create a public school within Kiryas Joel, it was found that "Satmarer want their school to serve primarily as a bastion against undesirable acculturation . . ." (*Board of Education of Monroe-Woodbury v. Weider*, 527 N.E. 2d 767 [1988]). See *Grumet v. Board of Ed. of Kiryas Joel Village School District* 618 N.E. 2d 95 109.

81. In *Monroe-Woodbury v. Weider*, public school authorities asked the Court to declare that Monroe-Woodbury was legally prohibited from providing special education services outside the district's public schools.

82. 62 USLW 4665, 4677.

83. The *Yoder* case, involving the Amish of Wisconsin (see note 78) was ultimately resolved by a Supreme Court opinion so narrow that it became an exception to prove the rule that a diversity of cultures cannot find sustenance through schooling unless the structure of public education is changed. See chapter 5.

84. "Forty Years after Brown, Segregation Persists," *New York Times*, May 18, 1994, p. B-7. Segregated schools are defined as those which are predominantly attended by African American and Hispanic students. Fifty-four percent of Hispanic students attended segregated schools in 1994, the year *Goals 2000* was enacted.

85. The essence of the *Brown* decision was the constitutional condemnation of forced separation of the races in schooling (see Pat Lines, "Equal Choice Plan for Eliminating School Segregation," 56 *Texas Law Rev.* 1245 [1978]). Where minority-race families voluntarily choose to educate their children with others of the same race, the schooling they seek is neither condemned by the Constitution, nor weakened by the shared heritage of the classmates. Similar schooling choices by the Satmars, the Amish, Christian fundamentalists, an artists' colony, or any other voluntarily formed community school are generally regarded as an expression of community vitality.

86. Jonathan Kozol, *Savage Inequalities: Children in America's Schools* (New York: Harper, 1992). Though there have been many studies of school funding in the past twenty years, the first, most comprehensive, and most thoughtful study of funding inequalities in schooling is John Coons, William Clune, and Stephen Sugarman, *Private Wealth and Public Education* (Cambridge: Belknap Press of Harvard University, 1972).

87. *Brown et al. v. Board of Education of Topeka*, 347 U.S. 483, 493. (1954)

88. 62 USLW 4665, 4677.

89. Richard Kluger, *Simple Justice: The History of Brown v. Board of Education* (New York: Vintage Books, 1977), 409.

90. The creation and survival of an African American community in the face of overwhelming brutality is chronicled by Vincent Harding, *There Is a River* (New York: Harcourt Brace Jovanovich, 1981).

91. *Plessy v. Ferguson*, 163 U.S. 537, 550 (1896). The case dealt with a law requiring separate railroad coaches for blacks and whites. Its application to public schooling was declared unconstitutional in *Brown*.

92. The closing of public schools and the provision of scholarships for white students to attend private segregated academies in Prince Edward County, Virginia, was not invalidated by the Supreme Court until 1964, in *Griffin v. County School Board*, 377 U.S. 218.

93. "Aftermath of '54 Ruling Disheartens Browns," *New York Times*, May 18, 1994, p. B-7.

94. Legal resistance to school busing used to overcome neighborhood segregation was massive, and not tamed by the Court until 1971 in *Swann v. Charlotte-Mecklenburg Board of Education*, 402 U.S. 1. When the focus of efforts to desegregate schools shifted to northern states, the Court stepped back from its commitment to equal educational opportunity and announced that desegregation could only be ordered where law or other racially motivated acts had created the segregation. See *Keyes v. School District #1*, 413 U.S. 189 (1973).

When whites fled to the suburbs of metropolitan areas whose city schools were segregated, the Court was willing to protect the white flight by disallowing school desegregation remedies that included suburbs with the inner cities, *Milliken v. Bradley*, 418 U.S. 717 (1974). When African Americans have reacted to this court-approved continuance of school segregation by asking for "equal" resources for their "separate" schools, they sometimes have been victorious (*Milliken v. Bradley II*, 433 U.S. 267 [1977]), but such remedies have been limited, largely ineffective, and are under attack by some districts seeking to end federal court supervision of the desegregation process, as in the voluminous litigation involving Kansas City and the state of Missouri. See Charles Lawrence, "Segregation 'Misunderstood': The *Milliken* Decision Revisited," 12 *USF Law Rev.* 15 (1977).

Even where African American or other minority students attend integrated schools, segregation is often perpetuated by a system of "tracking" and ability grouping based upon racial myths and self-fulfilling prophesies about the interests and abilities of minority students (see Anne Wheelock, *Crossing the Tracks: How "Untracking" Can Save America's Schools* [New York: New Perspectives, 1992]).

Chapter Two. School Wars

1. *West Virginia v. Barnette*, 319 U.S. 624, 642 (1943).

2. Id., 641.

3. In *Why Johnny Can't Tell Right From Wrong* (New York: Simon and Schuster, 1992), William Kilpatrick makes a strong case for renewing character education as a central part of schooling. He distinguishes character education from the "values clarification" programs of the 1960s, which he calls the "failed philosophy of moral education" (15). He argues forcefully that "morality, reli-

gion, story, and myth are bound together" in the "human face of principle" (143), and that "when schools stop contributing to the fund of shared moral knowledge" (122), the common culture and individual consciences are diminished.

The book is an important and useful one for parents, teachers, and independent schools. But as a guide for public school bureaucracies or culture warriors it would be problematic at best, for it does not deal effectively with coercive government intervention in the diverse ways that Americans define character, morality, religion, and conscience, or with the diversity of stories and myths that contribute to the constant redefining of our common culture.

4. "The Politics of Virtue: The Crusade Against America's Moral Decline," *Newsweek*, June 13, 1994, pp. 31–36.

5. "Right and Wrong," *Wall Street Journal*, Sept. 11, 1992, p. B-6.

6. Haynes Johnson, *Divided We Fall: Gambling with History in the Nineties* (New York: W.W. Norton, 1994), 309.

7. Stephen Bates, "Can Schools Teach Values?" *New York Times*, Education Life section, Jan. 8, 1995, pp. 16ff.

8. "State Bill Addresses Schools' Teaching 'Morally or Religiously' Sensitive Issues," *Daily Hampshire Gazette*, March 2, 1995. p. 1.

9. Amitai Etzioni, "Humanizing and Civilizing: Common Ground, Not Divisive Issues Should Strengthen Character Education," *Education Week*, June 8, 1994, p. 44.

10. National Commission on Excellence in Education, *A Nation at Risk: The Imperative for Educational Reform* (Washington, D.C.: U.S. Government Printing Office, 1983).

11. There is nothing new in this. In *Schooling in Capitalist America: Educational Reform and the Contradictions of Economic Life* (New York: Basic Books, 1976), Samuel Bowles and Herbert Gintis studied the demands that business and industry placed upon public schooling in the late nineteenth century. Many of the expectations imposed upon schooling involved obedience toward authority and the re-creation among students of the hierarchic attitudes prevailing in industrial capitalism. Modern business leaders have modern business needs and have drafted standards for what modern worker/students should know. See Michael Apple, *Cultural Politics & Education* (New York: Teachers College Press, 1996). In 1995, business leaders became frustrated when the pace of school reform did not produce the results they desired. See "Business' Enthusiasm for Reform Seen Flagging," *Education Week*, June 14, 1995, p. 11. At Education Summit II (March 26–27, 1996), business and state governors tried to revive reform efforts consistent with their economic goals.

12. The March 26–27 summit meeting was closely coordinated with most *Goals 2000* policies, and was in part an attempt to add impetus to the *Goals 2000* reform effort. While emphasizing state initiatives and controls rather than federal programs, the participants embraced the business-technology agenda for reform of schooling through comprehensive standards imposed by governmental bodies upon individual students, teachers, and schools. The summit meeting was widely reported by the press and had a substantial presence on the Internet, including its own World Wide Web page, www.summit96.ibm.com.

13. David Tyack, *The One Best System: A History of American Urban Education* (Cambridge: Harvard University Press, 1974), remains one of the best histories of public schooling. See also David Tyack, Thomas James, Aaron Benavot, *Law and the Shaping of Public Education, 1785–1954* (Madison: University of Wisconsin Press, 1987).

14. Alexis de Tocqueville's *Democracy in America* was first published in 1835.

15. The economic squeeze and insecurity felt alike by older Americans on fixed incomes and baby-boomers at risk of being down-sized out of their jobs have strained not only the ability but the willingness of many people to support the education of other people's children. Tax revolts, the rejection of school bonds, and the refusal to equalize school funds between wealthy suburbs and poorer inner cities are some of the results. They are all aggravated by the school wars, which make investment in public education seem of dubious worth.

16. Russell Chandler, "Robertson Moves to Fill Christian Right Vacuum," *Los Angeles Times,* May 15, 1990.

17. Reported by People for the American Way (a civil libertarian clearinghouse) in "The Religious Right and School Boards, 1992 and 1993: Executive Summary" (Washington, D.C.: People for the American Way, 1994), 5.

18. See People for the American Way, "Attacks on the Freedom to Learn," 1993–1994 Report" (Washington, D.C.: People for the American Way, 1994), 26.

19. See People for the American Way, "The Religious Right and School Boards," 3; George R. Kaplan, "Deceptions and Fallacies of the Religious Right," *Education Week,* Nov. 2, 1994, p. 60; Gerald W. Bracey, "The Right's Data-Proof Ideologues," *Education Week,* Jan. 25, 1995, p. 48.

20. Mary Walsh, "Christian Coalition Puts Education at Heart of Election Agenda," *Education Week,* Sept. 28, 1994, p. 10. See David Cantor, *The Religious Right: The Assault on Tolerance and Pluralism in America* (New York: The Anti-Defamation League of B'nai B'rith, 1994).

21. Lonnie Harp, "Fervor Spreads to Overhaul State Agencies," *Education Week,* March 8, 1995, p. 1. The proceedings of Education Summit II made it clear that the nation's governors intend to concentrate as much power over schooling as possible in the governments they administer.

22. For an explanation of why Christian fundamentalists oppose even exposing their children to beliefs that contradict fundamentalism, see Nomi Stolzenberg, " 'He Drew a Circle That Shut Me Out': Assimilation, Indoctrination, and the Paradox of a Liberal Education," 106 *Harvard Law Rev.* 581 (1993).

23. People for the American Way, "Attacks on the Freedom to Learn," 5–28.

24. Peter West, "Accuracy of 'Censorship' Report Is Questioned," *Education Week,* Sept. 7, 1994. p. 3.

25. "People for the American Way Defends Censorship Report," Letters to the Editor, *Education Week,* Sept. 28, 1994, p. 41.

26. As the information in the next few pages should make clear, the education establishment is not the sole creature of teachers' unions, and it is not dominated by them. Their role is important, but they are joined by many other associations and interest groups who are equally committed to, and benefited by, the education establishment's continued control of American public education.

27. The figures and other information reported in the next few pages come from: U.S. Department of Education, National Center on Education Statistics, *Digest of Education Statistics;* U.S. Census Bureau, 1992 Public Employment document # GE/92–1; Association of American Publishers Annual Statistics; telephone and mail information received from NEA, AFT, PTA; "School Reform Networks at a Glance," *Education Week,* Nov. 2, 1994, pp. 34ff; Myron Lieberman, *Public Education: An Autopsy* (Cambridge: Harvard University, 1993); Current Index to Journals in Education; ERIC; Educational Testing Service Annual Report; American Association of Colleges for Teacher Education 1993 Briefing Book; and Thomas Sowell, *Inside American Education: The Decline, the Deception, the Dogmas* (New York: Free Press, 1993, in which a chapter title similar to this one can be found, but in which the attitude toward school reform and the nature of school problems is totally dissimilar.

28. For an exhaustive examination of textbook publication and the education establishment, see Suzanne de Castell, Allan Luke, and Carmen Luke, eds., *Language, Authority, and Criticism,* (New York: Falmer Press, 1989).

29. Both unions have adopted school reform goals and strategies, partly in order to remain players in the *Goals 2000* struggle. At this writing they are still considering a merger.

Chapter Three. *Goals 2000*

1. In 1799, Samuel Knox received an award for his essay: "Best System of Liberal Education Adapted to the Genius of Government of the United States." (The essay can be found in *Essays on Education in the Early Republic,* ed. Frederick Rudolph [Cambridge: Belknap Press of Harvard University, 1965].) Knox's proposal called for "establishing a system of national education," based on "some uniform and approved plan or institution" (308), avoiding the many "inconveniences and disagreeable consequences" of diversity of modes of education (310), and advancing, among other goals, the interests of the technology and industry of the day. The plan was to be administered by "a board of education incorporated under sanction of the united authority of the states" (319).

Knox's plan, which of course was not adopted, might easily have been called *Goals 1800.* It even included a section entitled "On the Advantage of Introducing the Same Uniform System of Schoolbooks into a Plan of Public Education" (323). Thus it is that the more things change, the more they remain the same.

2. The language of legislation does not provide a complete picture of how the government agencies empowered or created by that legislation will actually operate or administer the law. The next federal administration may make something very different out of the *Goals 2000* Act than the Clinton administration has thus far. Amendments to *Goals 2000* may appear to change it substantially but may turn out in operation to be merely cosmetic. One official of the U.S. Department of Education—a holdover from the Reagan/Bush era—told me privately that *"Goals 2000* is a placebo." Other insiders have suggested that it represents the most fundamental change in education policy in this century in the United States.

Chapter 3 is not meant to describe how *Goals 2000* has actually been administered in its first two years. Rather it seeks to describe the structure of the Act and the assumptions about schooling and education reform upon which it is based. The *Goals 2000:* Educate America Act is both symptom and cause of many of the maladies that affect public schooling in the United States. Understanding and correcting those maladies require an understanding of the *Goals 2000* legislation enacted by the 103rd Congress.

Some of the history leading up to the adoption of *Goals 2000* and some of the evaluation of it after adoption can be found in: Chester Finn, Sara Lightfoot et al., "National Standards for American Education: A Symposium," *Teachers College Record* 91, no. 3 (Fall 1989); Marshall Smith et al., "A National Curriculum in the United States?" *Educational Leadership* 49, no.1 (Sept. 1991): 74–81; Marshall Smith and Jennifer O'Day, "School Reform and Equal Opportunity: An Introduction to the Education Symposium," *Stanford Law and Policy Review* (Winter 1992–93): 15–20; Theodore Sizer et al., "Standards and School Reform: Asking the Basic Questions," *Stanford Law and Policy Review* (Winter 1992–93): 27–35; A. Lockwood, "National Standards: Who Benefits?" *Focus in Change*, no. 11, National Center for Effective Schools (Summer 1993); Michael Apple, "The Politics of Official Knowledge," *Teachers College Record* 95, no. 2 (1993): 222; Sonia Nieto, ed., "National Curriculum Standards," *Educational Forum* 58, no. 1 (Summer 1994).

3. Some educators consider curriculum to be the specification of all the detailed lessons, examples, exercises, and so on that go into a particular course—the method of teaching. *Goals 2000* standards for content do not specify these details, though they often give examples or suggested topics for schoolwork. But the standards do specify the content of what every child is expected to learn and will be tested on, leaving the method of teaching this content to the teachers. For purposes of analyzing *Goals 2000* and its effect on freedom of intellect and belief, the specification of what students must learn is more important by far than the specification of details of teaching methods used. The use of the term "curriculum content standards" in this book refers to the prescription of what children shall learn and rather than how teachers shall teach.

4. Other countries have national systems of education, most notably South Africa, Japan, Great Britain, and France. A comparison of these systems with that of the United States would no doubt be interesting and useful for appreciating the benefits and drawbacks of such systems in their particular cultural settings. The conditions differ markedly among these nations, however; and a comparison among them would have to account for differences in diversity and homogeneity of population, the availability and cost of parental choice within each system, the legal/constitutional tradition concerning individual liberty in general and freedom of belief in particular, and the social/historical realities in which each national system was established.

The following may be helpful starting points for those interested in pursuing this matter further:

South Africa: Timothy Curtin, "The Political Economy of Education in South Africa," *African Affairs* 92 (1993): 417; Linda Chisholm and Ben Fine, "Context and Contest in South African Education Policy: Comment on Curtin," *African Affairs* 93 (1994): 233; Curtin's rejoinder, *African Affairs* 93 (1994): 249; *London Times Education Supplement,* Sept. 8, 1995, and Oct. 28, 1994.

Japan: L. Edward Schoppa, "Zoku Power and LDP Power: A Case Study of the Zoku Role in Education Policy," *Journal of Japanese Studies* 17, no. 1 (1991): 79.

Great Britain: Simon Longstaff, "Democratic Education and the Curriculum Safety-net," *Journal of Philosophy of Education* 23, no. 1 (1989); Neville Bennett and Charles Desforges, "Primary Education in England: A System in Transition," *Elementary School Journal* 92, no. 1 (1991): 61; Charles Winch, "A Defence of Educational Standards," *Journal of Philosophy of Education* 30, no. 1 (1996): 57; *London Times Educational Supplement,* Jan. 20, 1995, and Sept. 1, 1995; John White, "Two National Curricula—Baker's and Stalin's: Towards a Liberal Alternative, *British Journal of Educational Studies* 36, no. 3 Oct. 1988): 218.

France: Kathryn Anderson-Levitt, Regine Sirota, and Martine Mazurier, "Elementary Education in France," *Elementary School Journal* 92, no. 1 (1991): 79.

There are also brief comments about most of these nations' systems of school standards in Diane Ravitch, *National Standards in American Education: A Citizen's Guide* (Washington D.C.: Brookings Institution, 1995). On the all-important issue of school choice where national standards are in place, see Charles Glenn, Jr., *Choice of Schools in Six Nations* (Washington, D.C.: U.S. Government Printing Office, 1989), which covers Britain and France and four other countries.

5. Title I, section 102 (3)(A).

6. Title III, section 316 reads: "Notwithstanding any other provision of this title, standards or State assessments described in a State improvement plan submitted in accordance with section 306 shall not be required to be certified by the Council [the National Education Standards and Improvements Council created by the Act to certify national and state content standards]." But this assurance runs counter to the entire weight of the process created to ensure that state and local standards are consistent with national standards. In 1996, amendments to *Goals 2000* eliminated the council and its powers. Approval of state plans then became a function of the secretary of education and, ultimately, the National Education Goals Panel.

7. By mid-1996, only five states had not signed on to *Goals 2000:* Alabama, Oklahoma, Virginia, Montana, and New Hampshire. See Mark Pitsch, "To Placate Conservatives, Measure Alters Goals 2000," *Education Week,* May 1, 1996, p. 19. The 1996 amendments to the Act made it possible for local school districts to join the *Goals 2000* program (with state education officials' approval) directly in those states not signed on to *Goals 2000.*

8. Section 3 (a)(9), Definitions

9. See section 220.

10. See section 309 (b)(3)(A)

11. See sections 306 (c), 317 and 231 generally, and in particular 231(4). One of the purposes of the "Leadership in Technology" section (which includes sec-

tion 231) is stated as providing federal leadership and a national strategy "so
that no school system will be excluded from the technological revolution; . . ."

12. See sections 502 and 504 (d).

13. See Title IX generally, and sections 912, 931 (d).

14. Section 3(a)(7) of the Act contains the following definition of opportunity-
to-learn standards:

> the term "opportunity-to-learn standards" means the criteria for and the basis
> of, assessing the sufficiency or quality of the resources, practices, and condi-
> tions necessary at each level of the education system (schools, local education
> agencies, and States) to provide all students with an opportunity to learn the
> material in voluntary national content standards or State content standards;

This strategy is intended to reduce the glaring disparities in resources available to students in each state and reflects the political difficulty of using another, more effective strategy for resource equalization—directly ordering the
equalization of resources in each state under the powers granted Congress by
the Fourteenth Amendment.

15. See the 1996 Omnibus Appropriations Act, Conference Report accompanying HR 3019. Liberals in Congress were apparently willing to permit the
elimination of the opportunity-to-learn standards by the 1996 amendments because these standards were so weak. For a discussion of this and other amendments to *Goals 2000* that are mentioned in chapter 3, see Pitsch, "To Placate
Conservatives," 19.

16. Section 203 sets out these powers. In its original form it referred to section 216, which required the National Education Standards and Improvement
Council (NESIC) to submit the criteria and standards it approves to the secretary
of education who in turn would publish them in the *Federal Register* "for the
purpose of obtaining public comment." Because the 1996 amendments to *Goals
2000* eliminated NESIC, the secretary of education, along with the goals panel,
exercises much of the approval power NESIC might have exercised if it had not
been eliminated.

17. Alexis de Tocqueville described the irresistible force of voluntary government standards in 1830, a time when government was not nearly as pervasive
as it is now: "[Because] a government can only dictate strict rules, the opinions
which it favors are rigidly enforced, and it is never easy to discriminate between
its advice and its commands" (*Democracy in America*, vol. 2 [New York: Vintage Books, 1945], 117).

18. Section 306.

19. The Department of Education, along with private grantors, professional
associations, and university-based grantees, has already begun the process of
assisting in the development of the national content and performance standards.
The National Council of Teachers of Mathematics, a private group, published
math standards in 1989. Development of standards for the other subject areas
was virtually complete by spring 1996. For a discussion of the mathematics
standards, see *Journal of Research in Mathematics Education* 23, no. 5 (1992).
For a discussion of the American history standards, see chapter 1.

20. Section 213 (a)(2). The requirement that fair and democratic processes be

used by the council in certifying standards, including openness to public input, might be appropriate in a society not committed to protecting the formation and expression of beliefs from majority control. But as long as the United States adheres to the principles of individual and cultural freedom contained in the Constitution, section 213 (a)(2) of the Act, like the entire *Goals 2000* process, is nothing but an invitation to special interest groups to fight with each other over whose worldview will become orthodoxy in government schools.

21. Section 213 (e). The generality requirement itself is suspect, since its looseness leaves to federal, state, and local administrators the individual decisions that will determine how much freedom will be permitted teachers, students, and families. The burden is thus placed on individuals to contest restrictions imposed by state authorities, a scenario that suggests endless politicking and litigation against the power of the state as individuals pursue claims for intellectual and cultural freedom. Because this type of struggle has met with very limited success under the conditions prevailing before *Goals 2000* was enacted, the concentration of power created by the Act can only make prospects grimmer for educational freedom.

22. Section 213 (b).

23. Section 213 (f) requires that state assessments be consistent with state standards, which in turn have probably been certified by the national council. But there is protection covering the use of these assessments. The states must wait until 1999 until they can make these tests the basis of "decisions regarding graduation, grade promotion, or retention of students." See section 213 (f)(1)(C)(ii).

24. The Act had been administered for two years and forty-five states had participated in comprehensive school reform without a single member having been appointed to NESIC.

The 1996 amendments provide an alternative to submitting state plans to the U.S. secretary of education for approval. Though the old approval method remains in effect, a state may according to the alternative method submit an assurance from its governor and chief state school officer that the state has a completed plan that meets the requirements of the *Goals 2000* Act. This seems to be a distinction without a difference, since the Act's requirements remain. Furthermore, by the time these amendments were passed and were signed by the president, twenty states had already submitted their plans to the secretary and had had them approved after review and feedback from "experts." (See H.R. Report 446, 103rd Cong. 2d sess. [1994] and the amendment contained in the conference report on H 3019, Doc. 537, 104th Cong., 2d sess. [1996].)

25. If all of *Goals 2000* were repealed, the creation and attempted imposition of systemwide content standards might be privatized. Some conservative and liberal groups have already produced competing standards in various subjects and are preparing to do battle over whose version of history or economics or science or arts should be adopted by state or local school authorities.

This might seem to be in the best tradition of intellectual freedom and the marketplace of ideas—an abundance of views from which independent thinkers and thoughtful communities may choose. But *Goals 2000* is based on, and has reinforced, the idea among both the public and the Education Empire that standardized education, approved by state if not federal government, is necessary and desirable. So forcefully has the tide shifted away from individual educational liberty and toward government control of school content, that a repeal of *Goals 2000*—unaccompanied by a re-constitution of schooling—would have scarcely any effect on the power of states or the behavior of local education agencies.

26. Many of these state standards will differ from each other in only minor ways, because national standards created with federal help, if not approval, will already exist and would be troublesome to revise.

27. Section 301 is a listing of congressional "findings" about the need for systemic reform. Drawing from the language of the military-industrial complex, the findings also state that "federal funds should be *targeted* to support State and local initiatives, and to *leverage* State and local resources for designing and implementing systemwide education improvement plans" (emphasis added).

28. *Education Week* of May 4, 1994, reported that only $105 million was appropriated for the fiscal year ending September 30, 1994, but that the president requested $700 million for FY 1995 (which began October 1, 1994) and planned to ask for $1 billion in each succeeding fiscal year. Since then a Republican-dominated Congress has moved to eliminate all funding for *Goals 2000* but has succeeded only in trimming it and slightly altering the appearance of the legislation.

29. This is one of the very few places where nongovernment schools are mentioned. The state panel, according to section 306 (b)(1)(D), must include a representative of "private schools in which students or teachers participate in Federal education programs." However, section 1020 prevents private schools from receiving any Title III funds or any indirect benefit from these funds except for teacher and administrator training based on certified standards (section 310). The 1996 amendments eliminated specific requirements for the membership of state panels. Whether this will eliminate or enhance the presence of independent schools on the panels is unclear.

30. Section 316 states that standards and assessments included in a state improvement plan "shall not be *required* to be certified by the Council" (emphasis added). The states are nonetheless required to include content and performance standards in the plans they must submit to the U.S. Department of Education for approval in order to get funding. That the states are not required by law to seek council certification of these standards seems entirely without legal significance or practical impact on the existence of individual education freedom.

31. Title III, section 306 (c). There are several other requirements for the state plan, such as parental and community involvement in its design and implementation. Those who remember President Lyndon Johnson's War on Poverty know that even the strongest federal commitment to community participation seldom yields more than another layer of local bureaucracy and power-seeking. In a half-hearted attempt to address the enormous disparities in resources available to schools in each state, *Goals 2000* required that a plan consider "opportunity

to learn" standards (section 306 [d-m]) as a way of helping some schools acquire the resources to meet the demands set out by the content standards in the state plan. In 1996, even this requirement was repealed.

32. Section 308.

33. In the 1996 amendments to *Goals 2000*, local education agencies (school districts) in the five states that had not joined the *Goals 2000* reform process were given the ability to apply directly to the federal government for funds and participation in *Goals 2000*, provided that they received approval from their state government. (See Conference Report, House 3019.) This provision would seem to increase the level of compliance with *Goals 2000* among the few states not participating.

34. Section 306 (h). The requirement of parent and community involvement in the state and local panels that draft and implement the required reform plans might be read as a form of bottom-up participation. But even if these outnumbered community participants could overcome the accumulated power of experts, bureaucrats, and politicians in drafting plans consistent with the national curriculum, those really at the bottom of the national education pyramid, dissenters from systemic and monolithic reform, would be left without any meaningful participation or protection from the effects of *Goals 2000*.

35. The exception is found in section 310 (a)(1), which requires that upon request states inform private schools of the content standards and other reform requirements established for public schools, and in section 310 (a)(2), which requires in section 310 (a)(2) that a state or local agency using Title III funds for teacher or administrator training provide in its plan "for the training of teachers and administrators in private schools located in the geographical area served. . . ." Section 319 also contains some congressional findings about private education, the responsibilities of various levels of government, and an affirmation about local control. But even if these toothless statements were believable, they apply only to the federal government's direct authority and leave state governments free to ride roughshod over dissenters of any stripe.

36. The reauthorization of the Elementary and Secondary Education Act, the single largest federal aid program, already requires the use of standards. In 1995, the debate over how the rules affecting these standards would be written provided yet more evidence that *Goals 2000* is already becoming a monolith and that ideological conflict will follow the attempt to standardize schooling wherever it goes. See Mark Pitsch, "New Title I Rules Focus on Standards and Assessment," *Education Week*, May 10, 1995, p.16.

37. See "National Curriculum Standards," a symposium in *Educational Forum* 58, no. 4 (Summer 1994).

Chapter Four. Renouncing Our Constitutional Heritage

1. The Declaration of Independence reads, in part: "We hold these truths to be self-evident; that all men are created equal, that they are endowed by their Creator with certain unalienable Rights, that among these are Life, Liberty, and the pursuit of Happiness. That, to secure these rights, Governments are

instituted among Men, deriving their just powers from the consent of the governed, . . ."

2. The phrase is Alexis de Tocqueville's, drawn from *Democracy in America* (1835).

3. The phrase is drawn from *Pierce v. Society of Sisters of the Holy Name of Jesus and Mary,* 268 U.S. 510, a 1925 Supreme Court case that invalidated an Oregon state law that required all children to attend public schools. The Court ruled that parents had a fundamental right to satisfy compulsory school laws by sending their children to schools not run by the government, because the child is "not the mere creature of the state."

4. *West Virginia v. Barnette,* 319 U.S. 624, 638 (1943). Two histories of the conflicts that led to the *Barnette* case are, Leonard Stevens, *Salute! The Case of the Bible vs. The Flag* (New York: Coward, 1973); and David Manwaring, *Render Unto Caesar: The Flag Salute Controversy* (Chicago: University of Chicago Press, 1962).

The *Barnette* case (like others in this and later chapters) is used to evoke and help explain a central principle of constitutional democracy and the application of that principle to elementary and secondary education. It is not used to make legal argument on how the Court could or should evaluate *Goals 2000* or current school practices under the regime of local control. In fact, since *Barnette,* many of the cases decided in this area suggest that today's Court might approve some aspects of school indoctrination in the name of preserving the political, social, and moral values of the local community. See, for example, *Hazelwood v. Kuhl-meier,* 484 U.S. 260 (1988). That is why chapter 7 argues that it may be necessary to restate, in a constitutional amendment, how "We the People" want the rights of conscience and community to be applied to schooling.

Some scholars have sought to find in existing constitutional provisions significant limitations on government power to inculcate youth in public schools. See Robert Kamenshine, "The First Amendment's Implied Political Establishment Clause," 67 *Cal. Law Rev.* 1104 (1979); Tyll van Geel, "The Search for Constitutional Limits on Governmental Authority to Inculcate Youth," 62 *Texas Law Rev.* 197 (1983); Sanford Gottlieb, "In the Name of Patriotism: The Constitutionality of 'Bending' History in Public Secular Schools," 62 *NYU Law Rev.* 497 (1987).

For an argument that the First Amendment itself should be read as protecting individual rights of belief in schooling, see Stephen Arons, "Separation of School and State: *Pierce* Reconsidered," *Harvard Educational Review* 46 (1976): 76. For an argument that the *Barnette* principle is "fragile," see S. Shifrin, "Government Speech," 27 *UCLA Law Rev.* 565 (1980). See also Mark Yudof, "When Governments Speak: Toward a Theory of Government Expression and the First Amendment," 57 *Texas Law Rev.* 863 (1979), and Mark Yudof, *When Government Speaks* (Berkeley: University of California Press, 1983).

5. *Barnette,* 319 U.S. 624, 641.

6. *Minersville School District v. Gobitis,* 310 U.S. 586, 595 (1939). Justice Frankfurter's opinion denied the Gobitis family an exemption from the flag salute and pledge in spite of their claim that these ceremonies violated their

sincerely held religious belief that obeisance to such an image contradicted biblical commands. When *Barnette* overruled *Gobitis*, it ignored the religious freedom claim and rested the ruling upon the freedom of expression and belief generally.

7. The Witnesses cited Exod. 20: 3–5, which reads: "Thou shalt have no other gods before me. Thou shalt not make unto thee any graven image, or any likeness of anything that is in heaven above, or that is in the earth beneath, or that is in the water under the earth; thou shalt not bow down thyself to them nor serve them." In the *Barnette* case, the Witnesses offered a modified pledge of allegiance to the laws of the United States that are "consistent with God's law" and a statement of respect for the flag as a "symbol of freedom and justice to all." The substitute pledge was not acceptable to the West Virginia school authorities, and the conflict of conscience and state power again became inevitable.

8. *Minersville*, 310 U.S. 586, 600.

9. *Minersville*, 310 U.S. 586, 599. The constitutional guarantee to which Frankfurter referred was first articulated by the U.S. Supreme Court in *Pierce.*

10. The issue of religious freedom in the schools continues to be a thorny one for the Supreme Court and the country. There are two religious freedom clauses in the First Amendment, one protecting the free exercise of religion and the other preventing a government establishment (or aid or inhibition) of religion. In the past ten or fifteen years the interplay of these two clauses and changes in the Supreme Court have raised the possibility that fundamental changes in the separation of church and state may be on the horizon where schooling is concerned.

A review of the complex and sometimes inconsistent rulings of the Court in this area is beyond the scope of this book and not essential to its theme. It should be noted, however, that even if some judicially created "breach" in the wall of separation should permit religious exercises or ceremonies to become part of public schooling, that change would not solve the problem of restricted rights of conscience and community in schooling for anyone.

As chapter 7 argues (and as the retelling of the story of the *Kiryas Joel* case in chapter 1 suggests), a straightforward guarantee of freedom of intellect and belief in schooling is required to secure effectively the full range of these freedoms. A guarantee of equal funding for school choice for everyone is also required to secure freedom of conscience, whether religious or secular in origin. The constitutional guarantee of freedom of school choice would completely recast free exercise and establishment issues under the First Amendment. Compare George Dent, Jr., "Religious Children, Secular Schools," 61 *So. Cal. Law Rev.* 863 (1988).

Those wishing to read about the Court's possibly changing view of the religion clauses can consult, in addition to *Kiryas Joel*, the following cases: *Aguilar v. Felton*, 473 U.S. 402 (1985); *Wallace v. Jaffree*, 472 U.S. 38 (1985); *School District of City of Grand Rapids v. Ball*, 473 U.S. 373 (1985); *Witters v. Washington Dept. of Services for the Blind*, 474 U.S. 481 (1986); *Edwards v. Aguillard*, 482 U.S. 578 (1987); *County of Allegheny et al. v. ACLU, Greater Pittsburgh*, 492

U.S. 573 (1989); *Lee v. Weisman,* 505 U.S. 577 (1992); *Lamb's Chapel and John Steigerwald v. Center Moriches Union Free School Dist.,* 508 U.S. 384 (1993); *Larry Zobrest et al. v. Catalina Foot Hills School Dist.* 509 U.S. 1 (1993); and *Rosenberger v. University of Virginia,* 115 S. Ct. 2510 (1995). For an excellent discussion of these cases and the search for common ground in religious accommodation in public schools, see Rosemary Salomone, "Common Schools, Uncommon Values: Listening to the Voices of Dissent," 14 *Yale Law & Policy Review* 169 (1996).

11. *Barnette,* 319 U.S. 624, 634.

12. Id., 637.

13. Id., 633.

14. Id., 641.

15. Id., 640. Had Justice Jackson included competitiveness in a global economy in his list, he would have been predicting the future as well as writing about the past.

16. Id., 642.

17. Daniel Carroll of Maryland made the statement in 1791. It is quoted in *School District of Abington Township, Pa. v. Schempp,* 374 US 203, 231 (1963).

18. "70 Years after Scopes, Evolution Hot Topic Again," *Education Week,* March 13, 1996, p. 16.

19. See, for example, Michael Apple, "Do the Standards Go Far Enough? Power, Policy, and Practice in Mathematics Education," *Journal for Research in Mathematics Education* 23, no. 5 (1992): 412–431.

20. In Diane Ravitch's thoughtful book on national standards, *National Standards in American Education: A Citizen's Guide* (Washington, D.C.: Brookings Institution, 1995), she acknowledges the problem presented by government infringement on freedom of thought, though she does not, in my judgment, successfully resolve it. Taking into account the rationalist, marketplace-of-ideas conception of schooling she writes:

> The challenge is to pose issues and controversies without resolving them; to recognize that historic and scientific debates are always subject to investigation and evidence; and to acknowledge those instances where investigation and evidence have established conclusive facts. Diversity of opinion is a basic value in and of itself in a democratic society. If government-endorsed standards trample on freedom of thought or attempt to impose uniformity of opinion, they deserve to be short-lived. (20)

Ravitch's position fails to take account of misuse of the power to ask questions that others must debate; and would probably be an unacceptable response to the concerns of many individuals and groups who dissent from the mainstream worldview. See note 26, below.

21. In *Keyishian v. Board of Regents,* 385 U.S. 589 (1967) the Court ruled that the First Amendment "does not tolerate laws that cast a pall of orthodoxy over the classroom" (id., 603). The case concerned a public university and political loyalty oaths required of its employees.

22. *Barnette,* 319 U.S. at 641.

23. Paul Freund has written, "While political debate and division is normally

a wholesome process for reaching viable accommodations, political division on religious lines is one of the principal evils the First Amendment sought to forestall" (82 *Harvard Law Rev.* at 1692 [1980]).

The principle should apply equally well to culture wars that are not fought on religious lines. Wherever the deepest issues of belief become the subject of government regulation, the functioning and legitimacy of the political process itself is threatened as much as the freedom of belief.

24. A growing skepticism about the role of government in social life is not necessarily a reaction to the use of government schools to shape individual minds. But the two do seem to be related. Moderate citizens who see matters of conscience and individual freedom come under government control in the school wars might wonder whether government can be trusted to create programs that are fair and beneficial to all, or regulations that are reasonable and necessary to curb destructive behavior. By the same token, people whose philosophical individualism or self-interest make them hostile to any nonmilitary government activity may be able to point to the conflicts over conscience in schools to persuade moderate citizens that no government program or regulation in any sphere of life is acceptable.

The Constitution provides at least one principle by which to distinguish legitimate from illegitimate government activity. The principles of constitutional democracy in general, and the First Amendment in particular, prevent any government agency from infringing on freedoms of expression and belief except with the most compelling justifications. Permitting government control over these freedoms may ultimately render all democratic self-government illegitimate in the minds of many people. By using majoritarian politics to do the *wrong* things, we may make its use to do the *right* thing increasingly difficult.

This book is, therefore, not an argument to privatize all government functions. Nor is it an argument for exaggerated individualism in a complex, interrelated world. Rather it argues for keeping truly private matters—for example conscience and voluntary community—from government control, so that truly public matters such as defense, environmental protection, social welfare policy, and nondiscrimination requirements can be handled effectively by government.

25. Some communities of belief—for example the Amish, the Satmarer, and some Christian fundamentalists—even object to such exposure, claiming that it undermines religious freedom and community beliefs. See Nomi Stolzenberg, " 'He Drew a Circle that Shut Me Out': Assimilation, Indoctrination, and the Paradox of a Liberal Education," 106 *Harvard Law Rev.* 583 (1993).

26. Along with these input requirements go more subtle means of influencing attitudes and beliefs, such as those implicit in the hidden curriculum of school hierarchy, student obedience, and the gender organization of work and play in the classroom. Since children learn as much from what they observe and practice as from what they are taught explicitly, these subtle influences matter to parents and teachers. And since lessons embedded in classroom structure have an element of coercion about them (children who join a discussion without first raising their hand and being called on by the teacher may find themselves excluded from the discussion until they accept the teacher's rules of discussion

and the hierarchy of age), the hidden curriculum may be a mix of input and output requirements.

27. *Pierce,* 268 U.S. 510, 535. The state of Oregon had enacted a law that required public school attendance of all children, effectively outlawing private schools. Though the input requirements of public schools were few and relatively unrestrictive, the Constitution still gave every family the right to choose something different. In making this ruling, the Court did not forbid the state government from imposing "reasonable" regulations on private schools. But later cases made it clear that those regulations could not be used to make private schools so similar to public schools that the constitutional right to choose a nongovernment school was effectively eliminated. The Court's ruling about parental rights referred to "the liberty of parents and guardians to direct the up-bringing and education of children under their control."

28. Laurence Tribe, *American Constitutional Law,* 2nd ed. (Mineola, N.Y.: Foundation Press, 1988), 1309.

29. Section 3 (a)(9), of the *Goals 2000:* Educate America Act. The idea of competency testing as the only reliable way to insure that content standards are being learned runs throughout the legislation. Section 213 (f) and section 220 in effect require each state to have a system of assessments (tests and other evidence of performance), but postpones until 1999 the use of these assessments "to make decisions regarding graduation, grade promotion, or retention of students . . ." or "relating to program placement . . . or employment."

30. The *Goals 2000* statute provides a mechanism by which statewide tests may be certified by the federal government, but does not require them to be so certified (see section 316 of the Act). Some of the early supporters of national standards, such as Chester Finn, continue to advocate a national competency test (telephone conversation with author, January 1995).

31. The problem for public debate is much broader and ultimately more important than the technical legal question of whether competency testing, as a means of enforcing official knowledge under *Goals 2000,* is so like the compulsory pledge of allegiance that it violates the Constitution. Readers should be aware that no argument is made here as to whether competency testing does or does not violate the Constitution. The argument is rather that such testing—as part of a comprehensive politicization of schooling—violates the general principles of constitutional democracy; and that, for this to be made into a politically and legally effective conclusion, the people should consider amending the Constitution (see chapter 7).

32. The question, of course, is "Who are the teacher's clients?" If the teacher's client is the government and its regulations and requirements, the teacher's professionalism is compromised by obligations to the bureaucracy.

33. In applying professional knowledge and skills with families, students of varying ages, and school communities, teachers face a complex task. At what age should a child's interests and desires be taken into account? What if there is a conflict between the parents' beliefs and the teacher's understanding of the subject matter? Suppose a parent seems overly controlling of the child's intellectual or spiritual development? How much should the control of schooling rest

in the hands of the family, the teacher, the community, the child? Since young children cannot, almost by definition, decide about their own education, who should decide?

It is beyond the scope of this book to enter into a discussion of the competing interests, rights, and abilities of all these participants in the schooling enterprise, except to argue, as this chapter does, that when any government claims such complete power over schooling as *Goals 2000* allows, it cripples the freedoms of conscience and community of all the other participants and makes the teacher's task impossible. To put the point in an analogous context, one could ask whether the Constitution would tolerate government intervention in the equally complex issues of guiding a child's religious upbringing.

This book therefore assumes that however the interests of children, parents, families, and teachers are balanced, the government has no role to play in controlling the content of a child's schooling. The balancing of interests (and of rights of conscience and community) among children, parents, teachers, and communities—and the question of who should decide—is treated with extraordinary insight and sensitivity by John Coons and Stephen Sugarman in their excellent book *Education by Choice: The Case for Family Control* (Berkeley: University of California Press, 1978). For a brief look at how the Supreme Court has handled one issue of parents and teenage children with potentially different views on schooling, see *Wisconsin v. Yoder,* discussed in chapter 5.

34. For a specific discussion of teacher professionalism as being at the center of school reform needs, see Stephen Arons, "Constitutional Implications of National Curriculum Standards," ed. Sonia Nieto, *Educational Forum* 58, no. 4 (Summer 1994): 353.

35. Neil Postman and Charles Weingartner, *Teaching as a Subversive Activity* (New York: Penguin, 1971).

36. Dewey goes on to state:

Until the democratic criterion of the intrinsic significance of every growing experience is recognized, we shall be intellectually confused by the demand for adaptation to external demands. . . . Educators have to be on their guard against ends that are alleged to be general and ultimate. (*Democracy and Education* [New York: Free Press, 1944], 108–9)

37. Some aspects of this systemic reform will not be in place for several years, but all are mentioned and supported by the *Goals 2000* legislation and essential to its basic formulation and purpose of "promoting coherent, nationwide, systemic education reform" (section 2 of the Act).

38. *Webster's Third New International Dictionary* defines "totalitarian" as an adjective used to describe a "political regime based on subordination of the individual to the state and strict control of all aspects of the life and productive capacity of the nation. . . ." Replace the word "political" with "educational," and the word "nation" with "school system" and totalitarian becomes an apt adjective for the likely results of school reform under *Goals 2000*.

39. *The One Best System* is the ironic title of David Tyack's thorough and thoroughly interesting history of American schooling (*The One Best System: A History of American Urban Education* [Cambridge: Harvard University Press, 1974]). Also see David Tyack and Thomas James, "Moral Majorities and the

School Curriculum: Historical Perspectives on the Legalization of Virtue," *Teachers College Record* 86, no. 4 (Summer 1985).

40. The first purpose listed in the *Goals 2000* legislation is "promoting coherent, nationwide, systemic education reform" (section 2).

41. A recent and articulate expression of these views can be found in Deborah Meier, *The Power of Their Ideas: Lessons for America from a Small School in Harlem* (Boston: Beacon Press, 1995). The book is a reflection on the successful experiences of teachers, families, and children in a small, virtually autonomous public school in New York City.

42. The issues affecting centralization and decentralization of public schools are complex and fascinating; and there has been a lively debate about it in many academic and public policy forums for years. Consolidation of schools and school districts is an older manifestation of this debate. So too was the preservation of city/suburban school lines that hamstrung desegregation efforts. Newer ones include site-based management, charter schools, and public school choice.

To explore the complexities of the centralization versus decentralization debate and its consequences for education policy, see Tyll van Geel, *Authority to Control the School Program* (Lexington, Mass.: Lexington Books, 1976).

43. *Goals 2000* was conceived, presented to Congress, and initially implemented in part by appealing to the importance of systemwide reform and in part by stressing that federal and state governments could grant waivers from their school regulations upon application of local school districts. The waivers section of the Act is section 311.

44. See Friederich Hayek, "The Creative Powers of a Free Civilization" in his *The Constitution of Liberty* (Chicago: University of Chicago Press, 1960).

45. See Thomas I. Emerson, *Toward a General Theory of the First Amendment* (New York: Random House, 1966), in which he argues, among other things, that the free exchange of ideas among a diverse people is essential to political democracy and the most reliable way of attaining broader truths. To take one of these transient truths and fix it in a required curriculum systemically imposed around the country is to invert the process Emerson describes as essential to democratic self-government.

46. The language is drawn from the *Barnette* case.

47. *Goals 2000*: Educate America Act, section 2, "Purpose."

48. The crux of the problem of imposed goals for education may be the tendency of students and their families to ignore inner misgivings and accept these goals simply because they are required. This is one way that imposed goals might short-circuit intellectual and cultural diversity, reduce respect for the inner self, and make unity so thin that it collapses under the smallest challenge when it is not enforced by repressive means.

49. The language is drawn from the *Barnette* case.

50. The phrase "mere creature of the state" comes from *Pierce*, the 1925 case that first enunciated the constitutional right to send one's children to a private school. Later cases prevented the government from so regulating the private schools that, in effect, there was no real difference among schools available to parents.

51. *Goals 2000*'s commitment to systemic imposition of national or state

standards will create a system intentionally uniform in its most important aspects, thereby denying to those who cannot afford private schooling any meaningful choice of schools or their content.

52. Joel H. Spring has chronicled the interventions by state and federal authorities and national interest groups in education policy. See *The American School, 1642–1985* (New York: Longman, 1986), and *The Sorting Machine Revisited: National Education Policy since 1945* (New York: Longman, 1989).

53. In any conflict over official knowledge in schools, the multiplicity of competing voices makes it tempting to join the substantive debate over what children should know. It is important to consider the value and definition of a core of common culture, to evaluate Eurocentric versus other views of history and knowledge, to argue the meaning of cultural literacy, moral education, and the place of pluralism in the nation's spirit. It is important to argue about competing visions of individual truth and the nation's future, to discuss whose facts are really facts and whose are mere beliefs, to explore the ways in which schooling can be a vehicle for shaping culture and justifying ideology in an apparently aimless and alienating world. But when such debates, arguments, and discussions lead to government controls, basic freedoms are lost. Although the current substantive debate over knowledge and skills invokes the natural parental desire to make schooling an integral part of child rearing, it hides the fact that a shift of power over public schooling may ultimately frustrate that parental desire, turn the debate into a school war, and make the child into "the mere creature of the state."

54. Two examples from the school wars illustrate the point in education. First, in the Lake County, Florida, battle over American cultural superiority in the schools, the teachers' union condemned a local requirement as a violation of First Amendment rights. But in the same legal complaint, the teachers sought refuge in a state multicultural education law which imposed an equal, though substantively different, burden on the teachers' freedom to teach. Second, the Christian Right has repeatedly attacked texts and library books used by public schools on the grounds that these books impose upon students a worldview inconsistent with Christian values. But while claiming the right to educate their children by their own values, they have often sought to gain these rights by imposing their values upon all schoolchildren.

55. According to one consultant who wished to remain anonymous, the possibility of pursuing such a strategy under *Goals 2000* arose during the congressional debate, but its importance was minimized in an effort to avoid losing support for the bill from legislators unconcerned with equal educational opportunity. Nevertheless, the strategy was perceived in advance. The final copy of the Act contains language that appears intended to prevent the use of uniform content standards as the basis of such litigation that seeks "to provide equal educational opportunity for all students to meet high academic and occupational skill standards . . ." (section 2 [5]).

Section 213 (h)(2) reads: "Nothing in this Act shall be construed to create a legally enforceable right for any person against a State, local educational agency, or school based on a standard or assessment certified by the Council or the criteria developed by the Council for such certification."

56. One of the most important examples of this kind of litigation came in 1972 in *Wisconsin v. Yoder* 406 U.S. 205, when the Supreme Court upheld the First Amendment religious rights of Old Order Amish citizens who refused to send their children to any school after the eighth grade. The Court found that the state's compulsory school attendance law, though important to the economic and civic development of most children in the state, did not constitute a compelling justification for infringing the Amish right of religious free exercise. Under *Goals 2000*, this case might have been decided differently if national or state standards were seen as more compelling by virtue of the governmental support and national purposes which helped create them. In many cases involving local school impositions on the rights of conscience and community, the Court provided only marginal protection. For a further discussion of this and of *Yoder*, see chapter 5.

57. The connection between expression and formation of ideas and beliefs and opinions is discussed in Arons, "Separation of School and State," 76.

58. In Plato's *Republic*, only the elite (Guardians) were to receive an education by the state, and that education would be authoritarian—the only education offered and an education that trained its students in the character necessary for the continuation of the state. As Julia Annas put it, "it is undeniable that his educational system aims to impose on children a single set of values in such a way that they will not be seriously skeptical about them either at the time or later in life" (*An Introduction to Plato's Republic* [New York: Oxford University Press, 1981], 80).

59. When asked by the crowd whether the Constitutional Convention of 1787 had given birth to a monarchy or a republic, Benjamin Franklin reportedly replied: "A Republic, if you can keep it." Franklin, the founder of what is now the University of Pennsylvania, might wonder whether *Goals 2000* symbolizes a decision not to keep it.

60. Maxine Green, "The Arts and National Standards," *Educational Forum* 58, no. 4 (Summer 1994), 399. The statement is relevant to all the nine subject matters covered by *Goals 2000*.

61. In writing about the importance of protecting First Amendment rights, Thomas Emerson, one of the leading First Amendment scholars of the twentieth century, described the reasons for protecting these constitutional principles that might equally well apply to schooling:

> 1) as a means of assuring individual self-development, 2) as a means of attaining the truth, 3) as a method of securing participation by the members of the society in social, including political, decision-making, and 4) as a means of maintaining the balance between stability and change in the society. (Thomas Emerson, *Toward a General Theory of the First Amendment* [New York: Random House, 1963], 3)

62. When the current "received wisdom" changes—as it will at exponential rates—the nation will find itself saddled with outdated schooling practices and content standards. Then a new round of government-driven systemic reforms will be foisted on schools, teachers, families, and students.

63. The connections between democracy and education have been the subject of debate and disagreement, curriculum designs and school reforms for many

years. In the past few years there has been a fascinating resurgence of this debate among academics and educators; and it has important implications for the standards of education that might be required by government or adopted voluntarily by individual teachers, schools, or communities.

In one of its manifestations, the debate revolves around whether fundamentalist religious families or dissenting communities of any kind should be obliged to include the liberal values of tolerance and democratic citizenship in the schooling their children receive—even if these values conflict with the beliefs of those families or communities (see Stolzenberg, "He Drew a Circle That Shut Me Out"). The debate includes the question of whether public schools should be required to teach these liberal values as one means of ensuring the continued existence of democracy and the preservation of the religious and other freedoms on which dissenters rely. This debate has special overtones in a pluralistic, multicultural society. The following are comments by three of the most thoughtful scholars arguing for the inclusion of liberal values in the school curriculum:

> The basic question of principle is, Do families have a moral right to opt out of reasonable measures designed to educate children toward very basic liberal virtues because those measures make it harder for parents to pass along their particular religious beliefs. Surely not. (Stephen Macedo, *Ethics* 105, no. 3 [1995], 468–96)

> As we have seen, tolerance requires noncoercion for ways of life that differ from one's own without violating general public principles. It is hard to believe that tolerance, so understood, can be cultivated without at least minimal awareness of the existence and nature of those ways of life. So the state may establish educational guidelines pursuant to this compelling interest. What it may not do is prescribe curricular or pedagogic practices that require or strongly invite students to become skeptical or critical of their own ways of life. (William Galston, *Ethics* 105, no. 3 [1995]: 516–34)

> Nor do parents have the right to pass on their own religious beliefs if that entails exempting their children from an education for liberal democratic citizenship. . . . Parental convictions that conflict with teaching children civic virtues must be tolerated but they should not be publicly subsidized by schools. (Amy Gutmann, *Ethics*, 105, no. 3 [1995]: 576–77)

From the perspective of this book—in which the argument is made for a school *structure* that reflects and respects the principles of constitutional democracy—two observations can be made about the debate over inclusion of liberal values in the state or national standards applied to public schools:

First, although the preservation and passing on of the values of democratic citizenship are surely important to the preservation of democracy itself, it is by no means clear that governments do or should have the power to require such teaching. That was the message of the *Barnette* case, which did not question the goals of the pledge of allegiance but did question the means used by public schools to attain those goals, the compulsory confession of belief. The argument for government requirements concerning the teaching of liberal values does not necessarily involve similar confessions of belief. But one ought to pause before embracing any schooling mechanism that may infringe so directly on the freedom of conscience, belief, and opinion of families and teachers. Furthermore, the strength of civic virtues in young minds is likely to be stronger if a child sees them practiced in school and society rather than merely taught didactically in the classroom.

Second, assuming that governments do and should have the power to require the teaching of the values of democratic citizenship (e.g., through content standards such as those created pursuant to *Goals 2000*), that power should not extend to other, less compelling kinds of requirements. There may be a handful of school standards that are so crucial to the preservation of constitutional democracy that their requirement by government would be an appropriate overriding of the freedom of intellect and belief. First Amendment jurisprudence contains several examples of "compelling justifications" for infringements on freedom of speech and even freedom of religion. But under *Goals 2000*, no such compelling justifications are required and there are literally hundreds of content standards that governments assume the power to make without any justification other than distrust of the nation's parents, teachers, and school communities and disrespect for their freedom of conscience.

Should the supporters of government-required schooling in democratic citizenship carry the debate, it might therefore be possible to allow them to have their means as well as their ends; but without granting to governments the plenary power to require content in all areas of schooling. Wherever a compelling justification could convincingly be made for a government content requirement, it could be adopted. Otherwise the presumption of constitutional democracy would be that the government has no power to make content requirements, especially under a regime like *Goals 2000*.

For a thoughtful and thoroughgoing response to Gutmann and several other advocates of democratic citizenship education, see Stephen Gilles, "On Educating Children: A Parentalist Manifesto," 63 *University of Chicago Law Rev.* 937 (1996). See also the articles cited at note 4, above. For a consideration of similar issues as they affect independent schools, see Neal Devins, ed., *Public Values, Private Schools* (New York: Falmer, 1989), especially chapter 12, "State Control of the Private School's Curriculum," in which Tyll van Geel considers the problem of racist teaching in segregationist academies.

64. The U.S. Constitution is silent on the subject of universal, compulsory, public schooling, which did not exist in 1789. This has generally been interpreted to mean that government power over schooling resides with the states, many of whose constitutions specifically mention public schooling. But the idea that such state power includes manipulation of intellect and belief of children through content requirements in public schools violates the spirit of constitutional democracy, as the *Barnette* example illustrates.

Chapter Five. The Legacy of Local Control

1. Charles Glenn, Jr., *The Myth of the Common School* (Amherst: University of Massachusetts Press, 1988), explores the origin and development of the com-

mon school in Europe and the United States as a mechanism for forging common loyalties and attitudes among the masses.

2. Retelling the stories of these three cases and the others referred to in this chapter is not meant to be a statement of the current law in these areas; nor does it constitute an argument that the Constitution can or should be read differently than the Court has read it. Instead I try to evoke the principles of constitutional democracy in an accessible way and to support the book's general argument that changes in the Constitution are necessary if conscience and community in public education are to be respected and protected. Readers interested in the current state of the law in these and other areas of schooling will benefit by consulting Louis Fischer, David Schimmel, and Cynthia Kelly, *Teachers and the Law*, 4th ed. (New York: Longman, 1995) and David Schimmel and Louis Fischer, *The Rights of Parents in the Education of Their Children* (Columbia, Md.: National Committee for Citizens in Education, 1977).

3. *Pierce v. Society of Sisters of the Holy Name of Jesus and Mary* 268 U.S. 510, 534–535 (1925). See David Tyack, "The Perils of Pluralism: The Background of the *Pierce* Case," *American Historical Review* 74 (1968): 74–98.

4. 268 U.S. 510, 535.

5. Id., 534.

6. See *Farrington v. Tokushige* 273 U.S. 284 (1927) and *Ohio v. Whisner*, 351 N.E.2d 750 (1976), and Stephen Arons, "Six Cases in Search of a Theory: Government Regulation of Non-government Schools," *Threefold Review*, no. 1 (Summer 1989).

7. 351 N.E.2d 750, 770.

8. Some who oppose making the right of school choice universal claim that to do so would deplete the public coffers in order to subsidize private preferences. The reality is just the reverse. Those who attend nongovernment schools pay to pursue their own beliefs and they subsidize the public schools as well. If those children now attending nongovernment schools were to enroll in the public school system, local and state school taxes would increase by at least 10 percent.

It has to be recognized also that an increasing number of poor children have been attending parochial and independent schools, especially in urban areas. This is made possible by assistance from these schools themselves and by the proliferation of so-called private voucher programs that give no-strings-attached aid to poor children seeking to choose an alternative education. Nevertheless, all these opportunities combined are a mere drop in the bucket compared to the number of families that would like to have more choice in schooling. Economic discrimination remains the central fact of life for the exercise of *Pierce* rights.

9. Chapter 1 sketches a few of the many school conflicts that took place while the 103rd Congress was considering and adopting *Goals 2000*. Of the conflicts described, all but one was played out on the local and state levels. For some of the histories of school wars under the regime of local control, see note 20, below.

10. Michael A. Rebell, "Values Inculcation and the Schools: The Need for a New *Pierce* Compromise," in *Public Values, Private Schools*, ed. Neal Devins (New York: Falmer Press, 1989). Rebell's revised compromise would permit

government-required value inculcation only where democratic values were at stake and would provide vouchers for those wishing to choose a nongovernment school, but would limit the vouchers to those dissenters, mostly religious, whose dissenting beliefs were "sincere and deep-seated."

11. See Stephen Arons, "Separation of School and State: *Pierce* Reconsidered," *Harvard Educational Review* 46, no. 1 (1976): 76. The argument is that the *Pierce* decision could rest on the First Amendment if decided anew and that this basis of decision would bring with it all the principles developed by the courts for protecting freedom of belief and intellect. The result might be a requirement that states provide educational choice equally to all citizens, regardless of their wealth or point of view. The term used for such a change in the structure of schooling was "separation of school and state," an idea roughly paralleling the separation of church and state that simultaneously preserves free exercise of religion and requires government neutrality toward religious beliefs by prohibiting any laws "respecting an establishment of religion."

Just after *Goals 2000* was adopted, a school reform movement was initiated by the Separation of School and State Alliance (4578 North First St., Fresno, California) under the banner of "separation of school and state." It went considerably beyond the original idea by demanding not only that government at all levels be neutral toward the content of public schooling, but that government cease paying for public schooling and repeal the compulsory attendance laws. Unfortunately, instead of preserving the rights of conscience for all, this proposal would likely secure them—and schooling itself—only for the more privileged and successful in society.

12. *Wisconsin v. Yoder*, 406 U.S. 205, 210–11 (1972).

13. In a partial dissent, Justice Douglas complained that the individual Amish teenagers were not permitted to make their views known about the type of education they desired. The Court, however, apparently felt that if there were disagreements about schooling between parent and teenager, those could be considered in the family or in another, nonconstitutional case.

But Justice Douglas's opinion raised a significant issue. How much power should parents have over their children's exercise of freedom of conscience, expression, and belief? At what point do the rights of children come in conflict with the prerogatives of parenthood? What role should government play, compared to parents, in controlling children's schooling? Is there an appropriate analogy to religious upbringing, in which parents not guilty of abuse or neglect have virtually complete legal power, and the government may not intervene in the religious choices made by parents for their children?

This book does not analyze the extreme ideas that parents "own" their minor children, or that children's rights entitle them to be free of all parental control. Rather it assumes, as the Court in *Yoder* seemed to, that all such issues of religion and schooling between parents and children are best worked out in the absence of government power over religion or school content. For further consideration of this important issue see John Coons and Stephen Sugarman, *Education by Choice: The Case for Family Control* (Berkeley: University of California Press, 1978).

14. Recall from the discussion of *Goals 2000* in chapter 4 that although the

argument offered by Wisconsin for the compelling nature of its interest in power over the inculcation process in schools failed in *Yoder,* it might succeed in a case in which the state and federal legislatures had adopted content standards and declared them essential to preserving economic competitiveness and civic virtue. Recall also that advocates of democratic education as a requirement for public schools make their best case by basing the argument on the compelling interest the government has in preserving democracy (chapter 4, n. 63).

15. *Wisconsin v. Yoder,* 406 U.S. 205, 223 (1972).

16. After reviewing the history of the Amish community, the sincerity of their beliefs, and the effectiveness of their informal education for Amish teenagers, the Court concluded not only that compulsory schooling above grade eight would undermine the Amish community, but also that this was a showing of evidence "that probably few other religious groups or sects could make" (id., 236). Moreover, the Court conveniently ignored the fact that many groups with equally sincere beliefs might be undermined in the same way; and by restricting its decision to religious freedom claims rather than including all claims of conscience as had been done in *Barnette,* the Court closed the door on rights of conscience and community almost as soon as it had opened it.

17. *Wisconsin v. Yoder,* 406 U.S. 205, 236 (1972). Since the case arose at the end of the 1960s, it might be that the Court's use of the term "progressive" referred to the multiplicity of alternative schools, dissenting life-styles, and liberating countercultures that blossomed in that period. The Court didn't want to grant these sometimes threatening and historically unproven forms of dissent the same constitutional status it had granted the more traditional separatism of the Old Order Amish.

18. *Wisconsin v. Yoder,* 406 U.S. 205, 217. Perhaps the justices chose Thoreau as their example because in 1848 he had written in *Civil Disobedience:*

Can there not be a government in which majorities do not virtually decide right and wrong, but conscience?—in which majorities decide only those questions to which the rule of expediency is applicable? . . . Law never made men a whit more just; and, by means of their respect for it, even the well-disposed are daily made the agents of injustice.

19. In *Barnette,* Justice Jackson pointed out that "freedom to differ is not limited to things that do not matter much. That would be a mere shadow of freedom. The test of its substance is the right to differ as to things that touch the heart of the existing order" (319 U.S. 624, 642 [1943]).

20. See, for example, Stephen Arons, *Compelling Belief: The Culture of American Schooling* (Amherst: University of Massachusetts Press, 1986); Stephen Bates, *Battleground: One Mother's Crusade, the Religious Right, and the Struggle for Control of Our Classrooms* (New York: Poseidon Press, 1994); Martin Carnoy, *Education as Cultural Imperialism* (New York: David McKay, 1974); Joan DelFattore, *What Johnny Shouldn't Read: Censorship in America* (New Haven: Yale University Press, 1992); Robert Everhart, ed., *The Public School Monopoly: A Critical Analysis of Education and the State in American Society* (Cambridge, Mass.: Ballinger, 1982); David Nasaw, *Schooled to Order: A Social History of Public Schooling in the United States* (New York: Oxford University Press, 1979); Diane Ravitch, *The Great School Wars, New York City,*

1805–1973: A History of Public Schools as a Battlefield of Social Change (New York: Basic Books, 1974); William Ross, *Forging New Freedoms: Nativism, Education, and the Constitution 1917–1927* (Lincoln: University of Nebraska Press, 1994); Joel Spring, *Conflict of Interests: The Politics of American Education,* 2nd ed. (New York: Longman, 1993); David Tyack, *The One Best System: A History of American Urban Education* (Cambridge: Harvard University Press, 1974); David Tyack, Thomas James, Aaron Benavot, *Law and the Shaping of Public Education 1785–1954* (Madison: University of Wisconsin Press, 1987); Lawrence Cremin, *The Transformation of the School: Progressivism in American Education 1876–1957* (New York: Vintage Books, 1964).

21. The case was never retried. Upon seeing the strength of the Court's decision about the First Amendment and school libraries, the local board, whose membership had changed, decided to rescind its actions.

22. *Board of Education, Island Trees Union Free School District No. 26 v. Pico,* 457 U.S. 853, 872 (1982).

23. Id. Emphasis in the original.

24. Id., 865. That this statement was not necessary to the Court's opinion in *Pico* does not lessen its significance as an indicator of ongoing ambivalence. In *Bethel School District No. 403 v. Fraser,* just four years later, the Court permitted a school official to censor the contents of a student's campaign speech for class president and ruled that

> the role and purpose of the American public school system . . . [is to] "prepare pupils for citizenship in the Republic. . . . It must inculcate the habits and manners of civility as values in themselves conducive to happiness and as indispensable to the practice of self-government in the community and the nation." (478 U.S. 675, 684 [1986])

The Court did not say how to resolve community differences over what constitutes "the habits and manners of civility" or any other set of values a majority supports but a minority does not share. Neither did it claim that these particular values can be inculcated because they are of overriding importance under the Constitution, the test of "compelling government interest" that is usually used to justify overriding First Amendment rights.

25. The situation became even worse for student and teacher freedoms of expression when the Court handed down its ruling in *Hazelwood School District v. Kuhlmeier,* 484 U.S. 260 (1988), in which it ruled that censorship of a school newspaper by a high school principal was constitutionally permissible if the newspaper's publication was at all related to the school's curriculum.

26. There was, of course, a community of resistance to oppression among African slaves in the United States, but it was a community maintained in spite of the law and culture of slavery as laid down by whites. An eloquent and moving description of this resistance culture is Vincent Harding, *There Is a River* (New York: Harcourt Brace Jovanovich, 1981).

27. The phrase is drawn from Paolo Freire, *Pedagogy of the Oppressed* (New York: Herder and Herder, 1978): "men . . . cannot be truly human apart from communication, for they are essentially communicative creatures. To impede communication is to reduce men to the status of 'things.' "

As early as 1705, the Virginia colony adopted legislation defining African slaves as property—inheritable like land, salable like cattle, and without the legal status of personhood. The chilling origins of this and other laws of black slavery during the growth of the political philosophy that led to the white Declaration of Independence is described in A. Leon Higginbotham, *In the Matter of Color: The Colonial Period* (New York: Oxford University Press, 1978).

By the nineteenth century the dehumanization that lay at the core of slavery in the United States could be described clearly, especially by those whites who benefited from it but privately opposed it:

> With slavery . . . the end is the profit of the master, his security and the public safety; the subject, one doomed in his own person, and his posterity, to live without knowledge, and without the capacity to make any thing his own, and to toil that another may reap the fruits. . . . such services can only be expected from one who has no will of his own; who surrenders his will in implicit obedience to that of another. Such obedience is the consequence only of uncontrolled authority over the body. . . . The power of the master must be absolute, to render the submission of the slave perfect. (*State v. Mann*, 13 N.C. 263 [1829])

28. The information about the struggle leading to *Roberts v. Boston* is taken largely from Derrick Bell, *Race, Racism, and American Law*, 2nd ed. (Boston: Little, Brown, and Co., 1980), 364–71.

29. *Plessy v. Ferguson*, 163 U.S. 537, 550 (1896). The lone dissenter in *Plessy*, Justice Harlan, saw through this lie:

> What can more certainly arouse race hate, what more certainly create and perpetuate a feeling of distrust between these races, than state enactments, which, in fact, proceed on the ground that colored citizens are so inferior and degraded that they cannot be allowed to sit in public coaches occupied by white citizens? That, as all will admit, is the real meaning of such legislation as was enacted in Louisiana. (163 U.S. at 559)

30. See C. Van Woodward's, *The Strange Career of Jim Crow*, 3rd ed. (New York: Oxford University Press, 1974).

31. 347 U.S. 483, 494 (1954).

32. 347 U.S. 483, 493. The Court emphasized the psychological and educational effects of school segregation and rejected the *Plessy* ruling that had blamed the victims of segregation. By stressing these intangible educational harms over the tangible differences in resources available for schooling black children, the Court may have left the impression that these children would learn better in the presence of whites. But it makes more sense to read the case as a response to the clear intent of all acts of coerced racial segregation to stigmatize blacks while depriving them of resources equal to those provided to whites. The debate over the core meaning of *Brown* has gone on for over forty years. See Derrick Bell, ed., *Shades of Brown: New Perspectives on School Desegregation* (New York: Teachers College Press, 1980).

33. This resistance was perhaps encouraged unwittingly by the Court itself when, in its implementation orders, it allowed local courts to move only "with all deliberate speed" and commanded them to take into account "varied local problems." *Brown v. Board of Education II*, 349 U.S. 294, 298 (1955).

34. *Cooper v. Aaron*, 358 U.S. 1 (1958).

35. *Griffin v. Prince Edward County Board of Education*, 377 U.S. 218 (1967).

36. *Green v. County School Board of New Kent County*, 391 U.S. 430 (1968).

37. The Court refused to accept most of the resistance and approved, with some limitations, the use of remedial attendance zones, integration goals, and intradistrict busing to remedy a history of racial segregation in schools. See *Swann v. Charlotte-Mecklenburg Board of Education*, 402 U.S. 1 (1971).

38. *Moses v. Washington* 330 F. Supp. 1340 (1971). The district court struck down the tracking system in this case, but on narrow grounds not applicable to most systems of homogeneous grouping even when they have racially discriminatory effects.

39. Bell, *Race, Racism, and American Law*, 399.

40. See Charles R. Lawrence III, "Segregation Misunderstood: The *Milliken* Decision Revisited," 12 *U.S.F. Law Rev.* 15 (1977) for the most perceptive among many commentaries analyzing and criticizing the Court's reasoning.

41. The phrase was Justice White's.

42. Laurence Tribe has written:

The Court offered no explanation in *Milliken* for why it thought district boundaries were sacrosanct—a conclusion especially puzzling in the wake of the Court's repeated rulings that neighborhood school assignments enjoy no such sacred status as emblems of local autonomy and community control of public schools. (Laurence Tribe, *American Constitutional Law*, 2nd ed. [Mineola, N.Y.: Foundation Press, 1988], 1495)

Perhaps the 5–4 majority simply couldn't be honest about the retreat from the *Brown* ruling and the victory of local control over the principles of equal education opportunity.

43. The Court required plaintiffs in metropolitan cases to prove not simply the existence and effects of segregated schooling, but also that segregation was the intended result of racially motivated actions taken by suburban school districts. The severity of this test and its preference for intent over effects as a test of legally remediable segregation has continued to protect segregated schooling in almost all metropolitan areas.

44. *Milliken v. Bradley*, 418 U.S. 717, 740–741 (1974). The Court ignored arguments found in the dissent that local control could be exercised by the parents of children attending a school regardless of where those children's residences happened to be.

Local control is also attractive to members of the black community who see in segregated schools the silver lining of being able to wrest control of their children's education from hostile whites. This would have been a powerful argument against metropolitan desegregation plans—especially given the insulting and inaccurate implication of *Brown* and some integrationists that black children cannot learn as well in the absence of white children—if equal resources were available for *voluntarily* chosen black schools. But they are not. As Justice Douglas observed in his dissent in *Milliken*, "When we rule against the metropolitan area remedy we take a step that will likely put the problems of the blacks and our society back to the period that antedated the 'separate but equal' regime of *Plessy v. Ferguson*" (418 U.S. at 757).

45. It was common in the early public debates over school desegregation—

and in more abstract discussions of equality and liberty that accompanied them —to regard racial equality for blacks as being in opposition to individual liberty for whites. The suggestion was that the freedom of whites was at odds with the rights of racial minorities to equal treatment. In a sense, this argument persists in the current debate over affirmative action.

This alleged liberty right of whites referred in fact to the power to use government to discriminate actively or to protect private discriminators from the requirements of the Fourteenth Amendment. More important, the argument based on the allegedly inevitable opposition of liberty and equality is unconvincing because liberty and equality are *not* in opposition in schooling. It is the equality of liberty that matters—that all citizens are equally entitled to exercise the freedoms and privileges of citizenship; and that no citizen's liberty should come at the arbitrary expense of another's. In this sense, equality and liberty must go together. Martin Luther King put the matter more clearly when he said that no one is free unless all are free. To explore the interrelationship of liberty and equality in schooling, see Stephen Arons and Charles R. Lawrence III, "The Manipulation of Consciousness: A First Amendment Critique of Schooling," 15 *Harvard Civil Rights/Civil Liberties Law Rev.* 309 (1980).

46. The book is the earliest, most complete, and most intelligent exploration of the complexities and inequalities of school finance mechanisms. See John Coons, William Clune, and Stephen Sugarman, *Private Wealth and Public Education* (Cambridge: Harvard University Press, 1970).

47. Federal aid makes even less of a dent in the inequalities created by basing school funding on local property taxes.

48. These figures are drawn from Jonathan Kozol, *Savage Inequalities: Children in America's Schools* (New York: Harper, 1992), appendix table 4, p. 237.

49. For over twenty years experts have researched and argued the question of whether or how much disparities in school funding influence the quality of education. This is an interesting intellectual exercise irrelevant to the issue of whether a state should be permitted arbitrarily to fund some children's schooling at a lower level than other children's. If the funding didn't matter, why would so much energy be expended by Americans trying to move to wealthier school districts, preserve the inequalities they thereby benefit from, and resist attempts to create metropolitan-wide school desegregation plans? To put it another way, if money doesn't matter, why is there so much resistance from wealthier districts to equal funding for all children?

50. The case is discussed at length in Kozol, *Savage Inequalities*, and the consequences of the inequalities it approved are eloquently described.

51. *San Antonio Independent School District v. Rodriguez*, 411 U.S. 1 (1973).

52. Anatole France, *Le Lys Rouge* [1894]. English ed., New York: Boni and Liveright, 1917.

53. California appears to be one of the success stories. But almost immediately upon reforming its school finance system so that there was no more than a three hundred dollar per pupil annual funding spread from wealthy to poor districts, the state's tax cutters reduced the overall level of spending on public schooling to nearly last in the nation. As a result, poor districts continued to be

poorly funded, along with the 95 percent of California districts within the three hundred dollar spread. See Kozol, *Savage Inequalities,* 221.

54. One of the purposes attributed to *Goals 2000* by its liberal supporters is the elimination of inequalities in schooling by requiring that all students meet the same high standards of performance. But it was recognized that this goal would be unattainable unless something was done to help poor school districts get the resources denied them by discriminatory state finance systems. The "opportunity standards" were therefore added to *Goals 2000* as a substitute for actually requiring the equality of school funding that federal and state courts and state legislatures have been unable to produce. Chapter 3 points out that the standardization of schooling is an ineffective and destructive means of achieving these ends and that the opportunity standards are a weak substitute—now repealed—for directly addressing these inequalities (see chapter 3, n. 14). It was not surprising that the opportunity standards were one part of *Goals 2000* that the supporters of local control were initially anxious to repeal.

Chapter Six. Conscience and Community

1. Robert Nisbet, *The Quest for Community* (London: Oxford University Press, 1969), 246.

2. Because, at bottom, most school wars are struggles to gain government power and use it for ideological ends, many parents have been caught in the middle. They are forced by the realities of power either to join the culture wars on behalf of their own beliefs or to disengage from the most important issues of their children's schooling, leaving the field to others. It is debatable whether the common school has ever been successful in creating a common culture rather than imposing a one-sided order. See Charles Glenn, Jr., *The Myth of the Common School* (Amherst: University of Massachusetts Press, 1988).

3. The subversion of community may be direct, as in denying the Satmar community the public schooling funds to which they were entitled for education of their disabled children, or as in denying to urban African American communities the resources and control of the schools their children attend. The subversion can also be indirect, as when the possibility of real community is replaced by a bureaucratic, spiritless, shopping mall order that satisfies almost no one and frustrates almost everyone. See, for example, Arthur G. Powell, Eleanor Farrar, and David K. Cohen, *The Shopping Mall High School: Winners and Losers in the Education Marketplace* (Boston: Houghton-Mifflin Co., 1985).

4. This is the opinion of Robert Nisbet, whose work *The Quest For Community* ranks him with Tocqueville as an observer of American culture: "To this moment *Democracy in America* is regarded as the best study ever made of the American people, its institutions, culture, values, and social psychology. Few are the Americans today who, reading its pages . . . cannot say: 'This is how we are' " (Nisbet, *The Social Philosophers: Community and Conflict in Western Thought* [New York: Crowell, 1973], 421).

5. Tocqueville, as Nisbet points out, also wrote a brilliant analysis of the French Revolution in *The Old Regime and the French Revolution* in spite of

the fact that several members of his family had been victims of its bloody excesses. See Nisbet, *The Social Philosophers,* 421. For a discussion of the historical context of Tocqueville's work, see Philip Bradley "A Historical Essay," in Tocqueville, *Democracy in America,* vol. 2 (New York: Random House, 1945), 389.

6. *Democracy in America* contains both well-intentioned warnings and prescient predictions about what would result if this complex balance of forces were lost or destroyed. For example, thirty years before the Civil War broke out, Tocqueville warned that the United States was headed for such a conflict because of the persistence of slavery and the vastly different economic worldviews that prevailed in the North and South (vol. 1, "The Present and Probable Future Condition of the Three Races that Inhabit the Territory of the United States," 343–446); and he foresaw the rise of industrial tyranny and the creation of economic classes after the Civil War (vol. 2, "How an Aristocracy May Be Created by Manufactures," 168–72).

7. Alexis de Tocqueville, *Democracy in America,* vol. 2 (New York: Vintage Books, 1945), 109. Tocqueville first published the two-volume work in 1835 and 1840 respectively, based on his visit to the United States in 1830.

8. Tocqueville, *Democracy* 2:104. Tocqueville regarded individualism as "a mature and calm feeling" that leads the individual "willingly [to] leave society at large to itself" while attending to his or her own family and friends. But it is essential to Tocqueville's perceptions of the dynamics of democracy in America that he recognized that individualism tends to get out of hand, that it becomes excessive, and that if it is left unchecked by institutions that reinforce community it not only saps the virtues of public life, but "in the long run . . . attacks and destroys all others and is at length absorbed in downright selfishness." It is this selfishness, and the individual isolation that results from it, that leaves all individuals naked and powerless before a single, centralized government.

9. Tocqueville, *Democracy* 2:109, 111–12.

10. The right, or freedom, of association is guaranteed by the Constitution, in particular by the First Amendment. See Laurence Tribe, ed., *American Constitutional Law,* 2nd ed. (Mineola, N.Y.: Foundation Press, 1988), 1010–22. The freedom of association is fundamental to the existence of voluntary associations, which in turn are fundamental to preventing the kind of alienation and isolation that Tocqueville argued could lead to tyranny. The unbreakable connection between individual freedom and viable communities is commented on by Tribe:

> believers in the richness and diversity of a pluralist society, where a variety of voluntary private associations and groups operate simultaneously to maximize opportunities for self-realization and minimize the strength of centralized power, may begin to find comfort in the freedom of association. (1011)

11. Tocqueville, *Democracy* 2:115, 117. That the reciprocal influences of citizens upon one another were "null" in a democracy was the result, according to Tocqueville, of the fact that democratic equality of condition had severed the bonds of hierarchic societies. See e.g. his chapter "Of Individualism in Democratic Countries," which ends with the sobering observation that, "not only

does democracy make every man forget his ancestors, but it hides his descendants and separates his contemporaries from him; it throws him back forever upon himself alone and threatens in the end to confine him entirely within the solitude of his own heart" (106).

In another chapter, entitled "Of the Use Which the Americans Make of Public Associations in Civil Life," Tocqueville foresees the rise of a tyrannical, bureaucratically administered state in which entitlements and dependence on government far exceed participation in public life and in which individuals become easy to manipulate by those in power:

> It is easy to foresee that the time is drawing near when man will be less and less able to produce, by himself alone, the commonest necessaries of life. The task of the governing power will therefore perpetually increase, and its very efforts will extend it every day. The more it stands in the place of associations, the more will individuals, losing the notion of combining together, require its assistance: these are causes and effects that unceasingly create each other. (116)

It is tempting to see in the low levels of electoral participation among today's citizenry, in the harshness, superficiality, and lack of empathy in today's politics, and in the ease with which soundbites, talkshow attacks, and media hype are used by politicians to manipulate the electorate, a grim fulfillment of Tocqueville's warnings about the tyrannical effects of the collapse of communities.

Robert Nisbet saw something similar in the 1950s. Though he perhaps had in mind life in the Third Reich or behind the Iron Curtain, Nisbet's views, like Tocqueville's, seem as true today as when they were written:

> The individual who has been by one force or another wrenched from social belonging is thrown back upon himself; he becomes the willing prey of those who would manipulate him as the atom citizen in the political and economic realms. Given nothing but his own resources to stand on, what can be his defenses against the powerful propaganda of those who control the principal means of communication in society? (Nisbet, *Quest for Community*, 268)

12. Nisbet's central work is the extraordinary *The Quest for Community*. Like Tocqueville, Nisbet's view of individualism and community is based on the importance of a dynamic balance in the constitution of a society:

> He [the individualist] has been right in his contention that real freedom is bound up with the existence of autonomies of personal choice among clear cultural alternatives. Above all, the individualist has been right in his stress upon human *privacy.*
>
> "All freedom," wrote Lord Acton, "consists . . . in the preservation of an inner sphere exempt from state power." . . . Both freedom and the desire for freedom are nourished within the realization of spiritual privacy and among the privileges of personal decision. . . .
>
> But . . . it is the intimacy and security of each of these [small social] groups that provide the psychological context of individuality and the reinforcement of personal integrity. And it is the *diversity* of such groups that creates the possibility of the numerous cultural alternatives in a society. (246–47, Nisbet's italics)

Lord Acton's "inner sphere of privacy" protected from state power seems similar to Justice Jackson's "sphere of intellect and spirit" protected from government infringement under the First Amendment and to Tribe's "rights to shape one's inner life" free of government invasions. All three are formulations of the importance of individual conscience and, as Nisbet suggests, all three are inseparable from the existence of small groups, voluntary associations, and diverse communities.

13. A discussion of the myriad ways of understanding and defining individualism is found in Steven Lukes, *Individualism* (Oxford: Blackwell, 1973). See also Robert Bellah et al., *Habits of the Heart: Individualism and Commitment in American Life* (New York: Harper and Row, 1985); David Riesman, *Individualism Reconsidered* (Glencoe, Ill.: The Free Press, 1954).

14. Nisbet, *Quest for Community*, 269. Nisbet appears to adopt a view of human nature that holds that human beings are not born with a preexisting set of values and beliefs, but learn them from the environment of family and culture. This perspective is useful in understanding the importance to the constitution of democracy of providing for both individual conscience and community maintenance. But its grounding in ideas of human nature opens issues of philosophy which are beyond the scope of this book. The matter is introduced comprehensively in the context of political philosophy in Stephen Mulhall and Adam Swift, *Liberals and Communitarians* (Oxford: Blackwell, 1992), and the works ably analyzed there. Also very useful is Stephen Macedo, *Liberal Virtue: Citizenship, Virtue, and Community in Liberal Constitutionalism* (Oxford: Clarendon, 1990); John Hall, *Liberalism: Politics, Ideology and the Market* (Chapel Hill: University of North Carolina Press, 1987); and Nisbet, *The Social Philosophers*.

The jurisprudential discussion of similar issues of human nature and political philosophy can be found in an extraordinarily thought-provoking if occasionally obscure and inaccessible collection of articles introduced by Frank Michelman's "Law's Republic," and found in a symposium in 97 *Yale Law Journal* 1493 (1988). Among the most interesting of these articles are Derrick Bell and Preeta Bansal, "The Republican Revival and Racial Politics," 1609; Paul Brest, "Further Beyond the Republican Revival: Toward Radical Republicanism," 1623; and Kathleen Sullivan "Rainbow Republicanism," 1713. Readers interested in the articles in this symposium should be aware that the authors use the term "republicanism" not to refer to the GOP, but in the sense that the Constitution uses it when it guarantees a republican form of government in every state (Article IV, section 4), that is, to refer to the principles of constitutional democracy as understood in the political thought of the revolutionary era.

15. This was in essence the same perception that underlay the Supreme Court's decision in *West Virginia v. Barnette*, discussed in detail in chapter 4. West Virginia had sought to foster national unity by forcing every child to pledge allegiance to the flag. But the Court saw that "compulsory unification of opinion achieves only the unanimity of the graveyard," and that unity was more likely to arise from maintaining the constitutional principle of government respect for individual intellect and spirit.

16. Nisbet, *Quest for Community*, 232.

17. See Amitai Etzioni, *The Spirit of Community: Rights, Responsibilities, and the Communitarian Agenda* (New York: Crown Publishers, 1993). The book is a kind of manifesto for the communitarian movement, which claims to seek the restoration of moral, social, and public order "without puritanism or oppression" (1).

Another scholar, Robert Nisbet, saw the problem this way, in *Quest for Community:*

> One may paraphrase the famous words of Karl Marx and say that a specter is haunting the modern mind, the specter of insecurity. Surely the outstanding characteristic of contemporary thought on man and society is the preoccupation with personal alienation and cultural disintegration. . . . The widening concern with insecurity and disintegration is accompanied by a profound regard for the values of status, membership, and community. (3)

Nisbet then documents and analyzes the loss of community as a fact of modern life and as a central theme of modern thought in virtually every field. At one point he observes:

> It has surely become obvious that the greatest single internal problem that liberal democracy faces is the preservation of a culture rich in diversity, in clear alternatives—and this is a cultural problem that cannot be separated from the preservation of the social groups and associations within which all culture is nourished and developed. (256)

Among journalists, Haynes Johnson portrays the problem in *Divided We Fall: Gambling with History in the Nineties* (New York: W.W. Norton, 1994). In reporting on the hundreds of discussions he held as he traveled across America, Johnson observes that Americans "know America has failed to face up to long-festering problems . . . [and] that the breakdown of families, neighborhoods, and communities and the accompanying erosion of personal responsibility are symptoms of national decline" (36).

18. Etzioni, *The Spirit of Community*, 30 ff.

19. Nisbet, *Quest for Community*, 216.

20. Beliefs, values, and meanings are among the primary things protected from government infringement by the First Amendment to the U.S. Constitution and by the principles of constitutional democracy discussed in chapter 4.

21. It has been debated for centuries—but will not be debated here—whether law is capable of maintaining the moral fabric of a society in the absence of shared beliefs. The ancient Chinese philosopher Lao-tzu put the problem this way: "When the Way is lost; then come the laws." The matter can be further pursued in Roberto Unger, *Law in Modern Society* (New York: Free Press, 1977).

22. Murray Murphey, "The Place of Beliefs in Modern Culture" in *New Directions in American Intellectual History*, ed. John Higham and Paul Conkin (Baltimore: Johns Hopkins Press, 1979). Murphey claims that the absence of shared beliefs (the worldview that he defines as an "elaborate symbolically mediated cognitive system") renders individuals and groups disoriented:

> The world view does more than define what there is and provide a basis for action; it also provides the individual with a set of orientations toward himself and the world around him that are of fundamental significance for his psychological well-being. Without some stability and order in experience and

without normative and motivational orientations toward himself, other humans, and his natural environment, the human individual could have no security, no satisfying interpersonal relations, and no moral worth. Who may be loved and who must be hated, what one may be proud of and what one must be ashamed of, who is a friend and who is an enemy—these and hundreds of similar questions are answered for us by the worldview. Our ideas can domesticate the world and make us at home there, or they can leave us terrified strangers on an alien shore. (154)

23. Nisbet, *Quest for Community,* 279.

24. It has been argued that the importance of education to the preservation of democracy makes it legitimate for governments to impose the liberal values of democracy on students attending public schools. See Amy Gutmann, "Democratic Education in Difficult Times," in *Teachers College Record* 92, no. 1 (Fall 1990): 7. Gutmann's insistence that individual freedom and civic virtue (community) are mutually exclusive, and her consequent argument that some consciences must be infringed upon by government for the sake of preserving democracy, are refuted by Stephen Gilles in "On Educating Children: A Parentalist Manifesto," 63 *University of Chicago Law Rev.,* 937 (1996). The issue is also treated by Stephen Macedo in "Liberal Civic Education and Religious Fundamentalism: The Case of God v. John Rawls?" Ethics 105, no. 3 (April 1995): 468–96. See also Nomi Stolzenberg, " 'He Drew a Circle that Shut Me Out': Assimilation, Indoctrination, and the Paradox of a Liberal Education," 106 *Harvard Law Rev.,* 581 (1993). Even if it were decided that constitutional democracy in general or the U.S. Constitution in particular should be read as imposing the teaching of democratic values as a requirement in public schools, that would not justify imposing the hundreds or thousands of other matters of intellect and belief that are currently regulated in schools by governments at all levels.

25. In addition, many scholars have observed that the effectiveness of schooling itself is dependent upon the existence of a sense of community, both within the school and outside it. And just as schooling thrives in community, communities cannot be sustained, it has been argued, in the absence of effective schools. This important point is made with great care by Clifford W. Cobb in *Responsive Schools, Renewed Communities* (San Francisco: Institute for Contemporary Studies, 1992). See especially his introduction and chapter 13, "Community or Communities." Cobb makes the argument that a properly designed system of education vouchers would enhance the growth of community in schools and at large. His view of the rights of individual conscience, however, is somewhat different from that presented here.

26. The idea of describing the conditions under which schooling would be more likely to enhance conscience and community or to respect the principles of constitutional democracy is based on Cobb's *Responsive Schools, Renewed Communities,* which discusses "conditions of self-governance that would enable schools to become communities" (9) and "conditions under which people can take charge of their own lives" (12). Cobb argues that vouchers would create these conditions. Here I do not want to argue for any specific structure of public

education, but rather to set an expanded set of conditions that would have to be met by any structure of schooling that aims to honor conscience, community, and the principles of constitutional democracy.

27. Cobb in *Responsive Schools, Renewed Communities* suggested that the changing ways that Americans define community have meant that neighborhood schools can sometimes do more to create dissonance with emerging forms of community than to enhance them. If we want schools to be less dominated by destructive conflicts over beliefs and more characterized by the constructive conflict resolution that builds a sense of community, we must recognize, with Cobb, that "[i]n a community, people . . . work together on the basis of shared values. . . . those who seek an identity as part of a larger whole must invent community by voluntarily committing themselves to institutions or groups" (2).

In *It Takes a Village: And Other Lessons Children Teach Us* (New York: Simon and Schuster, 1996), Hillary Rodham Clinton echoes this idea about the shifting nature of how Americans define community: "The village can no longer be defined as a place on a map, or a list of people or organizations, but its essence remains the same: it is the network of values and relations that support and affect our lives" (13).

28. The use of proportional representation and voting in a democracy does provide a way to allow a diversity of different communities within one geographical area to be adequately represented in a legislative body.

29. The phrase is from *Barnette;* see chapter 4. A discussion of the relationship of schooling to diversity and consensus in a democracy is found in John Coons and Stephen Sugarman, *Education by Choice: The Case for Family Control* (Berkeley: University of California Press, 1978), which remains one of the most thoughtful and reasonable discussions of the basic issues underlying proposals for family choice in schooling.

30. See Cobb, *Responsive Schools*, chapter 13, "Community or Communities."

31. This is not an argument for refusing to recognize geographical communities as a basis for public schools; neither is it an argument for tolerating racism or other forms of invidious discrimination in the provision or operation of schooling. Racism will remain a problem to be struggled with no matter what structure of schooling is adopted.

Not long after *Brown v. Board of Education* made segregated schools unconstitutional, the argument was made that whites had a right to "freedom of association" that overrode the equal protection rights of African Americans. The argument was dismissed in law and in public opinion as an intolerable expression of racism. But the problem of differentiating racist exclusion from freedom of association which promotes group solidarity and the positive aspects of community is not easy to resolve in a society with such a long history of racial antagonism.

There is no substitute for vigilance, struggle, and constitutional oversight based on the compelling purposes of the Fourteenth Amendment when trying to subdue racism in schooling. Under the existing structure of public education,

70 percent of minority children attend segregated schools. Reducing racial coercion and discrimination in schooling may be more effectively accomplished where choice is guaranteed and equally available to all families. After all, it is racial minorities and the poor who are the disproportionate victims of lack of school choice now. See Tyll van Geel, "State Control of the Private School's Curriculum," and Stephen Arons, "Educational Choice as a Civil Rights Strategy," in *Public Values, Private Schools,* ed. Neal Devins (New York: Falmer Press, 1989).

32. If teachers are accorded the status they deserve as true professionals, they will be neither the bureaucratic agents of government at any level nor the blindly obedient servants of parents. They will establish with parents and students the same difficult but essential relationship of mutual respect that other professionals, such as physicians or attorneys, have with their clients.

33. See Jane Roland Martin, *The Schoolhome* (Cambridge: Harvard University Press, 1992).

34. Some advocates of a separation of school and state would prevent the government from supporting or regulating schooling, presumably on the theory that public funding must inevitably be accompanied by government regulation of schooling. The same fear of uncontrollable government intervention in schooling leads these advocates to favor the abolition of compulsory attendance laws. Both these positions seem not only unnecessary for the protection of conscience and community, but destructive of it. The matter is dealt with in chapter 7 and at chapter 5 n. 11.

35. *West Virginia v. Barnette,* 319 U.S. 624, 638 (1943).

36. See the discussion of *Barnette* in chapter 4.

37. The argument is sometimes made that parents and families have a guaranteed voice in school policies under the present public school structure. The whole school system is subject to democratic control, and therefore every voter is entitled to a voice in school policy. This "voice" option has been compared with the "exit" option, namely, leaving the school that the family cannot sufficiently influence and going to one more in keeping with the family's beliefs or more open to the family's concerns.

Myron Lieberman (*Privatization and Educational Choice* [New York: St. Martin's Press, 1989]) makes a very telling comparison between voice and exit:

> The parent who can exit enjoys a tremendous advantage over one who must organize a community or state campaign to change a policy. . . .
> Voice is much more effective when an exit option is also available. For most parents, voice is especially crucial because there is no exit option; paradoxically, however, although the absence of exit renders voice more important, it also lessens the attention school officials pay to voice. (150–51)

Equal educational choice is therefore a prerequisite of equal power and participation in the school community, as well as of freedom of conscience in matters of schooling.

38. This way of thinking about the importance to community building of voluntary participation and individual rights of conscience is based in part on an understanding of the process of mediation. In mediation, which is among the

best examples of the constructive uses of conflict, each disputant is asked to help find common ground and a reorientation that will transform conflict into consensus. Mediation may not be appropriate in conflicts involving constitutional law or the application of fundamental principles of human rights. But where it is appropriate, the extraordinary success of the mediation process and of the agreements it often produces lies in the fact that no disputant can be forced to agree to a proposed resolution or be penalized by mediators for not agreeing to it. This equalizes the power of disputants in the mediation and allows them to take more risks and explore possible resolutions more freely. It is harder to bring people together to find common ground than it is to impose an order from the outside. But agreements that result from voluntary compromise and finding common ground are more reliable and meaningful; they build trust and community.

Selected Bibliography

There are selected bibliographies on specific topics presented where they seem most useful, in the endnotes throughout chapters 1–6. For example, a brief bibliography of histories of public schooling appears in note 20, chapter 5; several references concerning national education standards in Europe, Japan, and South Africa appear at chapter 3, n. 4; and several references dealing with the debate over democratic education appear at chapter 6, n. 24.

The selected bibliography below contains only those items that seemed most interesting, useful, or challenging for thinking through the ideas presented throughout this book. Some of these items are not specifically cited in the endnotes, but were nevertheless influential as the book took shape. Some are the sources of references in the endnotes, but nevertheless appear again below because of their general importance. All are recommended as worthwhile reading. The bibliography is in two parts—books and articles, and a special section on some of the literature that deals with various school choice and other reforms that might help secure an equality of individual liberty in schooling.

General Books and Articles

Ackerman, Bruce. *Social Justice in the Liberal State.* New Haven: Yale University Press, 1980.

Apple, Michael. *Official Knowledge: Democratic Education in a Conservative Age.* New York: Routledge, 1993.

———. *Cultural Politics & Education.* New York: Teachers College Press, 1996.

Barber, Benjamin. *An Aristocracy of Everyone: The Politics of Education and the Future of America.* New York: Ballantine, 1992.

Bell, Derrick. *Race, Racism, and American Law.* 2nd ed., Boston: Little Brown, 1980.

Bolt, Robert. *A Man for All Seasons.* New York: Random House, 1962.

Brown, Richard. *Revolutionary Politics in Massachusetts: The Boston Committee of Correspondence and the Towns, 1772–1774.* New York: Norton, 1976.

Bowles, Samuel, and Herbert Gintis. *Schooling in Capitalist America.* New York: Basic Books, 1976.

Cantor, David. *The Religious Right: The Assault on Tolerance & Pluralism in America.* New York: Anti-Defamation League, 1994.

Cobb, Nina, ed. *The Future of Education: Perspectives on National Standards in America.* New York: College Entrance Examination Board, 1994.

Coons, John, and Stephen Sugarman. *Education by Choice: The Case for Family Control.* Berkeley: University of California Press, 1978.

Coons, John, William Clune, and Stephen Sugarman. *Private Wealth and Public Education.* Cambridge: Belknap Press of Harvard University, 1972.

Devins, Neal, ed. *Public Values, Private Schools.* Stanford Series on Education and Public Policy. New York: Falmer Press, 1989.

Dworkin, Ronald. *Taking Rights Seriously.* Cambridge: Harvard University Press, 1978.

Emerson, Thomas I. *Toward a General Theory of the First Amendment.* New York: Random House, 1966.

Everhart, Robert, ed. *The Public School Monopoly: A Critical Analysis of Education and the State in America.* Cambridge, Mass.: Ballinger, 1982.

Freire, Paolo. *Pedagogy of the Oppressed.* Translated by R. Ramas. New York: Seabury Press, 1970.

Gatto, John. *Dumbing Us Down: The Hidden Curriculum of Compulsory Education.* Philadelphia: New Society, 1992.

Gilles, Stephen. "On Educating Children: A Parentalist Manifesto." 63 *University of Chicago Law Review* 93 (Summer 1996).

Giroux, Henry. *Ideology, Culture, and the Process of Schooling.* Philadelphia: Temple University Press, 1981.

Glenn, Charles, Jr. *The Myth of the Common School.* Amherst: University of Massachusetts Press, 1988.

Godwin, William. *An Inquiry Concerning Political Justice.* 2 vols. New York: Knopf, 1926.

Gumbert, Edgar, and Joel Spring. *The Superschool and the Superstate: American Education in the Twentieth Century, 1918–1970.* New York: Wiley, 1974.

Hall, John. *Liberalism: Politics, Ideology, and the Market.* Chapel Hill: University of North Carolina Press, 1987.

Hayek, Friederich A. *The Constitution of Liberty.* Chicago: University of Chicago Press, 1960.

Hofstadter, Richard. *Anti-Intellectualism in American Life.* New York: Knopf, 1963.

Kaplan, Michael. "Civil Disobedience, Conscience, and Community: Thoreau's 'Double Self' and the Problematic of Political Action." In *The Delegated Intellect: Emersonian Essay on Literature, Science, and Art in Honor of Don Gifford,* edited by Donald Morse. New York: Peter Lang, 1995.

Karier, Clarence. *The Individual, Society, and Education: A History of American Educational Ideas.* 2nd ed. Urbana: University of Illinois Press, 1986.

Kilpatrick, William. *Why Johnny Can't Tell Right from Wrong.* New York: Simon and Schuster, 1992.

Lawrence, Charles R., III. "The Id, the Ego, and Equal Protection: Reckoning with Unconscious Racism." 39 *Stanford Law Review* 317 (1987).

———. "Promises To Keep: We Are the Constitution's Framers." 30 *Howard Law Journal* 937 (1987).

Lieberman, Myron. *Public Education: An Autopsy.* Cambridge: Harvard University Press, 1993.

Liggio, Leonard, and Joseph Peden. "Social Scientists, Schooling and the Acculturation of Immigrants in 19th Century America." *Journal of Libertarian Studies* 2, no. 1 (1978): 69–84.

Macedo, Stephen. *Liberal Virtues: Citizenship, Virtue, and Community in Liberal Constitutionalism.* Oxford: Clarendon Press, 1990.

McCarthy, Rockne, James Skillen, and W. Harper. *Disestablishment a Second Time: Genuine Pluralism for American Schools.* Grand Rapids: Christian University Press, 1982.

Mill, John Stuart. *On Liberty.* London: Parker & Son, 1859.

Miller, Ronald, ed. *Educational Freedom for a Democratic Society: A Critique of National Goals, Standards, and Curriculum.* Brandon, Vt.: Resource Center for Redesigning Education, 1995.

Mulhall, Stephen, and Adam Swift. *Liberals and Communitarians.* Oxford: Blackwell, 1992.

Murphey, Murray. "The Place of Beliefs in Modern Culture." In *New Directions in American Intellectual History,* edited by John Higham and Paul K. Conkin. Baltimore: Johns Hopkins University Press, 1979.

Nieto, Sonia, ed. "National Curriculum Standards." *The Educational Forum* 58, no. 4 (Summer 1994).

Nisbet, Robert. *The Quest for Community.* London: Oxford University Press, 1969 (reissue).

Ravitch, Diane. *National Standards in American Education: A Citizen's Guide.* Washington, D.C.: Brookings Institution, 1995.

Salomone, Rosemary. "Common Schools, Uncommon Values: Listening to the Voices of Dissent." 14 *Yale Law & Policy Review* 169 (1996).

Sizer, Theodore. *Horace's Compromise: The Dilemma of the American High School.* Boston: Houghton Mifflin, 1984.

Spring, Joel. *Educating the Worker-Citizen: The Social, Economic, and Political Foundations of Education.* New York: Longman, 1980.

———. *Images of American Life: A History of Ideological Management in Schools, Movies, Radio, and Television.* Albany: State University of New York Press, 1992.

Stanley, William. *Curriculum for Utopia: Social Reconstructionism and Critical Pedagogy in the Postmodern Era.* Albany: State University of New York Press, 1992.

Steiner, David. *Rethinking Democratic Education: The Politics of Reform.* Baltimore: Johns Hopkins University Press, 1994.

Toqueville, Alexis de. *Democracy In America.* 2 vols. New York: Random House, 1945.

Tyack, David. "Ways of Seeing: An Essay on the History of Compulsory Schooling." *Harvard Educational Review* 46, no. 3 (1976): 355–89.

West, E. G. "Political Economy of American Public School Legislation." *Journal of Law and Economics* (October 1967): 101–28.

Wise, Arthur. *Legislated Learning: The Bureaucratization of the American Classroom.* Berkeley: University of California Press, 1979.

Witte, John. "Essential Rights and Liberties of Religion." 71 *Notre Dame Law Review* 371 (1996).

School Choice and Related Reforms

Arons, S., *Compelling Belief.* Amherst: University of Massachusetts Press, 1986.

Budde, Robert. "Redefining Education Governance: The Charter School Concept." Austin, Tx.: Southwest Educational Development Laboratory, Austin, 1996.

Chubb, John, and Terry Moe. *Politics, Markets, and America's Schools.* Washington, D.C.: Brookings Institution, 1990.

Clune, William, and John Witte, eds. *Theory of Choice and Control in American Education* (vol. 1), and *The Practice of Choice, Decentralization, and Restructuring* (vol. 2). New York: Falmer, 1990.

Cobb, Clifford. *Responsive Schools, Renewed Communities.* San Francisco: ICS Press, 1992.

Cookson, Peter. *School Choice: The Struggle for the Soul of American Education.* New Haven: Yale University Press, 1994.

———, ed. "The Choice Controversy: Current Debates and Research." Special issue of *Educational Policy* 6, no. 2 (June 1992).

Coons, John, and Stephen Sugarman. *Scholarships for Children.* Berkeley: University of California Press, 1992.

Finn, Chester, et al. "Charter Schools in Action: A First Look." Education Excellence Network of Hudson Institute, 1996.

Friedman, Milton. *Capitalism and Freedom.* Chicago: University of Chicago Press, 1962.

Gintis, Herbert. "The Political Economy of School Choice" *Teachers College Record* 96, no. 3 (1995): 492–511.

Glenn, Charles, Jr. *Choice of Schools in Six Nations.* Washington, D.C.: U.S. Government Printing Office, 1989.

"Just Doing It: First Annual Survey of the Private Voucher Movement in America." National Scholarship Center, Washington, D.C., 1994.

Lieberman, Myron. *Privatization and Educational Choice.* New York: St. Martin's Press, 1989.

Moe, Terry. *Private Vouchers.* Palo Alto: Hoover Institute Press, 1996.

U.S. Congress. *Parental Rights and Responsibilities Act.* HR 1946 and S 984. 104th Congress, 1st sess. (1995).

van Geel, Tyll. *Authority to Control the School Program.* Lexington, Mass.: Lexington Press, 1976.

Online Material

A great deal of interesting material is available through the Internet, especially by beginning at http://csr.syr.edu/ For example: Mauhs-Pugh, T., "Charter Schools 1995: A Survey and Analysis of Law and Practices in the States." *Education Policy Analysis Archives* (peer-reviewed electronic journal): http://seamonkey.ed.asu.edu/epaa

Index

Book titles and names of court cases appear in italics.

Marketplace of ideas, 31, 57, 85, 160
Marshall, Thurgood, 98
Martin, Jane Roland, 200
Michelman, Frank, 196
Meier, Deborah, 181
Mill, John Stuart, 24–25
Milliken v. Bradley, 116, 119, 165
Minersville v. Gobitis, 78–80
More, Thomas, xi–xvi, 8, 152–54
Mulhall, Stephen, 196
Murphey, Murray, 197
Myth of the Common School, 103,
    185–86, 193

Nasaw, David, 188
National curriculum
    in United States, 68, 71–73
    in other countries, 169–70
    See also *Goals 2000*
*National Standards in American
    Education: A Citizen's Guide*,
    170
Nation at Risk, A, 2, 49, 156
NDEA (National Defense Education
    Act), 63
Nieto, Sonia, 169
Nisbet, Robert, 126–29, 193, 195–96,
    197

Official Knowledge, 17, 182
Official knowledge, 12, 23, 25, 83–87,
    89–90,
Old Order Amish, 106–9. See also
    Community, Amish
Omnibus Appropriations Act, 72
*One Best System, The: A History of
    American Urban Education*, 2,
    51, 92, 167
Opportunity-to-learn standards, 68,
    171. See also *Goals 2000*
Orthodoxy in education, 81, 111–12
    pall of orthodoxy, 85, 177
    See also Official knowledge

Parents' (family) rights
    and children rights, 179–80, 187
    under *Goals 2000*, 74–75, 90, 96,
    174
    and government power, 93, 95–99
    to religious exemptions, 106–9
    See also School choice; School wars

Peloza v. Capistrano, 163
People for the American Way (PFAW),
    28, 55–57
Pierce v. Society of Sisters, 104–12,
    121, 136
Pitkin, Hanna, 158
Plato, 48, 99, 141, 183
Pledge of Allegiance, 45, 78–82
Plessy v. Ferguson, 41, 114
Political correctness and family
    values, 14
Politicization of schooling, 7, 11–12,
    30–31, 65, 85–86, 92, 96, 102,
    110, 123, 136
Politics-as-usual, 10, 147, 154
Postman, Neil, 90
Power over schooling, xv, 20, 24, 32,
    45, 64, 100, 106, 130, 136, 140,
    185
    denied states, see *West Virginia v.
    Barnette*
    shifted by *Goals 2000*, 4, 65, 68, 76,
    95–99, 142, 172–73
    See also Conscience, rights of
Private schools, 73–75, 79, 87, 104–5,
    133, 174, 179, 186, 200
*Private Wealth and Public
    Education*, 164
Privatization, 178
Public discourse, 77, 101, 123, 148,
    150. *See also* Conflict over
    schooling, tone
Public education
    under attack, 1–3, 9, 29, 43, 49, 52,
    57, 62, 123, 132, 156
    as character education, 48
    and community formation, 6, 36–
    39, 42–43, 106–9, 129–31, 182,
    198
    history of, 103, 180–82, 188–89
    majority control of, 7–8, 56, 85–86,
    96, 102, 140
    as moral enterprise, 11, 158
    preservation of, 9–10
    and public opinion, 47
    re-constitution of, 64, 82, 137–51
    revitalization of, 4, 62–63, 133
    saved from public schooling, 5, 14
    secular, 37–38, 109
    structure of, 6–7, 26, 32, 46, 50–51,
    76, 122, 137